COMPETITION CAR
SUSPENSION

COMPETITION CAR
SUSPENSION

Allan Staniforth

Haynes Publishing

First published by G.T. Foulis & Company 1988
Reprinted 1991
Second edition published 1994
Reprinted 1996 and 1997
Third edition published by Haynes Publishing 1999
Reprinted 2000
Reprinted 2002 (twice)
Fourth edition (colour) 2006
Reprinted 2008, 2009 (twice), 2010 and 2012

A catalogue record for this book is
available from the British Library

ISBN 978 1 84425 328 9

Library of Congress catalog card no. 2006921760

Published by Haynes Publishing,
Sparkford, Yeovil, Somerset BA22 7JJ, UK

Tel: 01963 442030 Fax: 01963 440001
Int. tel: +44 1963 442030 Int. fax: +44 1963 440001
E-mail: sales@haynes.co.uk
Website: www.haynes.co.uk

Haynes North America, Inc.,
861 Lawrence Drive, Newbury Park,
California 91320, USA

Printed and bound in the UK by Gomer Press Limited,
Llandysul Enterprise Park, Llandysul, Ceredigion SA44 4JL

Contents

Author's preface

PERHAPS THE MOST REMARKABLE thing about the past 20 years since this book was first conceived is not what has changed in racing cars, whether at the peak of the sport, or lower down the scale, but what has not changed in any fundamental way at all. Consider light alloy wheels, tyres, wishbone linkages, uprights and hubs, coils (or, rarely, torsion bars), push and pullrods, bellcranks, steering wheel and column

The author in his Austin 7 Special circa 1949 – used as an 'office car.' No problems with single headlight, no wind (or aero) screen, knife-edged wings or metal eagle badge. (Author)

connected to a rack and pinion, the ancient 4-stroke petrol engine, aerodynamic downforce from non-adjust (in motion) front and rear wings, predominantly flat undersides, simply operated multi-speed gearboxes, plate clutches, disc brakes, alloy callipers, driveshafts with inner and outer joints, basically simple hydraulic pressure lines – all still with us, though improved again and again in detail and materials. Think glassfibre, carbon in its many forms, beryllium, specialised alloys, metal matrix, honeycomb flat and shaped, wing shapes, with their positions and mounting brackets, inlet and exhaust valve metals, air valve springs, tyre rubber compounds, complex formulae for 'standard' fuel, low viscosity oils, engine management, fly-by-wire throttles, 'thinking' diffs, together with data logging and its ubiquitous handmaiden the computer, and perhaps above all, driver protection.

The total or partial disappearance of many of this latter group has nothing to do with any lack of ingenuity, perseverance or resources on the part of their creators, but largely by an endless succession of rule changes, often apparently conceived and imposed in both draconian and sudden, short-term fashion, and not infrequently requiring top class legal advice to understand and help implement.

True or false, there now seems to be a growing impression that anything truly ingenious, inventive, unconventional – or, dare one suggest such a thing, likely to benefit one or other team however marginally over another – is fated to die at the hands of the rulemakers. So the brains and the cash have been concentrated almost

55 years on … the author piloting his Magapin at Harewood in 2005. (Gashley)

solely on endless miniscule detail improvements, primarily aerodynamic, while
suspension in the sense of what this book mainly concerns appears to be slowly but
irrevocably disappearing in F1 at least. Only tyres, theoretically a control item for one
and all, remain as some cushion between the driver/car/power unit and road. Not
surprising then, the howls of distress and complaint when the rare street or less than
billiard-table-smooth circuit presents small surface imperfections somewhere in the
world.

Any sport needs a rulebook. How closely one should control the participants or
their equipment is open to debate, but if a huge showbiz content is involved, the
perception and opinions of the paying customer should surely be a consideration?

Four really major possible contributions to progress off as well as on the track – a
personal view – wing downforce directly into the wheel/tyre (Chaparral) downforce by
suction from existing cooling air (Brabham Fan Car) and fully computer-controlled
'Active' suspension (Lotus) were all emasculated or legislated into the nearest skip with
shameful haste. Brought painfullly up to date by Renault's successful updating of an
old idea (inertia damping) – legal for nearly 18 months, but not for long after it leaked.
At first accepted as legal, even the FIA experts suddenly could not agree, and the
argument went finally to the independent appeal court, chosen by the FIA, who gave it
the thumbs down. A painfully public squabble.

One might add sophisticated differentials 'green' fuels and regenerative braking to
an embarrassing (sad?) list.

Happily, there are still refuges within the sport where this book may well prove
useful as well as a decent read. They include Rally Raid and other cross-wilderness
events, long-distance sports cars, hillclimb and sprint cars, one-off hybrids, NASCAR,
rallycross, autograssing, trialing, a variety of historic, one-make and '70s to mid-'90s
GTs and single seaters, America's C and D class sports racers and the UK's Monoposto.

Not to mention the monoshock approach to front suspension which has not only
remarkably proved that a 4-wheeler can be improved under certain circumstances by
having one of them in midair – but has never been banned – and is now covered in
these pages. May you find them interesting – even helpful.

Allan Staniforth
July 2006

Acknowledgements

THE AUTHOR'S CONSIDERABLE GRATITUDE goes to those who have helped to make this book possible, as well as contributing substantially to his patchy technical education in their various ways.

Special thanks to:

Neil Barnett
John Beattie
Richard Blackmore
Sarah Blenkinsop
Frank Bott
Jim Boursos
John Bright
Keith Calver
Tony Cotton
Ryan Currier
Frank Dernie
Graham Easter
Clare and Miles Gardner
Tony Gilhome
Keith Gowers
Richard Hurdwell
Nigel Killerby
Simon McBeath
National Motor Museum, Beaulieu
Steve and Lynn Owen
Brian Redman

Jeremy Rossitter
Ray Rowan
Greg Simmons
Fred Smith
Graham Ashley Smith
Darell and Jacky Staniforth
Clive Spackman
Joe Ward
Reverend Barry Whitehead
Allan Warburton

and particularly:

David Gould
Trevor Harris
Gordon Murray
Ian Scott
Tony Southgate
Frank Williams
Peter Wright

Chapter 1

The reasons why

... an introduction

THE WHEEL AND THE AXLE are not quite as old as the average hill but they still go back a bit. The path from a slice of tree trunk to an F1 rear is a long one, well worthy of a story all to itself, but we shall be more concerned here with all the complexities of holding it on the vehicle, controlling how it does its job and utilising the small area where it touches the road to the very ultimate. In a word: suspension.

In the early stages of the evolutionary path suspension did not, of course, exist. It was sufficient that man had devised a means to transport, however laboriously, objects that had hitherto been immovable. But war and sport (the latter often a thinly disguised derivative of the former) were incentives to rapid progress. The Romans were a shining example. The Legions had carts and the Colosseum had chariot racing, without doubt the Formula One of the day. Neither appear to have used suspension

Roger Moran on his way to the 2005 British Hillclimb Championship driving a Gould GR55B – one of the latest of a line that began in an uncle's metalworking shop and a home garage some 30 years ago.

Ferenc Szisz drives the Renault 'Agatha' in the 1906 French Grand Prix at Le Mans. The hero riding mechanic has never been identified for certain. (LAT)

1906 Renault 'Agatha' front suspension with – far ahead of its time – what strongly resembles a 21st century piston damper.

2005 Renault R25 front suspension, with any hint of damper(s) buried out of sight within the carbon tub.

Fernando Alonso drives the Renault R26 in the 2006 Malaysian Grand Prix. Dotted line shows no wheel rise or fall despite the shattering impact of inner front onto concrete rumble strips. (LAT)

but the strong metal-tyred spoked wheel had already appeared in the form it would still be taking 2000 years later on the horse-drawn English brewery drays of the 19th century.

Why bother to explain or illustrate the past at all? Because nothing happens in a vacuum. Everybody except the first to do something (often much further back than one might suspect) is copying to some degree, even if unknowingly. History has an extraordinary number of instances of major inventions made by different people in different parts of the world at about the same time, within milli-seconds of each other if you think in cosmic terms, that is in millions of years. Bitter are the disputes and accusations within science and industry when this happens.

So it is that a glance back (in no way totally comprehensive) will hopefully show how history and the designers it left behind laid the groundwork. What died and what survived is a fascinating insight into the state of the art not readily obtainable in any other way.

Despite computers and huge budgets, it is still an art at the highest level. While cars undoubtedly now tend to work very much better 'straight out of the box' the legendary performer is still nurtured by secret and ferociously intense testing and changes between that well known box and the first grid. Assuming the engine is good and the chassis is as rigid as possible (quite separate problems) how the car handles, its ability to put its power down and behave in the way a world class driver asks of it is almost totally down to suspension.

Some would say 'or lack of it' as one design parameter is often to reduce movement to almost nil on the premise that if a problem is currently insoluble you eliminate what is causing it. Construing this as a bit defeatist, later chapters will be aimed at getting the best of both worlds. This is not to ignore aerodynamics but downforce still has to be reacted through a linkage of some sort to reach tyre contact patches.

With the fundamentals fairly firmly established, success can often stem from brilliant detail, ingenious installation or integration and simplicity. Better materials, refinements in small or sophisticated ways often give immeasurably better results than attempts to re-invent the wheel and its attachments.

At the top of the motor racing tree, as in virtually all highly technological fields, money is effectively unlimited with the most highly skilled of craftsmen, most ingenious and talented designers all working for the best dozen or so drivers in the world, welded together by the most able team leaders. It can be such a formidable combination that even in the top echelons there can still be second and third raters, relatively speaking. Characteristics include coming into the pits on the first lap, having gear knobs fall off, failing to tighten plugs or wheel nuts, blowing engines and fitting incorrect gears. Such things rarely happen more than once to the top operators.

In many ways engine power was the name of the game for years. Suspension with all its intricacies, unknowns and hopelessly interrelated variables was a bit of a slow starter, making little impression in America until the Fourties, in Britain until the Sixties (and, some wit might aver, at Ferrari until the Eighties). Taking our trip back into history, we find even well before the arrival of the internal combustion engine suspension was of major concern to certain vehicle builders. As still today away from the race track, the reason was comfort.

The leaf spring in a variety of forms from quarter to double elliptic, with the necessary pivoting shackles and location on the chassis and axle was of vital concern to the well-named 'carriage trade'. The wealthy have always, by and large, demanded the best, so far as they could distinguish it. Whether technically minded or not, the long distance traveller's backside told him more than his brain about the quality of his purchase whether of the vehicle or his ticket to ride.

The farm cart, trans-Prairie Conestoga wagons and early stage coaches all relied upon the solidly mounted axle. The Brougham, later stages and the Hansom cab were the leaders in the new generation of comfortable transport. Both the theory and the practice of the Ackermann angle approach to steering front wheels with reduced or minimum scrub were known before the first Benz stuttered into life.

It was sensible and obvious that the first engines were hung in or on horse-drawn carriages, needing only a bicycle-style chain drive to an existing axle. It took the pioneers no time flat to realise that a suspended axle, moving with road shock needed to move about known arcs or lines if the chain was not to break.

Probably the best of several solutions was to insert a chassis mounted cross-shaft to which engine power went first. This was located on the same line as the forward pick-ups of the rear leaf spring. A secondary chain then ran from the cross-shaft to the rear axle. When the axle rose or fell, both it and the chain moved about a common axis and thus followed the same path.

The front already had suspension and movable wheels linked to horse shafts. Reversing the linkage after the departure of the horse, and bringing it off one side rather than centrally gave the fundamentals of a remotely steered suspension that would survive for some considerable time. And these first cars were the racers of the day, from the moment contemporary sportsmen (and a few rare ladies) perceived that they had a brand-new instrument with which to compete against their fellows.

Goggles, cloth caps and helmets did not in those early days immediately indicate a racing driver. They were essential protection for any motorist sitting out in the open at the mercy of wind and rain. Racing cars emerged as a separate breed quite slowly, with emphasis on engine development and light weight. In many ways road and race car development ran parallel, cross-pollination at first improving the racers, then the racers improving the road versions.

A front beam axle with a leaf spring each side proved admirably suited to accepting the move of the newer multi-cylindered engines to the front, this in its turn requiring a clutch and gearbox feeding rearwards into a shaft.

Industry had driven a gear on a shaft by means of a pinion gear at right angles to it for more than two centuries. It offered a method of driving the rear wheels in enclosed oilbath conditions that was to totally oust the chain. (Not without a rearguard action by the famed Frazer Nash sports cars which were still being propelled via chain in the early Thirties.)

The new geared rear axle could also be both located and sprung very conveniently on a pair of parallel leaf springs. Pre World War One, this layout was becoming common both on road and track with little or no alteration for the latter, and there is a strong case that the passenger car industry, particularly in America pioneered many of the steps over the next 40 years. Independent front suspension, coil springs, the MacPherson strut, rear axles with varying degrees of sophistication in location, plus wider, fatter tyres for good measure were all road car developments. Virtually everything had one target – the soft ride.

What gave Britain and Europe such a golden opportunity – or urgent need – for improved roadholding was, as has been frequently pointed out, a road system of twists and turns and uphill and downhill rather than flat and straight lined. It spawned a tradition of sports cars in Aston Martin, Alfa Romeo, Bentley, Delage, Hispano Suiza,

Figure 1-1 *The Fifties D-Type Jaguar was a purpose-designed Le Mans racer with a monocoque centre section, and the rear suspension was hung from the back bulkhead as shown here. The axle was a production item located by (non standard) pairs of trailing arms and the springing medium was a single (centrally located) torsion bar which linked between trailing arm pivots.*

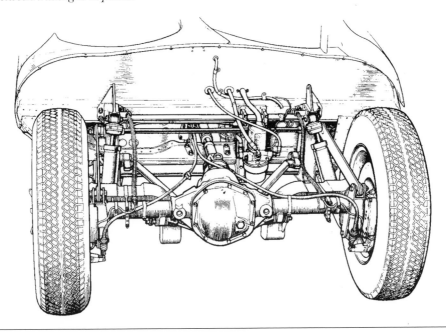

Bugatti, MG and a dozen others between the wars (not to mention the occasional sporting car from a mass manufacturer, notably Austin).

The inter-war sports car manufacturers shared two things – a constant struggle to get more engine power and reliability and a tendency to remain faithful to the beam axle with leaf springs. Improvements in handling came partly from a lighter body with a lower vehicle centre of gravity, and partly from much stiffer springing (leaf springs tightly bound with cord to increase the rate were a fairly common sight) limiting roll and unwanted wheel movements.

The precision of the handling and acceleration if not the comfort improved dramatically with this treatment over the saloons from which many sports cars drew their basic parts. A perfect example was the contrast between the dreadful roll-oversteering, gutless and almost brakeless early Austin Seven and the Nippy or more exotic Ulster from the same factory. Basically the same, they were a transformation in driving quality.

Only after World War 2, followed by space research releasing a torrent of technology, did the face of motor racing begin to change massively and rapidly. Commercial backing, the cash with advertising so contemptuously spurned in earlier years, did the rest.

What are now known as Sports-Prototypes (or Stateside, as Prototypes) were quick off the mark with the factory developed derivatives of the great sports cars of the period. From Napier, Delage and Renault to Alfa Romeo, Bugatti and Aston Martin, racing had previously been largely a two-man affair. Friction dampers remotely controlled by a riding mechanic, together with manually operated lubrication for the suspension – perhaps the true forerunners of late Eighties active suspension technician

Rear end of 1970 BRM P154 Chevrolet Can-Am car. V8 and light ARB. (LAT)

1970 BRM P154 Chevrolet Can-Am car in action in the hands of George Eaton. (LAT)

Rear end of 2004 Audi R8 with bodywork removed. Although not readily apparent in this picture, one development to deal with an early gearbox frailty was the ability to change the complete rear end, including box, driveshafts, wheels, tyres, brakes and suspension in some seven minutes – or less! (LAT)

with pits to car radio links and data logging to help modify computerised suspension settings!

The Sports-Prototype started life as a genuine sports car which, even in the early Fifties, an amateur could buy off the shelf and race competitively. However, at that time it quickly became apparent that cars which handled superbly at high road speeds showed painful shortcomings when really pushed to the limit. They rolled to extreme degrees, assumed odd wheel angles, tore tyres to pieces variously front or rear, outer edge or inner, had wheel twirling steering and what came to be known in every paddock bar as understeer, or oversteer, or both.

The amateurs – read anyone who did not own a factory – set about their own modifications as best they might. The factories – Jaguar for one with the C- and D-types – generally kept the engine and the bonnet badge while building another, vastly better handling car to carry the marque to victory. Spectators saw the familiar badge on a sometimes familiar, sometimes dramatically new body. Mostly they did not see redesigned 'production' suspension, different springs, new patterns of damper, the early experiments with independent rear suspension, racing tyres, reduced weight and sometimes double the production power.

Formula One had already embarked upon its single-minded approach to being the fastest thing on four wheels around a road circuit. But it had tended to always emphasise the engine and had been an affair of either countries (Germany with Mercedes and Auto Union – massive finance and power and horrific handling) or the rich talented customers of bespoke builders like ERA, Ferrari, the Maserati brothers, producing essentially light, narrow single-seater versions of sports cars, still with a preponderance of beam and solid axles and leaf springs, though with much experiment and refinement in location.

2004 Audi R8 in action during testing at Le Mans. British designer Tony Southgate made a major contribution to the aerodynamics. (LAT)

The true revolution in suspension began in both camps – when John Cooper put the engine in the back and combined it with transverse leaf springs, wishbones and anti-roll bars but questionable geometry, and Colin Chapman put coil springs and sophisticated wishbone control of wheel angles under the skin of his early sports racers (though they stayed front-engined for a curiously long time considering the magnitude of his thinking).

Chapman spelled out for the observant the needs and aims of racing suspension that have held valid for nearly half a century, being copied or adapted, modified or developed wherever cars race. They are covered later in greater detail but in broad terms might be defined as keeping the wheel and tyre vertical to the road surface at

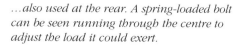

1934 Maserati 8CM front suspension with classic Andre Hartford adjustable friction disc dampers…

…also used at the rear. A spring-loaded bolt can be seen running through the centre to adjust the load it could exert.

all times, eliminating alterations caused by squat or nose-dive, road bumps or roll in corners and keeping the roll centre in one place and track constant.

Up to now perfection in all of these has proved impossible, but in the course of seeking it, all four wheels are independently sprung and connected through massive hubs to rigid links in pure tension and compression, which in their turn are attached to the vehicle via metal/metal spherical joints at rigid points in its structure.

None of these parts should be an ounce heavier than is necessary to deal with the forces involved, and when under load on the move should not allow the wheels/tyres to adopt unwanted toe-in or out or any other unplanned movements.

By the time of the mid engine era Sports-Prototypes were enclosed wheel, long distance versions of the Formula One sprinters and by the Eighties they had all finally arrived at five extraordinary similarities. Whatever else they did not share, almost every successful Sports-Prototype and Grand Prix car shared:

- unequal length wishbones to locate the wheel/hub unit;
- a coil spring to permit some degree of bump and rebound for the wheel;
- an oil or oil/air filled valved damper to control the spring's inclination to go ge-doing, ge-doing, ge-doing unless restrained;
- usually though not always an anti-roll bar of varying degrees of sophistication to reduce and control lean;
- effectively invisible, the geometry of the links, and the effect they have on the wheels as they swing through their various arcs.

The suspension systems of successful cars varied in detail, materials and complication but not in principle. Even the advanced and esoteric world of Active Suspension (see Chapter 6) was, in essence, exactly what has just been described. The only difference was that the coil and damper had been combined and given a new lease of life through a remote and virtually instantaneously adjustable hydraulic system. The mystery was, given the same basic layout, why did not all conventional systems work with the same degree of success? There is, at least for the time being, no answer to that. The number of variables is so great, with every alteration causing something else to alter, and so on and so on down the line, that as yet there are not enough hours in a racing day, week or season, even with computer assistance, to get it all together to a state of perfection. And even that statement assumes some definition of 'perfection', which happens to be lacking.

In the real world, designers and constructors are continually forced to strike a balance between conflicting targets. One man's idea of 'optimum' will rarely be that of another. Needless to say, some clearly get it more right than others, while the line between success and failure grows ever more fine. But the lure and challenge of being the best in the world, particularly at a Grand Epreuve or Le Mans, or Indianapolis are more than enough to ensure a long line of hopeful aspirants. Ahead of the reader lie no magic solutions, only a path of sorts through the jungle. To the would-be designer, a student of the art, the knowledgeable paddock prowler, or anyone else fascinated by the deceptive simplicity of Grand Prix, Le Mans and Indy cars all that follows is dedicated.

Suspension does not work in isolation any more than any other part of a racing vehicle. It cannot be mounted where the driver will sit or the crankshaft will revolve. Pullrods might be impossible to employ due to a lack of a point of sufficient strength on which to mount the necessary rockers. Space will always be at a premium, and available materials may limit what can be done though this will hardly affect those at the top of the tree. They operate in a world of effectively unlimited money just so long

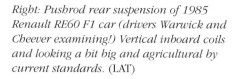

*Above: 1984 Renault RE50 F1 car front
pullrod suspension.*

*Right: Pushrod rear suspension of 1985
Renault RE60 F1 car (drivers Warwick and
Cheever examining!) Vertical inboard coils
and looking a bit big and agricultural by
current standards.* (LAT)

as they can balance on the edge of the financial precipice. Fall over the edge and they
are back to mild steel, glass fibre mouldings and second-hand rubber.

Strength and reliability with minimum weight are vital. Protection from heat may
prove essential. Complicated linkage with inevitable risk of failure may be forced upon
a designer. Some degree of alteration may save a team in mid season. Accessibility with
its partner, speed of replacement, may save a team in mid race (at least in endurance
events).

Though now growing rare, a radical technical change such as from cross-ply to
radial tyre could demand not only totally new suspension geometry, rather than simple
adjustments to increase static negative camber for radials, but a new chassis to accept
that suspension.

Aerodynamics can double or triple the weight of the car at high speeds, and
consequently the physical loads being fed into many components.

But all of these are still only peripheral complications to what is the heart of the
matter: getting the racing car to handle to the satisfaction of the best drivers in the
world. You might reasonably ask: 'What about the tyre, surely that is a vital aspect?'
Correct, but a separate subject: a good tyre will partially redeem poor suspension and
good suspension will be handicapped by an inferior tyre.

Top designers are not in search of half measures or less than the best that may be
achieved. That best must have at some future date things no more conceivable to us
than was the electric chair to Henry VIII. The developments of the future can be of no
help now. 'State of the art' is still an apt if somewhat glossy description of the best at
the time. Someone, somewhere is forever edging it forward.

It could be you.

Chapter 2

The springing medium

... springs and things

SUSPENSION BY DEFINITION means the vehicle is riding or hanging on something with give. It has to have some flexibility and a great deal of ingenuity has been expended on a wide variety of materials and methods of employing them over the years. As sci-fi's anti-gravity suspensors are not yet with us (though even these may appear within the lifetime of a schoolboy reader) we will examine those that are and the route that left the ubiquitous coil in the lead.

Leaf springs

This has supported and is still supporting a large part of the vehicle world from the milk float to the passenger car and commercial van and is seen on dozens of historic racing cars in our sphere. Ideas that really work are very often linked to the technology and materials existing at the time of their conception. They then become inextricably enmeshed in the industrial development of following years. The working

Rear suspension of 2006 Gould GR55. An interesting comparison with Renault on previous page. Note linear sensor rods checking coil/damper unit movement. (Gould)

Figure 2-1 *Leaf springs support the back end of the majority of road cars of all nations. This is an example of the rear leaf springs from a typical British contemporary mass-produced family car, the Ford Escort.*

1. Rubber bump stop; 2. Bump stop bracket; 3. 'U' bolts; 4. Nut; 5. Locking washer; 6. Shackle bar and stud; 7. Bushes; 8. Nut; 9. Locking washer; 10. Shackle bar and stud; 11. Insert; 12. Clamp insulator; 13. Clamp; 14. Rivet; 15. Nut; 16. 'U' bolt plate; 17. Nut; 18. Bolt; 19. Bush; 20. Locking washer; 21. Nut; 22. Rivet; 23. Clamp; 24. Clamp insulator; 25. Spring leaf; 26. Special bolt; 27. Spring assembly.

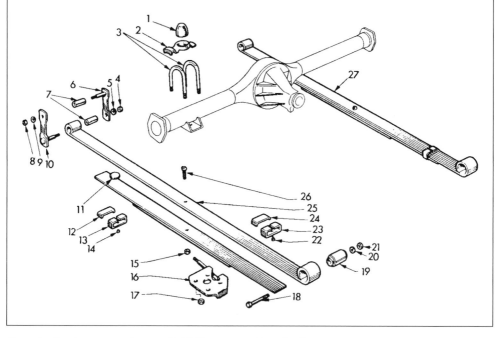

Front leaf spring suspension on 1934 Maserati 8CM Grand Prix car. Note rearward torque link to prevent leaf spring wind-up – ie, going 'S'-shaped under braking loads.

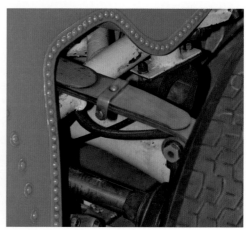

Rear leaf spring suspension on Maserati 250F Grand Prix car.

Designer John Cooper with one of his early/mid-fifties Cooper 500cc racers, using front and rear leaf-spring suspension. Visibly an ordinary road – probably Surbiton bypass where Cooper production was regularly tested! (LAT)

of iron and later steel had been known to man for centuries, and technically there are great similarities between a sword or rapier blade of the first quality and the resilient leaves of a cart spring. Lay such a blade on its side with an attachment bracket of some sort at either end, tie an axle to its centre and we could be looking at a stagecoach or a Ford Escort or even a late '60s Grand Prix car.

The cart spring had the early advantage of being able to be made by a blacksmith from available strips of steel and it had the incomparable plus of doing more than one job at once. This is still one aim of any good designer. The leaf spring if required located the axle in all three planes – fore and aft, side to side and when correctly tailored to its load, up and down as well. Crude as it might appear, it proved capable of very considerable refinement including multiple leaves, variable length and tapered leaves and if required even double and triple spring rate (for strength) could be achieved by differently arced leaves that only came into operation after a known amount of deflection.

The leaf spring's early use in competition appears to have pioneered at least two other refinements that had nothing to do with the quality of the metal. In the days when oil resistant rubber did not exist the springs were wrapped in neatly fitting leather gaiters filled with grease which both extended life and kept their rate constant. They could also be tightly cord bound which tended to put the rate up, stiffening the car and, in the days when a lot of racing and sports car roadholding came from flex in the chassis, perhaps improving its performance.

Sometimes the leaf spring was transverse, trapped in the middle (Austin Seven, Ford Prefect, Cooper Formula One), sometimes it was quarter elliptic, trapped at one end while the other flexed (Austin Seven rear). But always, commercially, it was cheap despite the weight of a lot of raw material. This latter, major, handicap may yet be eliminated by the use of composite materials. Plastic laminates radically reduce the weight. Costs and the problem of protection from stone damage are currently keeping them off the road car, but both would be irrelevant in racing terms.

A bigger barrier is the shape of such a spring and finding the space for a really compact installation with a low centre of gravity.

Torsion bars

These are a simple length of steel tube, bar or rod; in rod form, the equivalent of a coil spring before it has been coiled. Given suitable support at each end it will twist under a given load by a precise and calculable amount. At first sight even simpler to make than the leaf spring, it cannot achieve the multiple location tasks of the leaf. This, combined with a need for a high quality material extremely closely controlled on diameter, plus bearings, end fixings and lever arms made it a relatively late starter.

Yet it is more predictable and 'pure' in how it will perform, is unexposed to wear (if you don't count its molecular structure creaking and groaning and protesting) and appears easy to install. Or is it? Whether a round bar, square, laminated in strips, a tube or even a tube within a tube, it needs very strong anchor points, bearings in which to rotate and a lever of some sort through which it can be twisted under load. It does not want to contribute much to the vehicle design in other ways, and demands links all of its own to the wheels or axles.

Two main approaches to torsion bar links are generally used. With wishbones, the bar runs fore and aft and is joined (splined, clamped or welded) to the inboard end of the top or bottom wishbone. Thus the wheel may only rise or fall by twisting the bar

Figure 2-2 *The classic example of the torsion bar – VW Beetle rear suspension. The diagram shows:*

1. Axle shaft nut; 2. Brake drum; 3. Bearing retainer; 4. Oil thrower; 5. Oil seal; 6. Spacer (outer); 7. 'O' ring; 8. Shim washer; 9. 'O' ring; 10. Bearing; 11. Spacer (inner); 12. Pin (locating bearing housing to tube); 13. Bearing housing; 14. Bump stop bracket; 15. Bump stop; 16. Gaiter; 17. Axle tube retainer; 18. Axle tube; 19. Axle shaft; 20. Gasket; 21. Retainer plate; 22. Support bush; 23. Spring plate; 24. Torsion bar; 25. Damper.

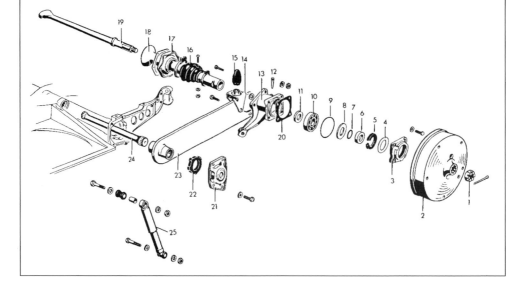

in its length. Mounting the bar across the car demands some sort of swinging link down to the axle/wheel, whether independent or solid. All this tends to induce complication, weight and cost. Cost horrifies the major manufacturer and weight appals the racing car builder, though the VW Beetle employed torsion bars, as did Auto Union, Mercedes and Porsche. Colin Chapman cunningly got the bar length he required into half the space by 'doubling back' a tubular one within itself. Unhappily it did not permit rapid or easy alteration, a severe handicap under race pressures. While factory development engineers can spend months getting it right for a road car, racing engineers do not have that time. Different circuits often demand radical changes; there are no optimum settings for a full season: spring rates are still being continually varied.

Consequently, torsion bars had a short life with Team Lotus and, one might say, no life at all when Porsche's previous commitment to bars was totally abandoned in the early Sixties for its World Championship Sports-Prototypes in favour of coils all round. Having said that, we now see a new lease of life for bars, very compactly employed by Barnard (Ferrari) and Head (Williams). With the banning of Active, both have used a similar approach of a tiny ultra-short bar acting both as spring and 'axle' of the bellcrank in a pushrod system.

Rubber

At first sight rubber is the perfect suspension medium. It can be compact, is controllable and light for the quantity needed, with a great deal of technical know how on its employment available. But…

Figure 2-3 *Rubber suspension, parts one and two. Early in 1963 a Cooper Formula Junior Single Seater appeared with Hydrolastic suspension but the experiment was not a success.*

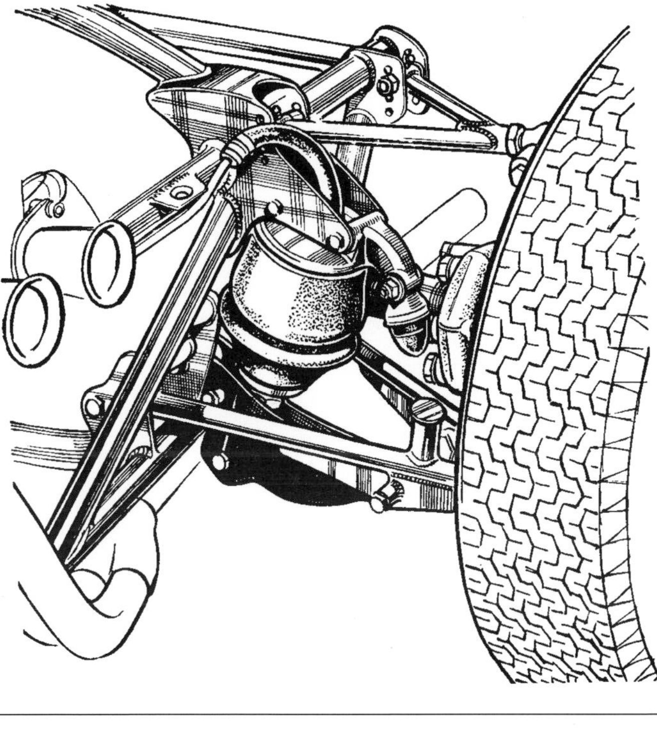

Figure 2-4 *Mini front suspension – another classic, with rubber cone springs. The diagram shows:*

1. Lower arm pivot pin; 2. Bushes; 3. Locknut; 4. Lower suspension arm; 5. Dust cover; 6. Ball-pin retainer; 7. Ball-pin; 8. Ball-seat; 9. Spring; 10. Shims; 11. Lockwasher; 12. Grease nipple; 13. Swivel hub; 14. Ring dowel; 15. Steering arm; 16. Lockwasher; 17. Retaining plate; 18. Thrust collar; 19. Sealing rings; 20. Upper arm pivot shaft; 21. Thrust washer; 22. Needle roller bearings; 23. Upper suspension arm; 24. Grease nipple; 25. Rebound buffer; 26. Bump buffer; 27. Rubber cone spring; 28. Cone strut; 29. Spacer; 30. Dust cover; 31. Knuckle; 32. Ball socket; 33. Shock absorber; 34. Upper mounting bracket; 35. Upper bush; 36. Sleeve; 37. Distance piece; 38. Locknut; 39. Tie-bar; 40. Tie-bar bushes; 41. Cup washer; 42. Locknut.

The rubber cone (27) was compressed by the top suspension arm (23) through a ball-ended steel knuckle (31) and metal cone (28). Plenty have run with little or no trouble for 50 or more years – impressive.

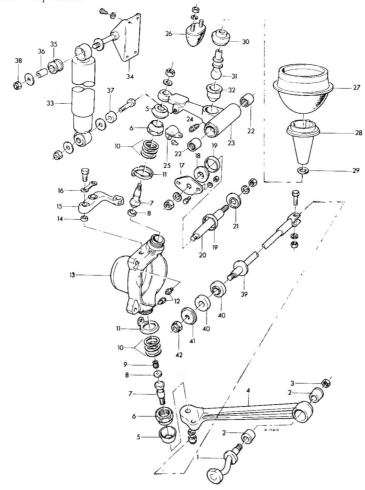

Figure 2-5 *However, one of the author's Terrapin single seaters used a unique 'rubber band' rear suspension, with success.*

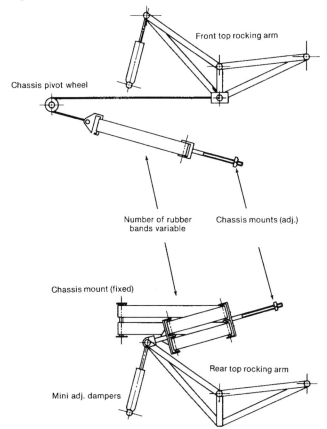

Front top rocking arm

Chassis pivot wheel

Number of rubber
bands variable

Chassis mounts (adj.)

Chassis mount (fixed)

Rear top rocking arm

Mini adj. dampers

Hesketh had a brief flirtation using rubber blocks that were barely more than massive bump stops and soon retreated. Minis are of course the classic example but even the great Issigonis had to devise leverages of the order of 5:1 because the rubber doughnuts of Alex Moulton, despite sophisticated contours and steel inserts permitted only minimal distortion. High leverages usually mean extra weight in the links and extra strength in the leverage points. Quite brilliant design (betrayed somewhat at the rear by production parts that guaranteed rust failure after a depressingly short period of time) overcame this for the Mini but an attempt by Cooper to adapt the Mini doughnuts for an early sixties Formula Junior car was barely more than a 'Racing Car Show special'.

Rubber has had no serious top level development, not because it would not work but probably because the steel coil spring won the battle for reasons we shall investigate in due course. It has been left to various stalwarts of the 750 Motor Club, Britain's grass roots source of a host of brains in the international race car design firmament, to employ rubber in a variety of ways. My own Terrapin Mk7 hillclimb car used Pirelli seat webbing (and Pirelli seat technology) in tension as does Reverend Barry Whitehead's RBS 4, a very successful club single-seater racing car. He has continued development through RBS 5, 6, and 7 is on the drawing board.

Employing rubber makes adjustment of both rate and ride height relatively simple. Using a light and adaptable wire and pulley system allows a designer to put the spring exactly where he wishes – a privilege still denied to the users of coils.

Air

Since it is all around us and free of charge, air appears to have quite a bit going for it, and it would seem at first to be a near ideal solution to the problem of springing. It has in fact worked well in commercial applications, particularly big trucks and buses operating on bad surfaces rather than the very good roads general throughout much of Europe and the USA. It also has natural rising rate.

The two major shortcomings of air springs are the heat generated under continual compression and the need to keep the unit or strut containing the air topped up to the correct pressures if they are not to have variability. Air compressors, even small alloy ones, are dead weight and power stealers. Seals, piping, pistons and their operating rods, and special valves all complicate the issue and add still more weight. Rubber bags, readily stowable under a double decker bus, pose serious locational difficulties in a single seater racing car.

Used as a spring, air needs damper control just like any other spring and the designer is then faced with the need for a separate yet similar unit using oil or a combined air/oil damper-cum-spring that has even more complexity and potential for trouble. Citroën has tamed this approach for road use and such a unit was the basis of the suspension that first graced the problem-dogged BRM V16 Grand Prix car of the early Fifties. We should not ignore the fact that Bilstein use precisely this union of air and oil with great success, but in dampers which are sealed and augment a leaf or coil spring that takes the actual suspension loads and forces. All in all, air seems more trouble than it is worth at present but it is not inconceivable that future 'active' suspension systems might find it has advantages over oil.

Oil

Oil has for long been the only fluid used for dampers and was adopted by Lotus to do this together with the job of the coil spring in the world's first computer controlled race car suspension system, the 'Active' system regularly raced on the team's 1987 99T Grand Prix car. Proving a considerable success, active suspension represented such a

Ayrton Senna on his way to winning the 1987 Monaco Grand Prix in the active suspension Lotus 99T. No detectable roll despite driver 'kerbing' over angled concrete of the corner's inner radius. (LAT)

mega-leap that it is dealt with fully in a complete chapter. Just like turbocharged race engines, active suspension was treated with everything from caution to derision until the day it started winning. But even before Senna's Honda-Lotus won the 1987 Monaco Grand Prix Williams publicly and McLaren privately had been at work on not dissimilar approaches, also employing oil as the springing medium.

Coil springs
So at last we come to the ubiquitous, near universal in racing, coil spring. Why and how has it achieved this position of quiet superiority over every challenger after nearly

Rear suspension coil-spring set-up on 1961 Lotus 18 Climax in which Stirling Moss won 1961 Monaco Grand Prix.

a century of racing car development? The answer lies in a list of virtues that seem to go on and on – it is light, compact, inexpensive, variable in rate, length and diameter, friction free and there is a mass of knowledge concerning its manufacture and use. What more could a designer ask?

The coil spring is normally made from a high quality round steel bar with an extremely accurate outside diameter. Heated, the rod can then be wound into equal coils, tapered, given varied diameter or spacing on the coils all to achieve different results in use. Final heat treatment gives it extreme resistance against failure or deformation in use, and its reliability is such that it is a 'fit and forget' part on literally millions of road cars.

Using the springing medium

Having chosen a springing medium, it remains to decide how best to use it and what form the spring will take; what will provide its specification be it coil, leaf, a rubber block or an oil strut governed by a computer chip. At least in its initial stages, this design problem is a relatively simple one governed by three factors:

a. The running ground clearance of the vehicle
b. The amount of suspension movement that is either required or can be tolerated
c. The wheel frequency that will provide or deal with a) and b) above.

Note that there has been no reference as yet to 'spring rate' – perhaps the commonest term bandied about in any discussion on suspension – as this is an end result, not a starting point in any design. In itself the rate – or strength if you prefer – is meaningless as it is totally modified by two things: the sprung weight of the vehicle and the leverage exerted by the suspension.

Low ground clearance causing sparking on 1990 Ferrari 641 F1 car. Replaceable lightweight titanium rubbing blocks supplied the dramatic fireworks, while protecting the car's underside from potentially disastrous damage. (LAT)

Low ground clearance on Audi R8 and almost no apparent suspension movement despite a violent inner 'rumble strip' of concrete teeth. (LAT)

The usual way of defining the strength of a spring in Imperial measurement is 'lbs per in of crush', or the weight needed to compress or deflect the spring one inch. Thus, a '150 lb/in' coil shortens by one inch under a load of 150 pounds. Metric units will be more familiar to many readers and are only ignored here due to the inflexibility of the author's well set mind ...

While ground clearance and suspension movement or length of wheel travel are definable by anyone who can read a tape measure or ruler, wheel frequency is slightly more complex. Quoted in Cycles per Minute (CPM) or Cycles per Second (hertz – Hz) it is the natural interval at which the wheel (or the vehicle to which it is attached) will bounce up and down without damping or friction in the suspension mountings. It can range from 50/60 CPM for big, softly sprung saloons to 400–500 CPM for a Formula One wing car at low speed and is covered in much more detail, together with relevant formulae in Chapter Eight.

So we can now retrace our steps to A and B above. Taking ground clearance first, this has been coming down and down with every passing year. The 'ultra low' racing cars of the Sixties with around 3.0 in clearance looked ridiculous in the Eighties when a Formula Ford car might have a setting of 1.75 in at the front and 2.75 in at the rear, even lower in the Nineties, while Formula One cars are now well under 1.0 in largely for aerodynamic reasons. Air flowing under the car spells trouble and drag, while discouraging the flow helps the creation of negative pressure beneath the car – downforce. So the needle noses of Formula One cars want to creep ever nearer the deck while rule makers raise and raise the permitted minimums, and the full width noses of Sports-Prototypes use splitters or scrapers as well as low clearances to help ensure that as much air as possible goes over the top rather than underneath.

Such tiny clearances dictate minimal suspension movement or the rubbing plates (or, worse still, the composite material of the tub or the rivets holding on the undertray) are all too soon seriously attacked by the tarmac as the full effect of downforce and, in the early stages, full tanks push the car nearer to the road. It is therefore clear why there are cries of distress and bitter complaint from teams when they arrive at courses with less than billiard table surfaces; particularly the American street circuits. A car designed from scratch for a specific ride height will have all sorts of problems if this has to be increased, as will become clearer in the following chapter.

Although you often see and hear the phrase 'put the packers in' an increase in ride height is more usually achieved by screwing up the threaded bottom collars that lie beneath the coils. In fact, this does not affect either the spring rate or the wheel frequency as is occasionally thought but it does affect both camber, the position of the wishbones in their arcs of movement and in consequence what the wheel will do in its new position of bump and droop. And these are highly likely to be bad news for driver and team, while adding insult to injury by taking time to adjust and reset. Packers are more likely employed to limit the stroke of the damper and reduce chances of grounding. The car goes solid before hitting the ground.

Our factors A and B are two sides of the same coin. If ground clearance will permit it, the more movement that can be permitted in the spring the more the designer can vary spring rates, reduce shock loadings into the chassis or tub and increase the potential life of all the suspension components. However, if the suspension has to operate within very small wheel movement distances (as with contemporary Formula One and Sports-Prototype cars) refinements including anti-dive and rising rate and bump stops will be needed to deal with the increases in loads or weight distribution under conditions of heavy braking or full tanks and these will be discussed in more detail at a later stage.

There are two other aspects of springing that come into action only when circumstances warrant it – the bump stop and the anti-roll bar. Bump stops can vary

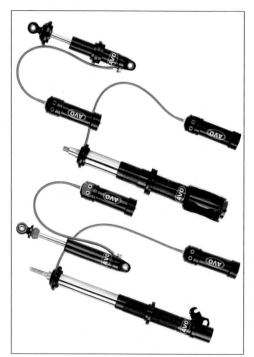

Left: AVO dampers with remote reservoirs. (AVO)

Below: An excellent view of what for many years was a classic anti-roll bar installation. Bent steel tube in chassis mounting blocks with a drop-link at each end to a lower wishbone or the upright itself.

from something looking like a kitchen doorstop designed only to prevent a damper closing totally and wrecking its delicate internal valving, to a most sophisticated rubber or plastic moulding that will provide known reactions to being crushed. Naturally, it is the latter which merits, and must have, real consideration. No driver or designer wants the rate of the suspension and wheel frequency to ascend into the stratosphere or go virtually solid in tiny fractions of an inch. It produces an instantaneous overload of the tyre on that corner and over or understeer to a gross degree.

Clearly, there is more than meets the eye to a bump stop and the two most commonly seen types are Silasto, an orange coloured plastic foam moulding with rising rate (ie, it gets stiffer the more it is crushed) and Aeon rubbers of varying shapes, hollow moulded internally which can provide a range of differing characteristics. Other specialised companies are moving into the field, particularly as the saloon car designer has special problems with violent variations in vehicle weight and load in varying places within the wheelbase plus a high comfort requirement, making race car criteria look relatively simple.

And so to the anti-roll bar, much misunderstood because it is not only difficult to understand precisely what it is doing a lot of the time, but also is a tricky device to install well, to control and vary, and to measure when the chassis or tub to which it is attached can never be totally stiff. Indeed, the chassis may well be so lacking in rigidity that the bar will override it and contribute nothing whatever to the suspension. Given that any decent racing car should have as rigid a chassis as technically possible, the anti-roll bar will normally do nothing when the vehicle is travelling in a straight line. In a corner any vehicle will lean outwards to some degree, whether it is a current Grand Prix car or a Citroën 2CV. The bar, normally a length of steel tube rather than a solid bar for various reasons, then begins to operate in twist.

Rear suspension of 2002 Williams FW24. Note the tiny rear anti-roll bar operated by adjustable links from the pushrod-operated bellcranks. (David Tremayne)

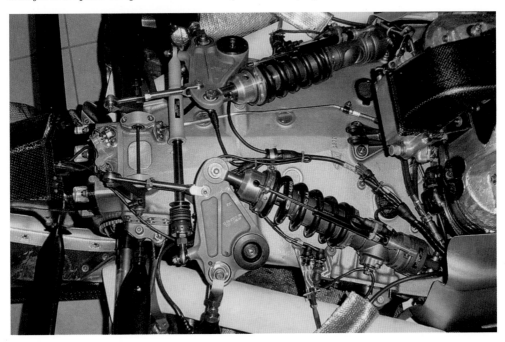

The anti-roll bar does three things. Firstly, with its connections to the suspension on each side, it resists roll: the suspension is being asked to allow rise at the outer wheel and fall at the inner but this cannot be achieved without twisting the bar. Secondly, the bar starts acting like an extra spring added to the existing ones, particularly at the outer wheel. Thirdly, it begins moving weight off the inner tyre onto the outer one, and the combined efforts of front and rear bars can move weight off the front onto the rear, and vice versa in any dynamic situation.

What is often not realised is that the anti-roll bar is a very powerful instrument and correctly dimensioned and fitted it can provide effects five or ten times greater than simply fitting stiffer springs. It has a rate calculable in lb/in and the car sees it partially as an extra spring. For those wishing to fit, design or redesign an anti-roll bar there is very full explanation in Chapter Eight including methods of calculation with the necessary formulae courtesy of David Gould, then an amateur designer/builder whose first honeycomb monocoque car took the British Hillclimb Championship outright in its debut season with anti-roll bars of his own calculation front and rear.

It is not always fully understood that the stiffest or most roll resistant end of the car receives the major part of any weight transfer. The weight can and does move diagonally and is the basis of 'tuning' a car to handle in a particular way.

It is interesting to consider whether the recent apparent total disappearance of a rear bar from certain Formula One cars indicates they are willing to accept the major weight transfer onto the outer front wheel, in search of increased rear grip at any cost?

Leaving such detail aside, the bar for many years was considered as a simple approach to under/oversteer problems and handling balance. Too much oversteer, or a need for more understeer and you slacked the rear bar, reducing the work the outer wheel had to do and consequently its slip angle, or else you stiffened the front bar, overworked the front tyre and made it slide a little on an increased slip angle.

The fact that an anti-roll bar is widely employed on road cars at the front to promote understeer and less sensitivity en route to the shops (often taking the form of an integral member of the front suspension to save cost and weight) strengthens the widely held view of what it does. However, in racing the approach can well be reversed. Stiffening the front bar can cure understeer, not make it worse, and vice-versa. There seem to be at least three possible explanations for this.

Firstly, the fact that racing tyres have made giant steps in recent years means that a given car might not be fully utilising, for instance, its front tyres. To put more load into them can raise the temperature, alter the contact patch shape or pressure distribution and simply improve grip rather than reducing it. Secondly, the car may be so badly out of balance in terms of the coils and bars fitted that one end or the other is taking a totally disproportionate amount of the anti-roll resistance of the vehicle as a whole. Without knowing it in precise terms, stiffening or softening bars may simply be balancing things out and helping the suspension work properly. Thirdly, there may be an aspect of the design that means that only the bar at one end is working properly, or at all.

While it might be easy to scoff that such things are impossible at top professional level, an analysis of one such vehicle showed that 81% of the car's total roll resistance was on the back, 19% on the front. Not only did this seem wrong but massive alterations to a more equitable split transformed handling – so it can happen.

In constructional terms one might say bars began life as tubes or rods bent at from 50–90 degrees at each end, mounted in alloy or nylon blocks on the chassis with links down to the bottom wishbones. These links normally had a slider so that the leverage being applied to the bent end could be varied. A major step which allowed anti-roll bars to become infinitely more precise and powerful was inboard suspension – the removal of the coil to a position where it was operated within the confines of the chassis by a

Figure 2-6 *Cockpit-adjustable anti-roll bar. The arm can be rotated by the driver via a simple linkage and is stiffest when the wide face is vertical and softest when it is horizontal. The bar mounts on the chassis and links to the suspension in the normal manner.*

Full Soft

Full Stiff

(B)   **PLAN VIEW**   (A)

90°

(A)

(B)

END VIEW   **SIDE VIEW**

Blade-type front anti-roll bar on BRM P578.

Figure 2-7 *The graph provides stiffness comparisons between solid and tubular bars while below it is one method of calculating anti-roll bar stiffness,* courtesy of Mike Pilbeam.

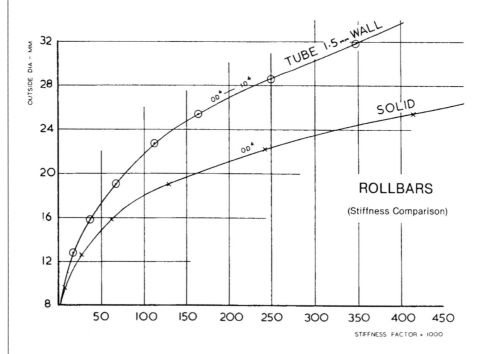

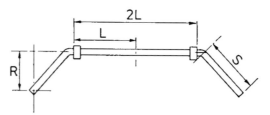

T = TRACK (INS)
K = FRACTIONAL LEVER ARM RATIO
$$\left(\frac{\text{MOVEMENT AT ANTI ROLLBAR PICKUP}}{\text{MOVEMENT AT WHEEL}} \right)$$
d = BAR DIAMETER (INS)
R = EFFECTIVE ARM LENGTH
L = HALF LENGTH OF BAR
S = LENGTH OF LEVER ARM
Q = STIFFNESS IN LB/INS PER DEGREE OF VEHICLE ROLL

$$Q = \frac{10^4 \times T^2 \times K^2 \times d^4}{R^2 \times L}$$

rocker arm of some type. What this made possible was a short, accurately dimensioned bar or tube rigidly mounted, without overhang and in proper bearings. The link to the suspension became short, convenient and permitted use of a blade adjuster.

A blade adjuster is a device of great subtlety, and of considerable difficulty to copy or assess, except by bolting them empirically to the bench and hanging a suitably calibrated spring balance on the end. The blade resembles a slice off a steel ruler. On edge it is rigid while flat it can be bent relatively easily. At intermediate positions (rotated via a spanner or a cockpit-adjustable remote control) it imparts a complex variable into the basic torsional strength of the bar. The blades can be used at both ends, or singly with a non-flexible version at the opposite end. The blades are tapered, in one or both planes, and sometimes stepped in thickness. By the nature of their installation they tend to skew as well as bend under load so that what is actually happening may well be calculable, but not by me!

A simple jig bolted to a really solid bench will allow a bar to be twisted with known loads – long lever fixed to one end and bathroom scales on the other – the results being plotted onto graph paper. Doing this simple experiment with an 'old fashioned' bent tube bar accorded very closely indeed with the calculated figures for its torsional stiffness. It was assumed that the bent ends were rigid, while a blade type would need a series of experiments with the blade adjusted to varying known angles.

Another aspect of the inboard linked bar is that it can be changed very conveniently and rapidly indeed. By making the outboard mountings, for instance, with a common sized spigot into a small bearing, a new and totally different dimensioned bar may be inserted without any other alteration. Various bars can be calculated and made at leisure, removing another unknown or variable on test. Knowing what a bar is doing, or what forces it is exerting is quite a different matter to knowing what you want it to

Gas dampers produced by Monroe with remote cylinders were used in Formula One by Williams on their 1986 FW11 shown below. Gas dampers were pioneered in Grand Prix racing by Renault working with de Carbon. Outside Formula One, Spax was and is a major supplier of competition gas dampers. A view of the internal design of a Spax unit appears on page 176. (LAT)

exert, under what degree of deflection and with what relationship to its opposite number at the other end of the car.

In the broadest possible terms any vehicle will have: A) a roll couple, and B) a total roll resistance and A/B will give a theoretical roll angle in a 1 G corner and for a variety of reasons the smaller the angle (probably) the better.

Formula One cars running without a rear bar also infers that some designers have obtained sufficient roll resistance from coils alone, eliminating another troublesome variable while persuading their chassis to perform well without the 'fine tune' abilities of a bar. This is not as unlikely as it sounds, for an excellent and reliable guide to the handling performance of a car has, for some considerable time, been that one near its best will be sensitive to small anti-roll bar adjustments. If it requires or is not even responsive to large adjustments, something else is badly wrong, needing to be located and corrected.

As tyres have virtually taken over a greater and greater part of the function of the suspension having flex and frequencies of their own (a major and separate study) they have permitted a further stiffening of springs especially on really good surfaces. Dampers, while being an integral part of any suspension system are not strictly speaking part of the springing, although a totally vital control on it, so they are covered in Chapter Nine.

So we come to 'rising and falling rate' or a suspension with characteristics in the spring or linkages that cause it to become harder or softer when loads are fed in. A moment of reflection will indicate that – at least in racing – there are a number of situations in which you need things to be harder with less deflection, but very few other than emptying tanks when extra softness is required.

To be more accurate, a rising rate is aimed at either keeping the wheel frequency steady or raising it in a controlled fashion. To do this, the spring rate must be varied. Two simple examples of what happens if you do not have it are: i) under heavy braking, weight transfer onto the front wheels causes the nose of the car to be squashed down and possibly scrape on the ground; ii) downforce increases the effective weight of the car, forcing it nearer the ground in a variable manner, normally linked to speed – the faster the car travels the greater the downforce and the lower it runs. In both cases suspension link movement takes place and wheel/tyre angle to the road is affected to a greater or lesser degree. And when you had Nigel Mansell 20 years ago on record suggesting that a variation of 1/8th inch in the ride height of his (1987) Williams FW11 could well be worth the gain or loss of 100 lb of downforce, the importance of trying to stabilise ride height as far as possible is obvious.

Putting aside Lotus 'Active ride', one of the paramount duties of which is to maintain a constant ride height under all conditions, much can be done through the coil, through the links or a combination of both. Taking the coil first, 'rising rate' is very often 'dual rate' – a simpler and poorer version. These are coils that have been more closely wound at one end in such a way that after a certain load has been applied they close up and go coilbound. The remaining coils becoming a shorter spring with a higher rate. The proper, more sophisticated, more difficult to calculate and manufacture and thus expensive ways are either to have coils variably wound or of tapered wire. In the former case the gaps between the coils reduce bit by bit in regular increments so that one coil at a time goes solid against its neighbour, steadily reducing the effective length and increasing the rate. In the latter case the wire from which the coil is made is tapered before it is wound. The thinnest and weakest parts go coilbound first, again producing a steady increase.

A combination of a steady rate coil and a progressive bump stop that will deal with the early, heavily loaded laps is a not an uncommon compromise. And it is as well to

The multiple Le Mans winning Porsche 956/962 mounted its spring/damper units in a vee above its transaxle and outboard at the front where it utilised progressive rate springs. Formed from titanium, these featured a variable wire diameter and a variable wind (and cost a fortune).

remember at the design stage that every suspension with a coil spring/damper unit leaning inwards from the bottom wishbone has modest but built-in falling rate with all its handicaps. Getting rid of this drawback was, initially a better argument for going inboard with rocking arms than any supposed help to the drag factor of a single seater racing car. The reasons are both geometric and aerodynamic.

The forces that a bottom link can exert upwards onto the coil are at their maximum when the two are at right angles to each other. The crudest of pencil sketches will show this. But as soon as that angle begins reducing when the coil begins to lean inwards the spring suffers a steadily increasing disadvantage. It is compressed less for given wheel movement, can only exert less force because of this and is seen by the

The latest 2006 Le Mans challenger from Audi, the diesel-powered R10 TDI has yet to reveal the secrets of its suspension design. (Audi)

Figure 2-8 *Unusual spring/damper mountings. Some years ago the McLaren M19 featured unusual suspension linkages to provide progressive spring rate increasing with the deflection of the wheel, as this diagram illustrates.*

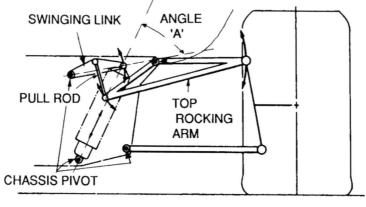

wheel as steadily weaker. The effect is very small to about 15 degrees of inclination, appreciable by 25 degrees and very seriously affecting wheel frequency by 40 degrees.

This is not to deny that the all conquering mid-Eighties Porsche 956/962 Group C car employed the traditional arrangement at the front. However, Porsche fitted a very sophisticated coil with variable wind and variable wire diameter in titanium costing around $12,000 a set at last enquiry, so it may well be more economic in the long run to lay out a suspension system to do the job for you.

That happens to be one advantage that pull/pushrod systems offer. As they all operate through a rocker of some type to reach the coil spring/damper unit correct design, with critical angles more than 90 degrees but closing and/or less than 90 degrees but opening and giving the coil an advantage over the wheel. McLaren employed this at a very early stage but for some reason abandoned it. On balance a pushrod system, if the structure of the car permits it, is likely to give fewer difficulties in achieving the objective, and is now almost universal in Formula One.

Surrounded by rockers and variously inclined units in the world of mid-Eighties Group C, ART's Tony Southgate took an elegantly simple approach at the rear when commissioned to produce a Sports-Prototype for the TWR organisation on behalf of Jaguar. The 'Jaguar XJR-7' had an alloy beam centrally mounted on the gearbox and long enough to reach to just inside each rear tyre. This was then triangulated downwards, back to the gearbox with a rod that gave a first impression that Southgate had employed a pullrod technique. He had not. Southgate mounted the spring/damper units vertically outboard, feeding the loads into the ends of the alloy beam. That gave him not only purity of motion with the minimum of trouble but also superb accessibility permitting the most rapid changes of unit, assuming only that the mechanics wear asbestos gloves for the job! While a requirement of such an approach is that the engine/gearbox unit must be able to accept the large twisting loads fed into it, the V12 block employed by TWR presumably could and did.

Southgate's later approach to the even more successful R8 for Audi can be found in Chapter 7.

Chapter 3

Location

... hanging it all on

EXCEPT TO THE MOST CASUAL and uninterested observer, there is clearly more than immediately meets the eye about the way the wheel and tyre are connected to the rest of a racing car. It is invisible anyway in a Sports-Prototype unless you have an entry to the pits during practice rather than the race, and even a full and unrestricted view of a Formula One car seems to tell one barely more.

Superficially, they all share remarkable similarities and some idea of what is happening once the vehicle is on the move, with the massive sideways forces of high speed cornering compressing, twisting and attempting to bend deceptively slender links, is needed if one is to have even a slight appreciation of the subtleties, compromises and audacities employed.

Bleeding the brakes of the 2002 Ferrari F2002 reveals much of the layout and complex load paths of the gearbox/rear suspension/rear wing assembly. (sutton-images.com)

A car leans outwards on corners and attempts to throw its occupants onto the pavement – as even WTCC racing drivers know (LAT) ...

As all drivers, spectators and aged back-seat passengers know, a car normally leans outwards on corners and attempts to throw its occupants onto the pavement. A full harness, wrap-round seats, and a lower centre of gravity will help make the sideways G-forces tolerable or to be ignored.

Roll angle, at the time of writing, appears to have been virtually eliminated in F1, not to mention pretty microscopic even in saloon cars as shown above. Apart from such complexity being vulnerable to failure and a source of extra weight, it may be that roll, however small, is a tiny but vital part of how a driver functions, especially at the highest level of sensitivity of the dozen or so best men in the world.

Suffice to say where we still have roll its effects are fundamental to what a car does in a corner. Being a projectile that needs relatively little skill to conduct in a straight line, the corners become the key and crux of success. At the heart of it all is the roll centre. As this is both invisible and prone to move about in various ways, we will try to define it as best we may.

Looked at from head on, a cornering vehicle is not only rolling but this rotation is clearly about some point or other in space. This being a situation where a picture is worth the proverbial thousand words, the geometric and static location of the roll centre for a variety of axle links and designs, and how it is plotted are shown in the accompanying diagram.

Figure 3-1 *Location of the static roll centre (RC) in various types of suspension.*

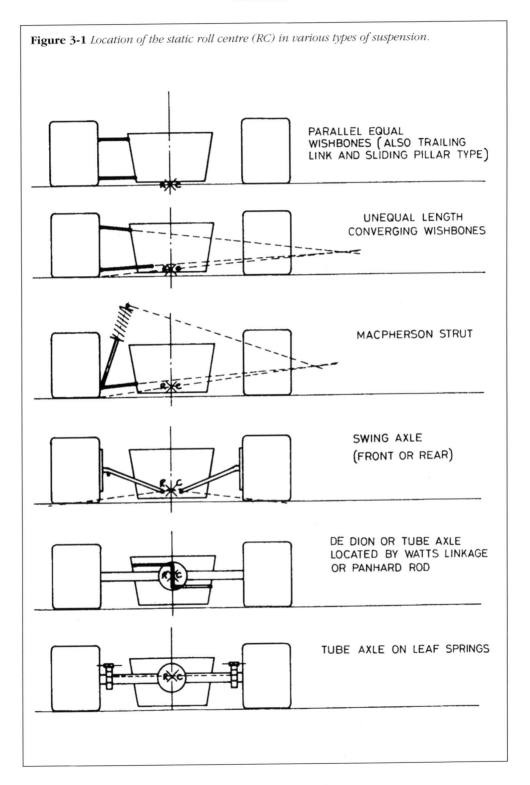

PARALLEL EQUAL WISHBONES (ALSO TRAILING LINK AND SLIDING PILLAR TYPE)

UNEQUAL LENGTH CONVERGING WISHBONES

MACPHERSON STRUT

SWING AXLE (FRONT OR REAR)

DE DION OR TUBE AXLE LOCATED BY WATTS LINKAGE OR PANHARD ROD

TUBE AXLE ON LEAF SPRINGS

Figure 3-2 *Design of the purest form of a pair of unequal length wishbones is taken as a head on view (opposite) of four points. Deviations from the four (anti-dive or skewed axes relative to centreline of the car) produce complex variations which need 3D computer graphics or actual car to measure, or predict.*

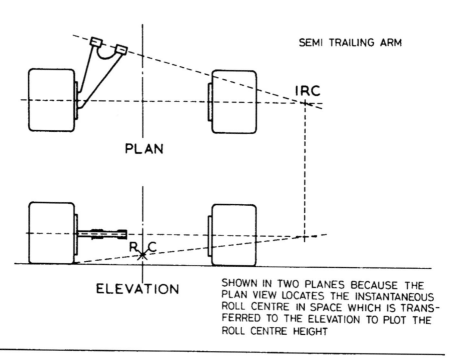

SEMI TRAILING ARM

PLAN

ELEVATION

SHOWN IN TWO PLANES BECAUSE THE PLAN VIEW LOCATES THE INSTANTANEOUS ROLL CENTRE IN SPACE WHICH IS TRANS-FERRED TO THE ELEVATION TO PLOT THE ROLL CENTRE HEIGHT

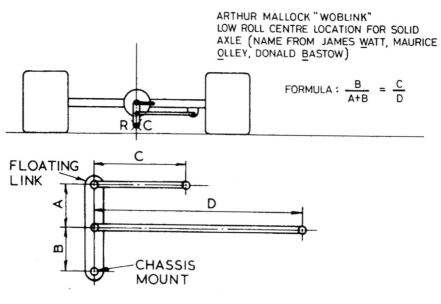

ARTHUR MALLOCK "WOBLINK" LOW ROLL CENTRE LOCATION FOR SOLID AXLE (NAME FROM JAMES WATT, MAURICE OLLEY, DONALD BASTOW)

FORMULA : $\dfrac{B}{A+B} = \dfrac{C}{D}$

FLOATING LINK

CHASSIS MOUNT

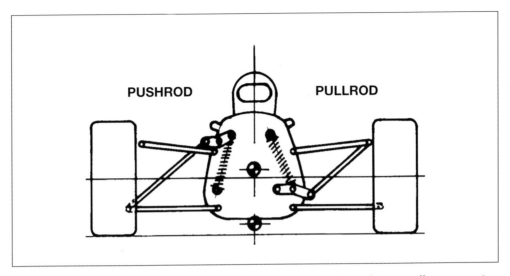

So far, so good, but roll then begins to alter various link angles as well as mounting point positions. These alterations can move the theoretical position of the roll centre both vertically and sideways to a greater or lesser degree.

Worse still, a plot of one side will put the roll centre in one place, and a plot of the opposite side appears to put it somewhere else. A practical (rather than mathematical or draughting) approach to what is happening to a roll centre is covered in Chapter Seven where the 'String Computer' will amuse or help the more involved reader.

However, if we accept that the roll centre cannot be in two places at once when the car has begun to roll, we appear to have a fixed geometric roll centre at rest, but a dynamic one when the vehicle is cornering that may move considerably both up and down by several inches or sideways, on occasion to some hundreds of feet – effectively infinity.

The bedrock first and last of my own suspension designs was to try and locate the roll centre as tightly as possible, keeping movement to the absolute minimum on the argument that if you did not have that as some sort of datum or starting point, what did you have? Thirty years on, it is possible both to use a computer to forecast roll centre movements, as well as, given accurate dimensions, to find out what it is doing in existing designs. What this has shown is that while the professionals have never spent much time shouting about it, they can and do take considerable trouble to locate the dynamic roll centre very well indeed, vertically in some cases within a few thousands of an inch – in practical terms, fixed. Movement of the roll centre is tied closely to roll angle, whether this be small or large and even if the car is going to only roll over 1 degree in a 3 G corner, which is more than most of us will ever experience in a lifetime, the roll centre movement and its effect on the suspension links needs to be as small and predictable as possible.

Experiment with the various layouts shortly to be considered soon showed that the various aims could not be simultaneously achieved. We can take those targets as:

a. keeping the outer or both wheels vertical in a corner, avoiding tyre lean,
b. constant track so that the tyres follow a straight line rather than a zig zag resulting from the contact patch moving in and out in sideways scrub.
c. constant camber angle thus avoiding the tyre going onto its inner edge in acceleration/braking bump or outer edge when 'going light' in droop.

Only a solid axle (or the lighter de Dion version) appears to achieve all three aims. In practice, due to tyre distortion and weight transfer, the solid axle does not manage it either, and its weight combined with other problems means it has no place in any contemporary Formula One/Sports-Prototype.

Attempting to achieve our three targets, it will be found that the searcher for perfection is in the middle of a triangle, trying to reach all three corners at once. As fast as he moves towards success on one, he moves away from it on the others. The first of a series of compromises will have to be made, and the three aims placed in an order of priority. Only then can a start be made to putting a dimension on the four points at each end that will dictate everything – pick ups for the upper and lower wishbones on the tub, and mounting points on the hub/upright at front and rear.

This will indicate how awkward it is, perhaps impossible, to start altering a car that has turned out badly, or gone downhill during the season. Teams could once upon a time alter brackets on a spaceframe, even on an alloy riveted tub, but pre-mounted structures with complex load paths inbuilt are singularly unamenable to being hacked about or having extra bits glued on.

In looking at the various ways, front and rear, that have been used to suspend the racing car, there are two outside factors – one at the front and one at the rear – that complicate the issue, and influence how it can and cannot be done well.

At the front, steering with all its variable movements on each wheel altering what should happen in an ideal situation (one wheel rising while the other falls due to caster angle, for instance). At the rear, the transfer of every scrap of power possible to the road via a contact patch at some distance from the mountings on the tub or shell, means that the links, which are also acting as the route by which forces to accelerate the car are being transferred, have a massive task quite separate from control of the wheel angle during cornering.

And both front and rear linkages need to be constructed in such a way that tiny and sensitive adjustments may be made quickly and accurately.

Front linkages

Beam axle (on twin parallel leaf springs or a single transverse spring with radius rods or steel cables to react brake torque). Heavy, high roll centre, outer wheel leans out in corners (goes positive), movements and shocks into one wheel reacted into the other. Despite these shortcomings it was still in use in racing and on most British road cars long after America had begun to develop independent wishbones in a major way on their road cars.

Split beam (on single transverse leaf with radius rods). Primarily this lowered the roll centre, put some static negative camber onto the wheels to compensate for going positive in roll, and was an easy and cheap means of modification to permit use of coil spring/damper units on the sports and sports/racing cars of the Fifties. It was good enough to grace a number of Chapman's Lotus models including arguably one of the greatest of them all – the beautiful, aerodynamic and hugely successful early Mk XI that came out of the Fifties.

Trailing arm (usually with transverse torsion bar as much for ease of construction as anything). This has really only one virtue, that of a low roll centre at ground level, together with a major shortcoming – wheels assume the same angle as the vehicle in roll and there is no way of eliminating this. Nevertheless, it was used on the BRM V16 Grand Prix car and carried Aston Martin to the first and until 1987 only World Sports Car Championship victory for Britain. Used on VW Beetles, its retention is a requirement of the regulations for Formula Vee – where performance is a triumph of courage and skill over design.

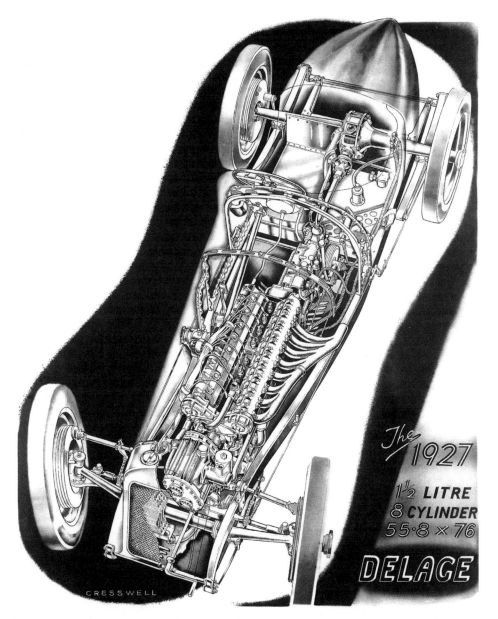

Cutaway view of a 1927 Delage, showing the front and rear beam-axle suspension. Propelled by a supercharged straight-eight 1½ litre twin-cam (!) and slowed by unique cable, chain and shaft-operated big-finned drums. (LAT)

Leading arm. Can be seen in action on the Citroën 2CV but is frankly more at home over a French ploughed field than at Paul Ricard as it has the same shortcomings as trailing arms, plus being even less suited to angled compression loads and steering movements.

Sliding Pillar. A contemporary anachronism, to coin a phrase, which can still be seen racing on the front of the Morgan.

Auto Union used trailing arm front suspension and adjustable friction disc dampers on their 1934 A-Type, seen here in the pits with Hans Stuck at the wheel. (LAT)

MacPherson strut on Peugeot 307WRC World Rally Car. An American design that now equips the vast majority of contemporary production cars all over the world. (Peugueot)

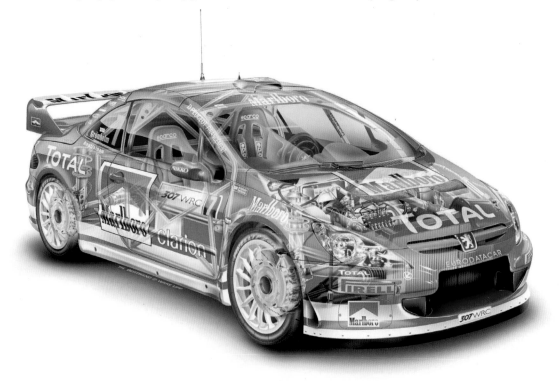

MacPherson Strut. A beautiful concept, which has been used in racing cars (early Lotus) and very much in rally cars of such high performance that they really count as racing cars. Has reasonably low and well controlled roll centre, but wheel angle is almost roll angle, unit is impossibly tall to fit into a really low car, and high braking forces are reacted by trying to break the unit in two and tend to lock its ability to slide in and out. Adjustment of camber and caster is far from easy. Combined with a leaf sprung driven rear axle or as front-wheel-drive unit it possibly equips more vehicles in the world than any alternative concept. As the Chapman Strut, seen in a non-steering rear version for the Lotus Elite and Lancia Stratos. Used on all four corners of the Toyota MR2 with a set of deceptively simple links that produced road handling which had every road-tester in the business searching for new superlatives.

Wishbones, equal and parallel. The roll centre is on the ground, certainly no bad thing but roll angle equals wheel angle in positive camber which we do not want. Despite this, the layout had a long lease of racing life, particularly on Cooper 500s and Cooper Bristols, using the transverse leaf spring as the top link. Not very rigid as the leaf bent sideways (ie fore and aft) under braking and acceleration and could impart some very peculiar movements to the upright and wheel. Good bump/droop control.

Wishbones, equal and non-parallel. Can be made to give low roll centres, always helpful in reducing part of weight transfer in cornering. Flirtations in Formula One with such a layout when tubs began to get really narrow and tall at the front and when suspension movement became almost nil in ground effect era. It fitted available mounting points very conveniently and tiny suspension movement meant its geometric shortcomings were also kept small.

Lancia D50 Grand Prix car of 1954 with equal and parallel wishbones.

2005 Renault R25 non-equal, non-parallel (just) wishbones and steering trackrod sharing an aerodynamic housing with top wishbone.

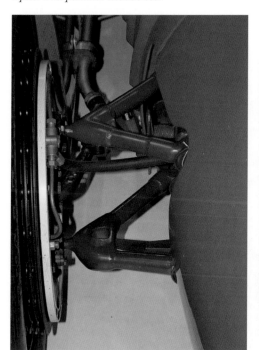

Wishbones, non-equal and non-parallel. Effectively the survivor everywhere because of its huge versatility. The wheel can be made to do anything the designer wishes but not, unhappily, all at the same time.

Variations on variations. Wishbones come in a variety of constructions, different to look at but all still the same in principle. They can be wide-based, narrow-based, multi-piece with left- and right-hand threaded adjusters for the benefit of caster and camber angles, and boxed or solid with an inboard section to produce a rocking arm.

For reasons of weight, strength and production in advanced metals they have become ever more simple and pure in shape: a simple V in elliptical cross-section tubing to sneak the last tiny fraction of aerodynamic efficiency with a spherical point at each corner used both top and bottom. Wishbones are also regarded as expendable being the first items to be wiped off in any accident, without damaging tub strong points, and also written off regularly, after every race in some teams, as part of a 'fixed life' programme for everything on the car.

One very curious variation that appeared (I think) early in 2005 on the McLaren F1 cars were top front wishbones that sloped upwards from the wheel to the tub before vanishing mysteriously within. They appeared at total variance with the long accepted geometry of arcs and roll centre intersection points, and unlike many more orthodox but readily visible variations on a theme, this was not copied immediately by everybody else either then or even two seasons later. Williams appeared to be the first to try it, and Ferrari among others, ignored it. The geometric implications were and are mysterious, but as they appeared in the later stages of Adrian Newey's talented presence at McLaren before departing for Red Bull it may not be unreasonable to suppose he might have both answers and excellent reasons.

One possibility is that with the F1 car now having virtually no visible movement in its 'suspension' but leaving the tyre to do it all, there is no longer any requirement for

2005 Red Bull RB1 cornering in the hands of David Coulthard. Note the top wishbone angle, with a noticeable uphill slope to the mountings on the tub. (LAT)

the specific wheel control during wishbone movement in the conventional sense. But what such an inboard pickup position does permit away from prying eyes is a stronger, stiffer location that removes unsupported sidewall bending stresses in the tub. Even in such a robust structure as an F1 monocoque, such a modification might provide a worthwhile increase in stiffness or alternatively lighter construction and resultant weight saving.

A good deal more intriguing, and barely more than rumour even a year later until exploding into a 'legal – no, illegal' internal but public FIA squabble in the 2006 German GP paddock was how perfectly it meshed with a possible solution to a problem that had been around since Dunlop first inflated a tyre, but had become serious once suspension 'went solid' in racing. Tyres are effectively undamped and able to bounce, vibrate or deform in a major way when hitting kerbing at high speeds doing singularly unwanted things to the contact patch. A device able to reduce or control this, may be in crude terms a substantial weight (ie 10 kg or so) sprung above and below in its own housing mounted vertically within the tub. Dampers once used to occupy this space but the wishbone mounting move fits uncannily with unavoidable need for a minimal vertical space to accommodate a relatively large rigid box container that at one time dampers would have inhabited until Aerodynamics and the needle nose squeezed them out. As they say, watch this space.

Rear linkages

Even more than at the front, a host of variations on variations during the long years of evolution to the present day.

Solid live axle. The original old faithful with a crown wheel, pinion and differential in the middle but located in a great variety of ways. Roll centre generally but not always somewhere in the centre of the differential and wheel angle mostly vertical. Too heavy and too high a roll centre for most serious racing except in the case of the Mallock U2 where the inimitable Major stayed faithful, fighting a 40-year battle to keep such an axle in the fray with ever more ingenious and successful linkages to get the roll centre down and control its movements. Variously located by: leaf spring; leaf springs plus Panhard Rod; leaf/coil springs with Panhard Rod and trailing links; coils with Watt's linkage; coils, trailing arms and various Mallock arrangements; sliding centre block with leaf/coil; torque tube with leaf or coil or Panhard Rod.

de Dion. Almost as old as the car and part of all early racers. It chassis-mounts the weighty differential and drive gears while the wheels have a tube axle connecting them, keeping them vertical under all conditions unless set with negative camber during construction, as Chapman did for the Formula One Vanwall. Offered the first chance of inboard brakes, a further drop in unsprung weight, and brake and drive torque reacted straight into the chassis. So good that development of the Count's original, circa 19th century version, was used by Chapman as mentioned and even a bolt-on-off version was tried by a Seventies Ferrari Formula One car. Offers choice of leaving the gearbox at the front or of making it integral with the final drive.

Swing axle. The first truly independently sprung driven rear wheels. Chassis mounted differential and driveshafts solid with the wheels. Looks hopeful but performs appallingly despite Professor Porsche's choice of it for the People's Wagon, the pre-war Auto Union racers and Britain's post-war Herald. High roll centre, excessive jacking with camber change, oversteer, wheels tucking under – what more do you not want? Mercedes three-quarters solved it with the well-known low pivot version on the legendary 300 SLR Mille Miglia winner but other, better solutions, blew it out.

Figure 3-3 *Panhard rod and Watt's linkage.*

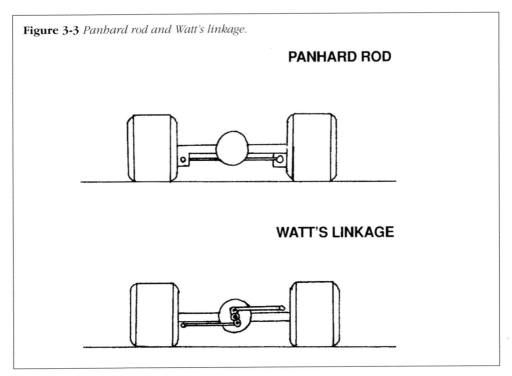

PANHARD ROD

WATT'S LINKAGE

Chapman strut. Colin's first solidified version of the MacPherson for rear installation. As at the front, penalised by height and far from easy adjustment, as well as a tendency to lock up under side loads.

Wishbones (or A-arms, or bottom/top links, or Z-frames) all with radius rods. Almost every variation that ingenious minds have been able to produce on the basic V of tubing with a multi-directional joint at each corner can be found on the back of some competition car somewhere. The rear has a special problem of its own, that of rear-steer, or the ability of the rear wheels, if not most carefully controlled, to alter their toe in/out angle and thus actually steer the back of the car. The forces involved, particularly when the sizes and grip qualities of slick tyres began to make big steps forward, rapidly became enormous.

The rear-steer forces proved capable of bending almost anything at the back of the car, or cracking chassis and gearbox casings, of tearing out their mounting points and of distorting complete rear frames. And if they couldn't break things they simply flexed the apparently inflexible. What this immediately permitted was some degree of toe-in/out to the wheel, however small. And at the rear, unlike at the front where a good driver may complain mildly but will more probably compensate almost automatically, toe in/out has a devastating effect on stability, feel and driver confidence.

Radius rods. The first move was to carry a long tube forward to a variety of mounting positions. Some gave effectively a perfect wishbone parallel to the ground and the centre line of the car, while some skewed up or down, in or out, or both. The resultant mix of arcs, pushing and pulling the rear upright here, there and everywhere produced cars that varied from good to bad to horrific.

Some designs were capable not only of causing toe in/out but also of track variation (scrub), front and backward lean and camber variation all from one bump in the road, and different on each side. Should anyone have needed some further complication, making the radius rods parallel and equal, equal but converging or diverging, or unequal while running uphill or downhill, produced mindboggling permutations.

One attempt to stabilise the situation a little was to use parallel bottom or top transverse links, some of which had one member which adjusted for static toe in/out. This link survived the test of time and is to be found on many current cars.

Driveshaft as one link. Lola's Eric Broadley, shortly followed by Lotus (on the 18) used this approach whereby the driveshaft carrying the power from gearbox to hub was given a second job in life as the top link while a very low mounted bottom A-frame, pointed end-in, with a radius rod did duty underneath. To complete the structure a top radius rod ran from the chassis rearward to a lug cast into the hub. Jaguar later used the system with short, compact twin double coil spring/damper units mounted on each side of the driveshaft. It worked, and does work well but from a racing point of view tied a designer to an unalterable top link with fixed length and pivot points, a finally unacceptable restriction.

The big clean-up

Designers within the car industry coming up against rear wheel steer problems were in most cases free to solve it rather brutally with skewed or inclined arms that fed in fairly violent understeer whenever the vehicle diverged from the straight and narrow. Not only were they not over concerned with the finer points, but they became

Classic rear suspension of the Sixties mid-engine generation: Lotus 49B, 1968. Note reversed lower wishbone, single upper link and upper and lower radius arms running from firewall bulkhead to upright.

1961 Lotus 18 Climax rear suspension, with a lower A-frame and twin radius rod locating the upright.

responsible for the many saloon and sports cars which behaved reasonably well on the road but earned unpleasant reputations when used for competition and thus pushed really hard. Curing these shortcomings – or trying to – made the name of many a modest tuning concern, and made many a works competition manager old before his time.

In the hard worlds of Formula One and Sports-Prototype racing the problem had to be solved and perhaps the biggest pressure and influence came as a by-product of Ground Effect. Within one season it was shown that getting air out of the ever-growing side air tunnels was even more difficult than getting it in. Cluttering the air exit route were not only the driveshafts but a hotch potch of links, bars, tubes and the coil spring/damper unit, still tending to be mounted leaning inwards from the bottom wishbones. The solution, which produced the contemporary layout, featured a hefty top rocking arm, later replaced by a push- or pullrod and linkage operating a coil spring/damper unit tucked neatly inboard beside or on top of the gearbox complete with the earlier mentioned toe-in/out link, plus a slim wide based pure V wishbone at the bottom with an outboard spherical joint that permitted camber adjustment, and made from elliptical tube. Loads went into very robust points on the engine/gearbox/tub.

Gone almost overnight were radius rods and all sorts of jointed links. When combined with truly massive cast or fabricated uprights enclosing giant hub bearings, the ability of the wheel to move other than up and down along a carefully pre-ordained path was reduced to almost nil. So elegant was the arrangement that even after venturi cars were banned, it permitted such a clean air exit at the rear of the car and on the approach to the rear wing, together with lightness, simplicity and strength that it may be some time before it is displaced.

Chassis pick-ups

Inextricably mixed with each other, suspension pick-ups and their layout were influenced over the years by the steady development of the chassis, as it progressed from girders to channel, to steel tube, to space frame, alloy monocoque tub, honeycomb tub, and carbon composite moulded car including stressed bodywork.

The major suspension loads emerge from the coil spring/damper units together with (in order of severity) the lower rear, the top rear, the front lower and the front top wishbones. A little reflection on how the latest tall, narrow outline, whether eggshaped or rectangular, of a current Formula One car encourages the use of a pullrod or pushrod with rockers and vertical coil spring/damper rather than a top rocking arm which must have its pivots awkwardly outrigged in space in some way, illustrates one example.

The loads cannot stop dead when they get to the chassis. They must be accepted with – preferably – no distortion of the structure. In a tub or chassis, rigidity combined with strength and light weight are all. Heavy chassis are a built in handicap that can never be removed, weak chassis break, usually at some critical moment, and flexible chassis defeat every single objective of the suspension designer.

Flexible chassis destroy the geometry, prevent anti-roll bars working properly or at all, permit constant disputes between front and rear of the car to escalate into a war that will wreck any hopes of the vehicle ever handling properly. As with tyre technology, chassis technology is a separate and complex subject but without rigidity the suspension designer is working with both hands tied behind his back.

In accord with the unbreakable rule that you never feed a load into an unsupported tube or panel, suspension loads have tended more and more to be absorbed directly into transverse bulkheads – either cast, machined from solid, or fabricated in tube or honeycomb sheet, which are then bonded, welded or riveted into the main structure.

Figure 3-4 *Inclined coils. Note that these calculations are primarily for the static situation when an angled coil is part of the design, thus reducing the coil rate as the car sees it. (Effective rate.) This can be considerable at steep angles. Any further loss from the suspension moving into bump will be small to negligible and can be ignored. 'Angle' is that between coil axis and that of the operating link (wishbone, bellcrank, push/pullrod).*

EFFECTS OF INCLINING COIL SPRING SUSPENSION UNITS.

Ideally coil springs need to be at 90 degrees to their operating mechanism and to stay as near that angle as practicable during suspension movement. When the angle alters, the effective rate of the coil alters, in most installations for the worse, giving a softening spring just when it is not wanted in bump, squat or nose dive.

Outboard, steeply inclined coils are still current under the skin of sports-prototypes, including the Porsche 962, and it is quite possible to lay out a rocking arm or push/pull rod design that will suffer from falling rate to some degree or other.

Up to 10 degrees either side of 90 degrees (ie. 20 degrees total arc) will not cause alterations worth bothering about. However, 25 degrees from the ideal rightangle is beginning to have considerable effect and 40 degrees alters things dramatically for the worse.

To obtain rising rate, the angle between the coil and its operating link needs to be more than 90 degrees and closing, or less than 90 degrees and opening. This can be very helpful in bellcrank mechanisms normally employed somewhere in push/pull rod systems.

The illustration simplifies the problem slightly (by considering the wheel as moving vertically, for instance) but will give a practical guide to the effects of inclination and angles within a suspension design.

It will be seen that although the load (100lbs.) does not alter and neither does the basic rate of the coil (100 inch/lbs.) because the chassis is moving downwards vertically while the coil swings about an arc, the chassis has to travel further than one inch to compress the coil one inch and thus reach equilibrium. When a further 150lb. of load is fed in (the bump force necessary to compress the coil a further 1.5 inches) the chassis must travel down further than a total of 2.5 inches to again reach equilibrium.

In our 40 degree example, the chassis moves down 1.376in. (a) for a static load of 100lb., with a further 2.42in. (a1) making 3.796in. for a total load of 250lb. (100lb. plus 150lb. bump).

$$Effective\ Coil\ Rate\ (static) = \frac{100}{1.376} = 72.67lb/in.$$

$$Effective\ Coil\ Rate\ (full\ bump) = \frac{250}{3.796} = 65.86lb/in.$$

Clearly if our design aim is a 100lb./in. coil rate we cannot get this as a constant. We can only take a rate of, say, halfway between static and full bump (ie. 69lb./in.) and work it backwards to find a coil that will give this compromise figure.

We can obtain this with the formula:

$$Required\ rate^2 \quad or \quad \frac{100 \times 100}{69} = 144.9lb/in.$$
$$\frac{}{ECR}$$

This coil will in fact now be harder in the static position (105.4lb./in.) and softer in full bounce (95.49lb./in.), but still a vast improvement over doing nothing and wondering why the rivet heads or exhaust system are being filed off the bottom of the car every time the brakes are applied.

How to discover the amount of vertical fall of the chassis (1.376 inches

and 3.796 inches in our example) mathmatically? Use the SIN Rule formula:

$$\frac{Side\ a}{Sin\ angle\ A} = \frac{Side\ b}{Sin\ angle\ B} = \frac{Side\ c}{Sin\ angle\ C}$$

Note that when solving this particular problem, angle C will always be obtuse and obtuse angles do not appear in SIN tables. What you will get will be an angle somewhere between nil and 90 degrees. This angle must then be subtracted from 180 to obtain the actual angle C. Sequence:

$$\begin{aligned} &if & \frac{Side\ b}{Sin\ B} &= \frac{Loaded\ coil\ length}{Sin\ unit\ angle} = Constant\ K. \\ & & \frac{Side\ c}{Sin\ C} &= Constant\ K. \\ &then & Sin\ C &= \frac{Fitted\ coil\ length}{Constant\ K} \end{aligned}$$

Obtain angle C as noted above

$$Angle\ A = 180 - (B + C)$$

$$\begin{aligned} &if & \frac{Side\ a}{Sin\ A} &= Constant\ K, \\ &then & Side\ a &= K \times Sin\ A. \end{aligned}$$

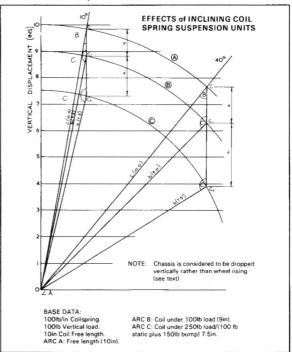

EFFECTS of INCLINING COIL SPRING SUSPENSION UNITS

VERTICAL DISPLACEMENT (INS.)

NOTE: Chassis is considered to be dropped vertically rather than wheel rising (see text)

BASE DATA:
100lb/in Coilspring.
100lb Vertical load.
10in Coil Free length.
ARC A: Free length (10in).

ARC B: Coil under 100lb load (9in).
ARC C: Coil under 250lb load/(100 lb static plus 150lb bump) 7.5in.

It is perhaps worth pointing out that the phrase 'the main structure' has for many years in Formula One (though to a lesser extent in Sport-Prototypes) meant the engine and transaxle case as well as the tub. Indeed, in many categories of contemporary single seater the power unit is more than a stressed member. It IS the car once you have moved aft of the rear tub bulkhead, with the front of the block being joined to the rest of the car with methods that must provide rigidity while still accepting the expansion and contraction of the power unit from cold to full running temperature.

The block and bellhousing have to deal with major torsional stresses, and should the engine not have been conceived originally with this in mind, the likelihood of mysterious engine failure is considerable. The rear suspension pick-ups tend to be on the gearbox or outriggers from it, either cast or fabricated. Looking around some cars, the unworthy thought sometimes occurs that a convenient threaded hole or flange had more to do with the location of a wishbone pick-up than the required geometry.

Make a mental note to see if that car wins, ever or never.

Methods of Spring Actuation

Ideally any coil should be mounted vertically, or to be more exact at a constant 90 degrees to the lever that will compress it. A moment's reflection on the arcs involved will show that this is technically impossible with a simple linkage, but it is normally possible to keep the 'lean' of the coil within plus or minus 10 degrees, or 15 degrees at worst. Within these limits, while the effective rate of the coil will be rising and falling (the dreaded 'falling rate', already discussed) it will not be by an amount sufficient to cause serious trouble.

Ignoring any spring type except the coil, currently almost paramount, there are three ways of utilising it.

Coil/damper acting directly on front lower wishbone on 1961 Lotus 18 Climax.

Pushrod front suspension on Ferrari F2000. Coil/damper units not visible but actually located horizontally fore/aft on ultra-rigid platform within carbon tub above driver's feet and legs.

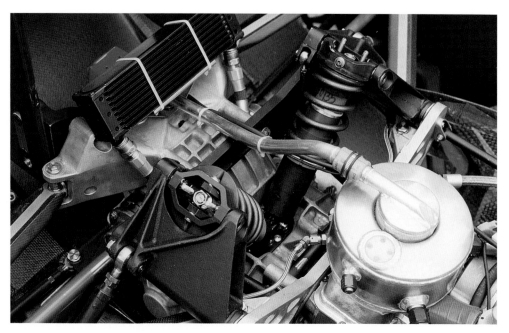

1986 Ferrari F1 car with neat combination of pushrod acting on a cast rocker, chassis-mounted to turn movements and forces through 90 degrees. (LAT)

1. Directly onto the axle, upright or wishbone. It then has to be inclined inwards to a greater or lesser degree to meet a top mounting on the tub or chassis. For many years this angle was quite large with units leaning in sometimes at 45 degrees, or even more. This not only reduces the effective rate of the spring in a major way, but introduces an unwanted variable in bump and droop, almost minimal in 2006. The earliest March cars took immediate steps to eliminate as much of this lean as possible by taking the top mounting as far outboard as a delicate, three-tubed support bracket would permit. Bringing the bottom mounting inwards, while apparently simpler puts very high bending loads into the bottom wishbone and also requires an ever more powerful spring because of the leverage effect, rising by a squared figure. At such extreme angles, the spring is also devoting an appreciable part of its strength to trying to pull the bottom wishbone out of the car, something we can do without.

2. Rocking arm. This was a very logical development that in one jump took the coil inboard out of the airflow, kept it more or less vertical and removed bending loads from the bottom link but at the cost of rather more difficult constructional methods and total reliance on the quality of the steel and welding.

The bearing on which the rocking arm must pivot tends to require a long expensive reaming tool or accurately machined housings to accept small self-aligning bearings and the necessary shaft and lubrication arrangements. When the wing car era was at its height, coils became so strong that an appreciable part of any suspension movement came from the top rocker arms bending!

The need to thread the driver's legs between the two coils at the front placed ever greater limitations on the leverages available as cars became narrower and narrower, although the rear stayed admirably suited to this design. The coil spring/dampers are tucked neatly down beside a gearbox or clutch housing; the casting often sculptured

Ayrton Senna on his way to winning the 1985 Belgian Grand Prix in the Lotus 97T with pullrod front suspension, and with a small modicum of roll. (LAT)

to take them. They are accessible with a low centre of gravity – and there they look like staying into the immediate future. But not at the front.

3. Push and pullrods. These opened a new era, not simply because they reduced still further, however modestly, the aerodynamic drag but they brought in a whole new era of control of when and by how much the coil was compressed by wheel movement and where it might be located. Ride height and corner weight adjustment became simpler than it had ever been as the rods had left hand/right hand threaded ends. Loosening two lock nuts permitted instant alteration in length. Imponderable bending was removed, and introduction of a skewed rocker, or even a further intermediate link allowed the coil spring/damper unit to be located in a variety of situations including horizontally if required.

Technically there appears to be little or no difference between pull and push versions, both employing slim tubes of about 0.75 in, in carbon fibre or quality steel in perfect tension or compression. In 1987, Lotus pushed while McLaren pulled, and often the rear is different to the front and it seems considerations of space, convenience and accessibility probably govern final decisions. 20 years on, pushrods appear almost universal, but this seems more a result of where coil/damper units need to be mounted than some mysterious geometric secret.

If one or the other integrates more easily into certain shapes or internal design of the main structure of the car and consequent load paths that is the one that gets used. Whether front or rear the rod usually takes the loads directly out of the hub/upright through cast lugs, or alternatively via brackets welded extremely close to the ends of the top or bottom wishbone reducing outboard end bending loads to the minimum. During 1987 Williams and Benetton pushed at the front while March pulled – but either could and have altered within weeks given a powerful enough reason.

Two interesting versions of changing the direction of operation and thus placing the coil spring/damper units where it is more convenient through the use and mounting of very skilfully contrived rocker mechanisms could be seen on the front end of the 1987 Ralt Formula 3000 car and the rear end of the 1987/88 Mercedes-Sauber. The former permitted the units to be located inclined in the front bay over the pedal box and hydraulic master cylinders while the latter placed the units horizontally pointing forwards along the side tubes of the engine support frame.

Twenty years later, the location of rear coil spring/damper units horizontally fore/aft was not only almost universal, but had filtered down the ladder to – for instance – seriously lower-priced OMS and Megapin motorcycle engine-powered single-seaters.

Uprights

If any item can be called more important than others in the suspension, the upright has a good claim. At its most advanced it is a marvellous piece of design having to cope with a singularly complicated mixture of loads, stresses and strains of a very high order, the rear obviously having an even tougher life than the front.

Among some of the criteria that must be reconciled into a shape that can be either cast or fabricated and then machined are the top and bottom suspension pick up points to accept a variety of bearings/spherical joints, brake calliper lugs that will neither crack off nor thrust the callipers into the inner rim of the wheel, torsional and bending stiffness in vertical and horizontal planes to resist cornering, wheel and brake/acceleration forces, and bearings and oil seals that will neither disintegrate nor melt in an oven-like environment. Many also incorporate air ducting to help vented discs to function. Adjustment of toe in/out, camber and caster is usually done through whatever pattern of joint is used on the wishbones, but not always.

The Porsche 962 for one has a method at the front where the top suspension pivot and steering arm are all contained in a separately machined alloy section. This is bolted to the top of the upright with a shimmed gap. Pre-planning and design ensures

Horizontally mounted rear coil spring/damper units on a 1999 Benetton B199. (LAT)

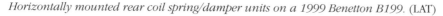

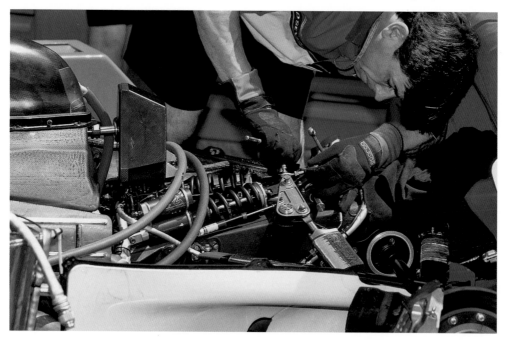

Horizontally mounted rear coil spring/damper units on the author's current Megapin single seater. Moving a bottom bolt one hole saves a complete strip to install a new coil. (Author)

The distinctive rear suspension and upright of a 1975 Lotus 77. (Phipps/Sutton)

that camber can be instantly adjusted by putting in or taking away shims, and the tracking of the front wheels is unaffected because the steering arm is adjusted at the same time. Crafty and widely borrowed.

Very many front uprights have a cast-in lug to which can be bolted two horizontal alloy plates. These not only form the steering arm, but altering their size or hole locations can provide different Ackermann angles, fine bump steer adjustment and a variable steering ratio without being forced to a complete change of rack and pinion. Three separate virtues stemming from a modest addition to the shape of the casting has to be good value.

Bearings

All the suspension parts we have so far considered have to be reliably attached to each other, very often with something able to accommodate movement in three different planes. Without wishing to labour the obvious, this will be most clearly evident at the front where both the top and bottom upright joints must be capable of allowing movement for the upright to rise and fall in bump and droop and also rotate when the driver turns the steering wheel.

For very many years plain bearings of machined brass and bronze with a steel pin down the centre were the only answer, all of which suffered lubrication and anti-dirt sealing problems. Front steering rotation was achieved by a king pin with bushed bearings often of top-hat form to provide a substantial thrust washer which had to deal not only with much of the weight of a front-engined car, but also the instantaneous shock loads from road bumps. An alternative was a coarse Acme thread in which the front wheels actually wound themselves up and down in going round corners.

Do not think we are talking vintage or historic here. The MG to almost the last moment of its life and BL's Marina saloon of the '80s enjoyed this archaic arrangement which happens to ensure unwanted dive angle as an extra handicap. There is still a time and a place for the accurately made plain bush, its much refined son the needle roller bearing, and its cheap and versatile grandson, the plastic moulded bearing, but the first low-priced major step forward to accommodate complex motions were probably the Silentbloc and Metalastik bushes.

These bushes had a steel outer housing and steel inner sleeve with rubber bonded between the two. Variations of rubber hardness, thickness, length and diameter could provide bushes ranging from not dissimilar to bronze to types with the flexibility to suspend a delicate instrument in safety. A new generation of racing and sports car builders embraced them with enthusiasm in the '50s. They permitted wishbones and links to move in double arcs that would have been otherwise impossible. But this very virtue ensured their days were numbered. Not, it might be said, in the motor industry in general where they became ever more sophisticated in design and application, but in racing where precision of movement became more important with every passing day.

What the industry saw as 'invaluable compliance' a racing man began to see as 'squidging about all over the place' and the moment the spherical joint was spotted in aircraft the days of the rubber bush were numbered. The spherical bearing or rod end is known universally and colloquially as a 'Rose Joint' because Rose were not only the earliest major manufacturer in Britain, but also controlled to some degree, import of foreign competitors such as the German Heim variety.

There are now a number of other high quality makers including Ampep, American Uniball and Japan's NMB, all on the same principle – a ball within a ball of varying qualities of steel, various diameter bore/thread combinations, high angular movement versions, male/female, left-hand threads and right, and almost all now have a tough wear-resistant plastic woven interliner between the metal faces of the inner ball and outer housing.

Spherical bearings made possible almost any variation on a suspension theme that might be envisaged by a designer. The range of sizes and materials is so wide that a compact basic guide and comparison is to be found in Appendix 4.

The basic circular types are normally lightly pressed into an accurately machined housing, with a circlip of some sort making certain they stay where they have been put. Then a bolt, pin or shaft runs through the centre ball to lock it into the other component.

Rod ends are more versatile, more easily attached by being screwed into threaded bushes and permit rapid length adjustment without dismantling by using LH and RH threads at each end of a link. In certain applications, the interliner may be more of a handicap than an advantage. The tightness it introduces through the method of manufacture, puts some amount of pre-load into the bearing – a 'stiction' – which has to be overcome before the bearing will move at all, and which was incidentally a shortcoming of the moulded 'Silentbloc' type of earlier rubber bush.

One example when 'stiction' is certainly not wanted is the use of a large diameter bearing in the support and installation of the steering column, often running at an awkward angle, skewed in two planes relative to the car. A non-interliner pattern needs to be employed here, and a similar type is normally fitted into the ends of coil spring/damper units for similar complete freedom of movement.

Despite the high quality and variety of materials including stainless steel available 'off the shelf' it is some indicator of the outlook of top level teams that they still think it worth the cost and effort to produce their own in even more exotic, aerospace-developed materials to save ounces for the same or superior strength.

Figure 3-5 *Diagram to illustrate two methods of achieving fine rod end adjustment, as described in the text.* (Darell Staniforth)

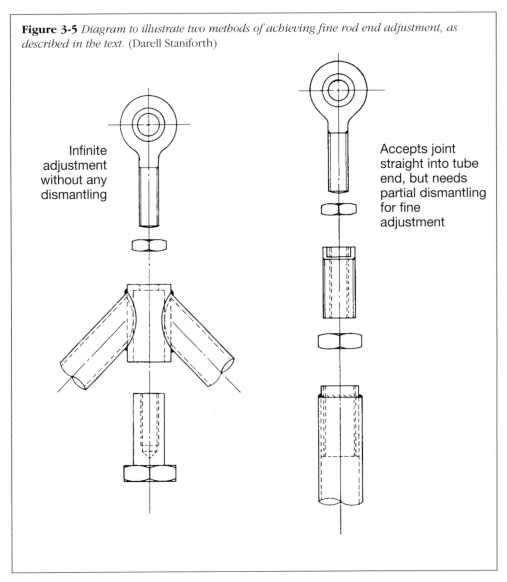

Infinite adjustment without any dismantling

Accepts joint straight into tube end, but needs partial dismantling for fine adjustment

As a further bonus, all the top quality units are effectively corrosion proof in a race environment, another safety and life factor.

Despite its almost universal usage and great convenience, the rod end with its threaded shank does have the shortcoming that the shank is often required to accept bending loads, when pure compression or tension is a far more effective way of utilising the weight of metal involved.

Much thought has gone into the detail of installing spherical bearings with ease of fine adjustment. Simple insertion into a threaded bush means no finer setting than half a turn (or half a thread) plus the need to remove the ball of the joint from its bolt or pin. March were possibly the first to produce a beautiful refinement still in widespread use, of a threaded sleeve within the main bush that can give a length adjustment literally to thousandths of an inch.

Both patterns, however, introduce a stress line into the base of one of the threads when the essential lock nut is tightened, and Tony Southgate produced his own version for the Jaguar XJR-6 where the receiving bush was split with a pinchbolt to lock the rod end. It took more time to make, lost the ultra-fine outboard adjustment but gave a tiny amount of extra strength and reliability for nothing.

A perfect view of a successful World Championship car in microcosm.

Within two more years, however, McLaren for one were eliminating the thread adjustability, welding them solid into the wishbone ends, and not too long after that John Barnard abolished some of them completely in favour of a thin flexible titanium plate. When this burst on a startled world he explained that while he expected everybody to copy it in due course he was not going to explain precisely – or at all – the virtues the idea conferred on his new Ferrari. Rigidity, reliability, a gramme or two saved, perfect load transfers into the structure? You tell me.

The McLaren and Ferrari approaches are only possible on a car built to aircraft (at least) standards of accuracy and rigidity, so that an installation of wishbones, and other links, upright and wheel would all be in precisely the correct position and angle, without any second chance. But keeping the spherical part of the joint meant that there was still some small freedom for a wishbone to bend or flex without locking a single plane joint solid.

Considering this at least hints that Barnard's approach may have achieved ultimate simplicity while injecting yet another tiny addition to the rigidity of the suspension and its effect on the tyre contact patch.

Although the costs of spherical joints will be infinitesimal in Formula One terms, they can add up to the biggest single item in the budget of a one-off, and the substitution of plain bronze down the motor racing scale. For those that are bought, a trudge through the catalogues for a money versus strength, versus weight comparison will normally prove very worthwhile. Smaller is lighter and can provide a comparable strength to a larger joint costing the same in a larger size.

Figure 3-6 *Southgate approach on extremely heavily loaded 1987 Jaguar rear suspension link to reduce locknut shear/tension loads.* (Miles Gardner)

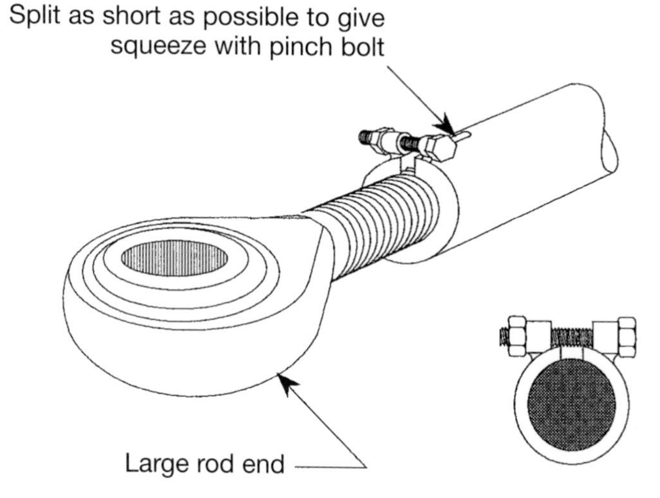

Split as short as possible to give squeeze with pinch bolt

Large rod end

Chapter 4

Ackermann Steering Angle

BETTER TO PUT MY CARDS on the table from the beginning as a total believer and convert to Ackermann steering angle, one of the very few things in the four-wheeled vehicle that is self-adjusting to the precise demand of varying circumstances with highly valuable pluses, forgiving and flexible in application, relatively easy to fit and forget, needing neither further adjustment nor lubrication and search as one may, no awful negative to weigh against its installation.

Having gone in so heavily, let us begin at the beginning. Supposedly conceived about the time of the Battle of Waterloo to deal with complaints from wealthy carriage customers who could not bear the unsightly furrows in their gravel drives left by horsedrawn carriages swinging in to decant passengers at the front doors of stately homes, the way had been wide open for some mechanism or geometry that would prevent a pair of pivoted steering wheels mounted on a common axle vying with each other for grip when forced to turn on identical radii.

Some years pre rack-and-pinion there came a certain Herr Langenspurger with an approach that worked. Also well ahead of his time in business acumen came Herr Ackermann, resident in Great Britain and so in a fine position to see its value, organise its legal protection and embark on its manufacture or the licensing of such toil by others.

What it achieved in essence was to enable a pair of wheels on the same axle to turn to two different angles when asked to go around a corner, matching themselves to the tightness of the turn, and thus eliminating what had been until then inevitable scrubbing and even tearing up of the surface on which the (often steel banded) 'treads' were rolling.

We have to accept at this point that later development, particularly with the arrival of the motor vehicle forced much deeper analysis of what went on in steering mechanisms, often providing the basis of bitter argument for and against, what might occur at certain angles and speeds, reaction with different rear ends and so on. Especially concerning very high speed circuit cars, the argument is often still that 'you don't need it because steering angles are small. And anyway the inner wheel is doing little or it is off the ground'. The decision to use or not to use Ackermann, whether as an F1 driver or a wet-morning commuter, has always seemed to me a simple one. Once on the move, any driver has normally only four tyre contact patches through which to handle any situation which may arise. Anything which can help the grip of those patches, however minimally, should be worth the most serious consideration, bearing in mind that a driver's level of skill in using this quartet (hardly bigger than the soles of two pairs of rubber boots) is the only real difference between us and the front row at Monaco or Dubai.

Figure 4-1 *Traditional drawing to establish angle (Ackermann) at which steering arm should be mounted. Strictly this will be correct only for a single chosen corner radius – but variations on either side will rarely be critical (see also text).*

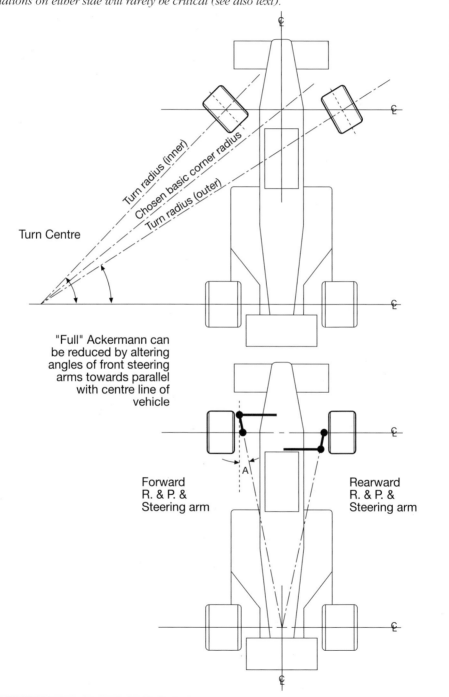

Turn radius (inner)

Chosen basic corner radius

Turn radius (outer)

Turn Centre

"Full" Ackermann can
be reduced by altering
angles of front steering
arms towards parallel
with centre line of
vehicle

A

Forward
R. & P. &
Steering arm

Rearward
R. & P. &
Steering arm

If it is capable of self-adjusting progressively and automatically from small to large or vice versa, dependent on the requirement at a given moment AND has no horrible snag ready to appear with or without warning, it seems to me senseless not to employ Ackermann.

You do not have to be Einstein to see that perfectly parallel wheels cannot get round a corner where the outer is unavoidably following a different (larger radius) path to the inner one without some dispute (ie, scrubbing) between them. In other words, your are giving 50% of the total front patch contact area a harder time than it might otherwise enjoy (see Figure 4-1).

Before going into detail, it should first be made clear that the usual approach of defining the angles of the steering arms for full Ackermann (lines drawn along the arms from the trackrod end, via the kingpin axis to intersect at the centre of the rear axle line) is valid ONLY in the following case. The rack and pinion itself must lie on a straight line joining the two trackrod ends to each other.

The situation is, in fact, the approximate normal layout of very many vehicles including road and rally cars, pre-1985/90 single seaters and most, but certainly not all, 'Locaterfields' and other kit cars. Trouble starts and gets steadily worse the further forward of that critical line the rack and pinion is positioned, manifested in a steady loss of the effect you thought you had achieved until it vanishes completely.

Particularly on more recent single seaters and sports-racing cars (including my own Megapin) many other design criteria, including space for legs, feet, pedals, steering column and really robust front bulkheads, force a less-than-perfect siuation in which the rack and pinion must perforce be mounted well ahead of the ideal. As Ackermann is effectively 'variable dynamic toe-out', increasing steadily the more lock that is applied, it deals automatically with corners of varying radius: the tighter the corner, the more lock needed, the more Ackermann divergence is available. It is of greatest value in the slowest, tightest corners, becoming of less importance and smaller magnitude the faster and more wide open the corner, as G-forces increase and weight transfer moves onto the outer wheel. The normal limitation in practical terms is then rack and pinion lock stops, though it is a separate problem to decide what combination of rack-and-pinion movement and steering arm length will be needed to get you round the tightest corner you are going to encounter. All others will look after themselves.

Being at the time unaware of quite how disastrous might be the results of mounting the rack 'out of line' competing in the car went on in happy ignorance that the handling, already good enough to win, might well be improved still further. My own interest was triggered anew when working on one of the all-conquering F3 Dallaras and noticing an apparently mystifyingly huge 'Ackermann angle' on a deeply curved steering arm. Even a check by eye suggested an immense amount of outset on the track-rod end. It had to be there for a good reason.

Dallara would surely not have gone to the considerable trouble of an ultra deeply dished wheel and a hub design that allowed location of the brake disc far outboard without thought and consideration. A check with the wheelbase/kingpin drawing approach on measured data from the vehicle itself indicated a required steering arm angle of 18 degrees. The most casual glance suggested something like double this figure. The problem was to establish accurately how much Ackermann was actually imparted between the two wheels throughout the range from straight-ahead to full lock. At least on paper it was to be hoped that it would be modest in gentle (high-speed) corners, but much increased in sharper bends (low speed). Not having the full access to the Dallara which would be needed for what might be a lengthy and fiddly night-time investigation, it was decided to check my own Magapin-Kawasaki hillclimb

Figure 4-2 *Establishing the angle sought is still a product of traditional 'lines to centre of rear axle' – see below. It is how it is used that alters – it becomes the required basic included angle between trackrod and steering arm.*

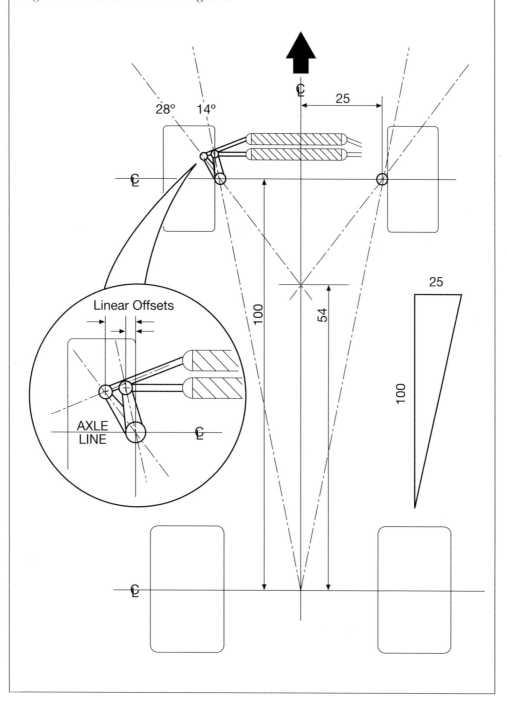

single seater, designed and largely built by Ian Scott, in which we had incorporated 'full' Ackermann from Day One (based on lines drawn rearwards along the steering arms to intersect at the centrepoint of the rear axle line). The arms were luckily adjustable if necessary by simply redrilling or making new from .125 (3 mm) alloy plate.

Preliminary planning had meant that the rack and pinion had finished up mounted a long way ahead of the axle line (some 9 in 23 mm) with the trackrods in consequence raked rearwards virtually parallel to the top wishbone forward arm. Other considerations required a short steering arm (2.75 in 70 mm) – see Figure 4-2. Many other cars have not dissimilar layouts, and our earlier concerns had been with rack length and its position vertically between the wishbone chassis pick-ups, guarding in good time against the dreaded bump-steer. In fact both cars were completed and running with reasonable turn-in for three seasons, without qualms – until the day we saw the Dallara. A rough check showed it to have at least double the offset that full Ackermann (henceforth referred to as AA) might require. After some attempts at drawing failed or were inconclusive, Ian suggested and sketched out a practical approach on the Megapin.

First step was a check with very carefully scribed lines on the workshop floor at full lock. Then came the shock. There seemed to be none.

Worse. There was if anything some anti-AA. The quickest 'fix' was to drill new holes in the steering arms to double the offset of the trackrod end. Eureka. At full lock it was visible even by eye that the two wheels were now turning differentially and putting on dynamic toe-out. It was time for much improved accuracy, seeking a reason and a cure. We discovered two things. Using the centre of the rear axle as the intersection point is ONLY correct if the complete rack and trackrods lie on a straight line – seen in plan view – from one trackrod end to the other. Move the unit back and you increase AA. Move it forward and you start to destroy it. My own location had more than managed this. However the original and basic angle calculation turned out to be still an essential part of a new approach in which it now became the required angle between steering arm and trackrod, ignoring any use of a rear axle centre point, as the way to create AA in an existing vehicle.

And the only way to achieve this is normally to swing the steering arm outwards moving the trackrod end joint ever closer to the disc, calliper, brake pipe, bracket, or what-have-you. Unfortunately, quite a lot of cars do not have this space available, and the only answers may be to live without AA, make a new front upright, or sell the car. Should you still be at the thinking stage, it cannot be emphasised too strongly that design and construction of your front upright should include the maximum practical TRE-to-disc dimension you can manage.

It might now be appropriate to consider how AA might best be quantified or defined if the 'rear axle intersect' is no longer valid, and there are at least four approaches that might be used. The objective throughout this discourse has been to keep it as simple as possible, staying well away from advanced maths or 3D computer programs. Those I have seen usually work to three or even four decimal places, of no value in an average team workshop where 0.2 of a degree will be infinitely more practical and achievable outside F1. For instance measuring across the bulge of a tyre wall (about 17 inches on an average medium slick) gives a dimension of 0.3 inches/per degree. Working to a tenth of a degree requires measurement to 0.03 in/0.75 mm – well within the capabilities of the human eye.

Relating this to the table (Figure 4-7) will demonstrate how practical it is to do your own research and settings without ever stepping inside McLaren or Williams. So how might it be defined?

(A) An alternative location of the intersect point. (B) Moving the trackrod end outwards transversely either as a linear distance or an angle. (C) The included angle between the arm and the trackrod. (D) A new intersection point at some distance ahead of the rear axle.

If we consider AA located in the traditional way as 100% we doubled this to 200% by increasing the linear outset approximately 0.6 in (15 mm) to 1.2 in (30 mm) by redrilling the plates and immediately began to produce wheel movements with that sought-after progressive toe-out, with a measuring method shortly to be outlined. Even more satisfying was the later on-track proof that what had seemed decent turn-in had improved in startling fashion, with the sharper and slower the corner the better even to the extent of a tailhappy tendency.

The next step was to try in a somewhat less suck-it-and-see manner a new and alternative way of designing full AA steering on any car where the rack and pinion

Figure 4-3 *Plotting actual wheel angles as fronts are turned into a right-hand bend.* (Ian Scott)

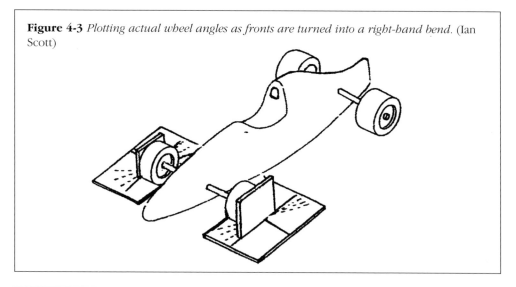

Figure 4-4 *Each line is the result of step-by-step rotation of the steering wheel.* (Ian Scott)

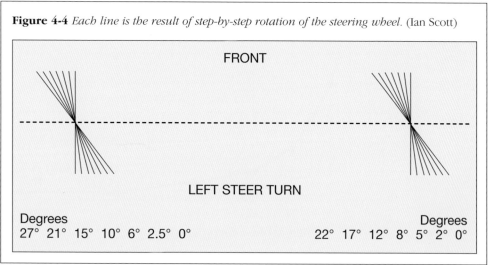

FRONT

LEFT STEER TURN

Degrees
27° 21° 15° 10° 6° 2.5° 0°

Degrees
22° 17° 12° 8° 5° 2° 0°

COMPETITION CAR SUSPENSION

does not lie in a straight line at 90 degrees to the fore/aft centre line. This was to ignore the traditional line from the kingpin to rear axle centre line and instead reduce the included angle between the steering arm and the trackrod. The only practical way to do this is to swing the steering arm outwards. The questions are 'where to?' and 'to what angle?'. Happily the angle you want is one you have already calculated but subtracted from 90.

As it happens the track/wheelbase ratio of very many cars calculate into quite a narrow bracket from 13 to 16 degrees. This figure, when subtracted from 90, is the angle you will be seeking between the trackrod and any modified steering arm. Unless you decide you cannot live without acquiring a computer programme for this task, it is hard to improve on the Ian Scott approach. It is not only cheap, easy and accurate but also automatically takes into account various small though uncertain effects involving caster angle, kingpin inclination, wheel offset and any track variation – see Figure 4-3. A cost of about £3 ($5) and his parts list are indicators of his economic approach.

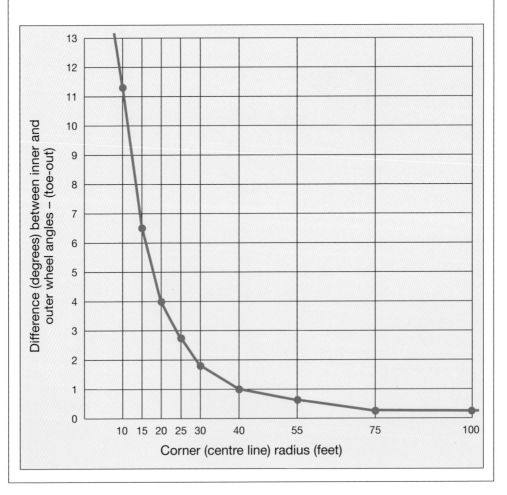

Figure 4-5 *Ackermann angle progression on a vehicle with: 1. straight line R & P installation; 2. Specific ('average') dimensions for wheelbase, track and steering arm.*

- 3 rectangles 2 ft by 2.5 ft hardboard or plywood
- 1 pen: black felt tip
- 3 ballpoints: red, green and blue
- decent protractor (90°, 180°, 360°)
- good quality kneeling mat
- a luxury addition to aid your research would be a steering arm capable of rapid adjustment in its mounted angle or alternatively predrilled holes to permit moving the TRE outwards or inwards when setting the static AA in relation to the disc or hub. Even without this you will still be able to analyse what AA effect – if any – you do have and the target dimensions to which the arm must be bent or refabricated in search of 100%.

Modus Operandi

1. Take the load off the front wheels by placing a spacer block under each front wishbone sufficient to avoid the tyres touching a marker board below.
2. Set static toe in/out to nil.
3. Centralise the rack and put a small marker on the steering wheel at 12 o'clock for reference.
4. Align each front wheel with the fore/aft and axle lines already marked on each board.
5. Place the 3rd board against one tyre wall and drop it vertically down to match the datum line on the floorboard and scribe on it a coloured line.
6. Repeat on the opposite wheel.
7. Proceed to move the rack in increments of – say – 0.125 in (3 mm) until the rack reaches its limit. At each step reset the 3rd (vertical) board, and scribe a new coloured line onto its base board.
8. Repeat on the opposite side using the same colour sequence – red, green, blue – to aid later identification and angle measurements.
9. Repeat the whole process but moving the steering in the opposite direction.
10. It remains only to measure and tabulate the angles of turn now marked in colour on the baseboard of each wheel to discover how much one has turned in relation to the other in both left and right corners to the limits of the rack (see Figure 4-5).

The results from the measuring system just outlined are not only listed but also graphed, a new method that makes visually very clear the degree of self adjust and progressive nature of the steering corrections it makes when a car is taken into a variety of corners (Figure 4-5).

Dynamic changes may well take everything into a whole new arena. Approaching and entering a corner the driver is making a series of extraordinarily quick and complex decisions about where he/she wants the wheels to point, all inextricably mixed with speed, road surface, attitude of the car, braking and thrust from the rear tyres. Because the differentials in steering angle at early stages appear small – 0.5–1.5 degrees – it is still a large percentage of the slip angle range in which most racing tyres will be working, perhaps 6–7 degrees at maximum before the inevitable degeneration moves into the dreaded understeer and does offer a potential advance in grip not to be sneered at.

To be free to deal with the future uncertainties any designer might be well advised to plan for easy variability in certain components at least in his prototype or even production if future vehicles are to be handled by a wide variety of driver talent. Maximum required lock will vary in different branches of the sport, but design in as much AA as there is physical space. You do not have to use it, but without it you may find yourself somewhere, sometime forced into a 3-point turn, not much help to a win.

The first move is to determine what you do have in terms of steering angle and then follow a new approach to obtaining AA successfully. This entails abandoning the traditional 'lines to the differential' method in favour of the angle between the trackrod and the steering arm. To establish this angle we use the 'traditional' (lines to the rear diff) method (see Figure 4-1). On a surprisingly large number of vehicles this gives a required steering arm angle of 13 to 17 degrees. We will use 15 degrees in any following examples which may be converted into a linear distance of outset depending on the length of the steering arm. Given only that the rack and pinion lies on a straight line, this works excellently and will produce a progressive and self-adjusting increase in dynamic toe-out in any corner of whatever radius – in a very tight one of the order of 30 degrees on the outer wheel and 40 degrees on the inner. So far, so good. Trouble begins as soon as the rack and pinion is located for whatever reason ahead of a perfectly straight mounting line. We know this steadily diminishes AA until finally reversing it completely. How to deal with this?

We subtract our calculated 15 degrees from 90 to give 75, the really critical figure in all of this. *It is the angle we must achieve between the steering arm and the trackrod.* Unfortunately, rack and pinion offset forwards causes this angle to open out, perhaps to as much as 85 to 90 degrees. We need to reduce this back to our calculated target of 75 degrees by whatever means may be open to us. The only way is to increase the steering arm angle by moving the trackrod end away from the centre of the car and the sad thing is it may prove impossible as there is not sufficient clearance before hitting the brake disc, calliper or some part of the upright. If this happens, you have to either accept reduced Ackermann, build a new front half onto the car, or sell the car. If you are dealing with the much rarer situation of a rack and pinion behind the axle line, the same rules apply with the single exception that you add the 15 degrees to the 90 (105) for the critical angle between the steering arm and the trackrod.

Figure 4-6 *Effects of variations/combinations of R & P ratios and steering arm lengths. R & P 'speed' is rack bar movement (in ins) for 360 degrees at steering wheel.* (Author)

STEERING SPEED			
R & P Ratio 1.5 (slow): road 2.5 (quick): race	**Steering arm length** 2.5–5 in	**Result**	**Notes**
Quick	Short	Ultra quick	But also heavy
Medium	Medium	Medium ◄—	Any of these three
Slow	Long	Ultra slow	different approaches
Quick	Long	Medium ◄—	could give identical
Slow	Short	Medium slow ◄—	results

Figure 4-7 *Some examples of variations in the relative angular movements of the wheels depending on R & P location and increasing the mounted angle of the steering arm.*

R & P POSITION	WHEEL ANGLES (DEGREES)							
STRAIGHT LINE with 15° ARMS –100% ACK.	OUTER	0	5	8	14	21	26.5	32
	INNER	0	6	10	16	23	31	40
	RELATIVE DIFFERENCE	0	1	2	2	2	4.5	8
3 in AHEAD of TRE LINE with 15° ARMS: MAJOR ACK. REDUCTION	OUTER	0	5	8	13.5	17.5	24	30
	INNER	0	6	9	15	20	26.5	32
	RELATIVE DIFFERENCE	0	1	1	1.5	2.5	2.5	2
6 in AHEAD of TRE LINE with 15° ARMS: TOTAL ACK. REVERSAL	OUTER	0	4.5	9	15	20.5	25.5	33
	INNER	0	4.5	8.5	14.5	20	25	30
	RELATIVE DIFFERENCE	0	0	-0.5	-0.5	-0.5	-0.5	-3
6 in AHEAD of TRE LINE 30° ARMS (200% ACK.) SOME RESTORED	OUTER	0	5.5	8	12.5	18	23.5	27
	INNER	0	6.5	9.5	13.5	19	25	30
	RELATIVE DIFFERENCE	0	1	1.5	1	1	1.5	3
6 in AHEAD of TRE LINE 40° ARMS (265% ACK.) ALMOST FULLY RESTORED	OUTER	0	4.5	9	14.5	18.5	24	28.5
	INNER	0	6	10	17	22	28	34.5
	RELATIVE DIFFERENCE	0	1.5	1	2.5	3.5	4	6

Assuming there is sufficient space available to relocate the trackrod end carrying out the necessary modifications to the steering arms may well be the most difficult part of the whole task unless you have a well-designed race-type situation of two horizontal alloy plates bolted to a lug on the upright. Road car designs with a bulky taperpin joint and a bolt-on forging needing machining or heat bending can verge on the impossible. Once achieved, you will find lines from the arms now intersect much further forward, perhaps level with the steering wheel.

A suitable label for how much 'extra' Ackermann is being employed can be angular or linear:

ie 30 degrees from 15 degrees = 200% or 1.280 from 0.670 = 191%

These differ slightly because one uses degrees and the other linear distance but using 'doubles' works as both are conversational rather than technical. And may this toil and dedication make you quicker – the object of the exercise!

Chapter 5

The winning package

...but there's always a problem

WHAT SEEMS TO BE A CONSTANT burden of the human condition – the rule that as fast as you get something right, something else goes wrong – could not be more apposite than in the situation surrounding suspension. As we have seen, there are more than enough difficulties trying to get it right in the first place, with some things that at present simply cannot be reconciled.

Having done the best we can, other parts and aspects of the car will now exert powerful effects on how it will perform, or even have to be modified in the light of actually getting out onto a track, for the track has to be a painfully different environment to the drawing office or the workshop. As the vastly experienced world-class sports car driver (and tester) Brian Redman often observed; 'Forget what it feels like or what it looks like. What does the stopwatch say? That is the only thing that matters'.

The current winning package in Formula One – the 2006 Renault R26. (Renault)

In 1967 Chaparral shocked European road racers by appearing on the Sports-Prototype World Championship trail with this giant adjustable wing above its sophisticated Chevrolet propelled (and GM Tech-assisted) machine. The support struts fed loads directly into the uprights but wing movement and such upright mountings were subsequently outlawed. (LAT)

Audi R10 in the wind tunnel. Rear wing mounted directly onto rear bodywork, and rules permit full width of car. Smoke trail appears to be confirming the flow at the adjustable (only at a standstill) flap. (Audi)

Excepting only reliability, that is a statement that brooks no argument. The points now to be considered may need fuller examination by the serious student than they are going to receive here; suspension, like any other aspect of the racing car, does not function in a vacuum. It is affected in a variety of ways once the car moves, by many of its other features, all finally coming back to the tyre contact patch.

Aerodynamics

Almost the only thing that can be said with any certainty about the airflow around a ground vehicle is that the faster it moves, the more powerful will be the effects – for

Ferrari V12 (below) was the first Grand Prix car (ahead by some hours of Brabham) to run with a simple rear wing: at Spa Francorchamps in 1968. Unrestricted ground effect tunnels came and went in due course but wings remained. In 1984 sporting 'winglets' (subsequently outlawed) for extra width ahead of the axle line was allowed by the regulations and seen at bottom on the Porsche/TAG-McLaren which also shows huge development in 'slipperiness' and airflow management from front to back. (Phipps/Suttton and LAT)

Gulf Mirage M6 Ford at Le Mans in 1973. Modest roll angle, even in a gentle curve. (Phipps/Sutton)

Although Mark Webber's 'kerbing' in the 2006 Williams has the inner wheels apparently airborne, neither wishbones, pushrods nor body angles indicate any suspension movement. (LAT)

good or bad. Although the earliest approaches concentrated on the concept of 'streamlining' reducing drag, the only area in which this has ever seemed to achieve much success is in pure record breaking with the full teardrop shape. Mercedes' efforts with all-enveloping Formula One cars for Fangio and Moss were finally abandoned in favour of open-wheel versions after showing barely measurable improvement over the open-wheel version and big susceptability to damage.

In the cut and thrust of normal racing, aerodynamic effects only came finally into their own with the harnessing of down-force, the reverse of the aircraft's wing lift, working through the suspension to increase tyre grip. But none of it came without the speed-sapping penalty of drag. Once regulations forbade direct mounting on the uprights, the suspension crushing force badly affected precise ride heights and the carefully set nose down attitude that primarily controls airflow around and below the car.

At the height of the ground effect era when, as Niki Lauda has written, maximum downforce could approach 5 G and a Formula One car 'weighed' well over two and a half tons at 180 mph, suspension in the conventional and current sense simply could not cope. There were no coils or mechanisms that could deal properly with both low speeds and high so the high took precedence; coil rates of 6000 lb/in came on the scene, dampers of iron-hardness controlled the tiny movements, and 'suspension' became virtually solid. What movement there was came from within the tyre carcass, itself built to provide wheel frequencies of around 400 cycles per minute, and flex in the top rockers. It was not too surprising that drivers complained of blurred vision and back trouble.

When it is realised that airflow affects the car's attitude and the car's attitude affects the airflow, the difficulties of reconciling one with another and integrating the result with the suspension will be seen more clearly, or perhaps less clearly.

Well into the 21st century, downforce is still with us, in Sports-Prototypes in the fullest sense with side venturi tunnels, and in Grand Prix cars with heavily, double or triple, flapped wings, underwings and skilfully employed hot air exits from radiators, turbo aftercoolers and the exhaust pipes themselves. A full time, highly qualified (often ex-aircraft industry) aerodynamicist was soon on the staff of any serious team, and those with the foresight and money already have 50 or more such experts with multiple wind tunnels in which to work – and ultimate G figures are still around 4.5–5 G despite constant new rules designed to reduce it.

But suspension has altered visibly, though movements are still small. Swing axle lengths shortened as top links altered from horizontal to visible downward inclination towards the chassis and then lengthened again as convergence reduced (see Chapter 8 for a longer discourse on cause and effect of SAL). Perhaps most intriguing, roll has virtually disappeared, as has bump and droop movement, leaving the tyre to deal with the forces both from the road and aerodynamics. Maintaining the wheel vertical appears to be an overriding requirement of the tyre if it is to put 700–800 bhp on the road through two rear wheels which is highly likely to remain even with some reduction in engine power.

Uprights

The geometric positions of the top and bottom pivots at the outboard ends are not so vital as those on the chassis, mainly because they can be integrated with the inboard ones which normally take first priority. The two main criteria are that, a) they do not contact the wheel rim – all too obvious until the day an alternative wheel or rim offset is fitted and to the consternation of one and all they foul it and begin to machine the wheel into two parts – and, b) the further outboard they can be contrived the more leverage of the wheel against the links can be reduced.

It is certainly not unusual to see clearances so tight that specially thinned bolt heads or totally recessed cap-screws are essential.

Brakes

Over the years these drift inboard and outboard at the rear, while staying generally outboard at the front. Either way they are something of a nuisance to install around the suspension but not serious obstacles though dissipation of the heat they generate is likely to be a different story.

Unsprung weight

This used to be an idol much worshipped at the expense of other things, but which has tended to sink into relative obscurity in recent years. In terms of a solid axle it is still a highly important consideration, because the sheer mass of 250/300 lb of steel casting, brakes, halfshafts, crown wheel and pinion, differential gears and cage puts enormous loads, strains – and thus heat generated – into dampers and mountings. However, when it is all independent, thin carcass racing tyres in combination with alloy wheels, callipers, dampers and hubs, plus carbon-carbon discs have not only massively reduced this but have also brought it down to a near 'standard figure' on each corner of between 40 and 55 lb. Any practical reduction on this makes a relatively much smaller difference to sprung weight and the consequent wheel frequency calculation is barely affected.

The 1985 Renault-Tyrrell was the last Grand Prix car of recent times to run inboard rear brakes. The following year Tyrrell joined its rivals with an outboard layout for aerodynamic reasons. Note the possibly unique box-girder top wishbones. (sutton-images.com)

Carbon fibre brake disc on a 2000 Williams FW24. Since this nearly all discs have been elaborately cowled for low drag/high cooling efficiency airflows thanks to thousands of wind-tunnel man hours. (sutton-images.com)

Wheels

Curious as it might sound, wheels are not really part of the suspension, except as tyre carriers, and in some areas of racing a poseur's delight. Leaving aside wood and cast iron, variations on the theme of a circle keep a mini-industry successfully in business for road cars in steel and alloy, spoked pressed, cast, one piece, in two halves and multi-section permitting variable offsets. This latter type gives the designer some elbow room in varying both the track and other clearances if desperate – but at a cost.

Wheels old and new. Left, a traditional wire wheel with screw-on eared nut and splined centre – essential equipment for Fifties World Championship cars. Right, a modern one-piece Formula One wheel in die-cast light alloy, also centre-lock, but on separate drive pegs. (LAT)

In 1986 Gordon Murray reached an all-time 'high' for wheelbase/track ratio for modern Grand Prix cars with the wheelbase of his 'lay-down' BMW-Brabham M12/13-1 – BT55. The radical car boasted a 120 inch wheelbase whereas the rival, highly competitive (upright-engined) BMW-Benetton ran a 106 inch wheelbase. Murray talks frankly about its problems in Chapter 7. (LAT)

In suspension terms, wheels are nonetheless the vital link between the geometry and the tyre contact patch, and as such have to have all those old virtues – lightness, strength and reliability.

Track/wheelbase ratios

Wheelbase divided by track has always had a fascination of its own, since the early days of around 2.5:1 (4 ft track with 10 ft wheelbase) to current karts with almost 1:1 (4 ft track and wheelbase). Present day racing cars have tended to stabilise more because of regulations combined with the shape of a human being, the volume of 190 litres or so of fuel, an engine, oil tank and a transaxle than because there is any 'perfect ratio'. The now mandatory rule keeping the driver's feet behind the front wheel axis is a major wheelbase factor.

Given overall width maxima as well, there is a very limited freedom to dispose the major components and ratios tend to be around 1.6:1 (5 ft track with 8 ft wheelbase). The usual restriction on track is maximum width and a reduced track is an invaluable aerodynamic help in terms of frontal area, but at a penalty in terms of roll leverage calculation, aerodynamic flow alterations and geometry restrictions. Limited freedom or not, Formula One certainly avails itself of various techniques to alter both dimensions and with them the handling of the car – a major interest with every new season's unveiling.

The baselines are that long slim cars have a smaller frontal area, tend towards improved stability at high speeds and are less inclined to dart about. Short, wider cars are not as fast in a straight line, are more twitchy but consequently are more sensitive and responsive on a tight course. Manoeuvrability is partly a function of the moment of polar inertia which in turn is related to the weight ahead of the front axle line and behind the rear and a short wheelbase helps the attainment of a low moment if the weight can still be kept within the axles.

In between these two extremes, whether handling, turning or speed are the priority, top drivers are as usual not only very sensitive to changes, but men of strong preferences in various ways.

For these reasons if no others, methods of varying track and wheelbase without having to go away and build another car may be regarded as well worthwhile. Ferrari for one, have used alternative sets of front wishbones that moved the front wheels forward or backwards as required, and a number of teams have achieved the same result with variable length alloy spacers inserted between the engine and gearbox. Variable offset wheels, as we have seen, can alter track.

The only clear thing seems to be that there is no clear answer – yet again – or any 'perfect' ratio at which to aim. More clear is that small alterations, as in so many other aspects of the design puzzle, can make major differences, for better or worse, in how a car will perform. Consequently, it will be worthwhile if at all possible to build in the ability to vary wheelbase and track, either between races, or better still while testing or in practice for an actual race.

Steering

While there have been innumerable approaches over the years, the mechanism with which the front wheels are pointed in the required direction has been distilled into a single component located in only two places. The rack and pinion, capable of great precision and infinite variation of sensitivity stands alone. As is usual in all parts that have stood the test of time, it is simple, can be made very light and strong with the correct materials and verges on 100% reliability.

From the days when it had an intermediate location somewhere between the top and bottom suspension arms, and was ahead of the driver's feet, it has finished up level with the top links, its rack-end pivots aligned exactly with the inboard pivots of the top wishbone. The only variation on this theme is that some designers have put it ahead of the top suspension (majority) where it is clear of just about everything, while some place it behind (Benetton, Ligier, McLaren at one time or another) where it tends to be perilously near the driver's shins.

In the latter position, it has a shorter, slightly lighter steering column, a factor instantly cancelled out if there is a need for a substantial universal joint moving through an appreciable angle, with proper support from a bearing that must itself be correctly held in an area often rather short of a suitable structure.

Should Ackermann angle be one of the aims, which in many cases it is not, the rearward location offers a much better chance of the steering arm avoiding a calliper, brake disc or wheel itself. However, it also forces a high mounting of the R & P for sensible clearance of the driver's shins. You sometimes see a rack so awkwardly mounted the driver has to thread his feet underneath even to reach the pedals. Appalling in foot safety terms alone.

Opinion is so divided that while John Barnard chose a high rearward rack with visible Ackermann for all his highly successful McLaren cars, it was instantly junked in favour of a forward mounting with little if any detectable angle by his successors when he left. In due course aerodynamics dictated that the trackrods should run alongside and just ahead of the top wishbone, both hidden within a common aerodynamic sleeve.

What even the rack and pinion cannot do is behave perfectly once the driver has begun to put on right or left lock, but unless it is giving serious bump-steer in the straight-ahead position, lesser imperfections do not appear to cause significant

Figure 5-1 *The three critical dimensions when planning a front hub.*

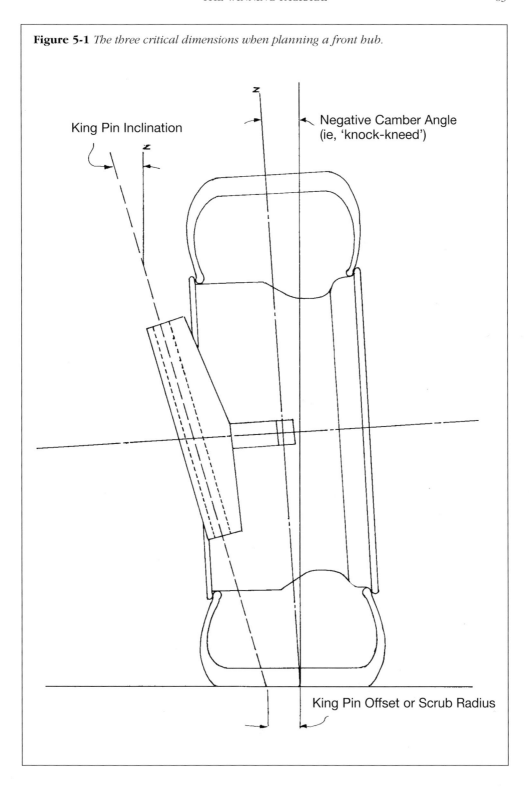

problems, probably dealt with by the driver automatically. Linked in with the movement of the front wheels in cornering are some implications of both the king-pin and caster angles so we shall consider them together.

King-pin inclination (or angle)

A useful approach to visualising what is happening during small movements in various linkages is to violently exaggerate the movement, either on paper or in your mind's eye. Contemplation of the illustrations should help clarify the following, which tends to be a bit heavy going in words alone.

Although actual King Pins are now to be seen mainly in museums, the name appears to be indestructible. That is more than can be said for the original parts which took the form of a piece of round bar, some four or five inches long and half to threequarters of an inch in diameter, gripped by heat fit or some sort of cotter in each end of a beam front axle. The hub was given two bronze bushes on which it pivoted around the pin to give steering movement to the front wheels. Lubrication and sealing against dirt frequently left much to be desired, and resulted in rapid wear.

The wear gave birth to the hallowed action by all second-hand car buyers with a pretence to mechanical knowledge, of gripping the top of the front wheel for a push-pull session. All too often the wheel rocked violently in and out indicating worn pin and bushes and was a useful and potent bargaining factor. This largely irrelevant tale aside, the angle of the pin was so arranged that a line drawn through it intersected the centre line of the tyre on the road. This provided 'centre point steering' with both lightness and lack of kick back through the steering wheel that is still a laudable aim, though now achieved with different and longer lived pivots.

In racing terms, the advent of ever wider tyres and the rims needed to mount them has forced a need to bury the hub ever deeper into the wheel. Accommodating a brake disc and single or twin callipers, together with the steering arm and top and bottom pivots for the wishbones, makes it even more difficult to achieve a perfect 'centre point' layout with universal 13-inch diameter rims totally dictated by available tyre sizes.

In practice it rarely is achieved. Whether it is or not, King Pin Inclination has the more important twin effects of putting (unwanted) positive camber onto the outer wheel in a corner, together with a slight lowering of the outer wheel and thus a small but possibly important increase in its corner weight. Traditionally, the inclination was of the order of 12 degrees, currently down to around 7 degrees, the less the better, down to zero were it possible to achieve 'centre point' at the same time.

Caster angle

Looking at the car in side view, the top pivot of the front upright will lie behind the lower one. The angle between the line joining these two pivots and vertical will normally be somewhere in the bracket of 2–6 degrees. Alternatively, the pivots are on the same vertical line but ahead of the hub – the 'tea trolley' pattern. Both provide the self-centre action that helps a car run true at high speed in a straight line, and will also pull the wheels back to straight ahead coming out of a corner.

This was well illustrated in TV pictures from Monaco when it still had the Gasworks hairpin, and a director with enough sense to put his viewers in the cockpit as drivers left the corner. Some of the cars, notably McLaren, had enough self centre to allow the drivers to simply allow the steering wheel to spin through their hands rather than indulging in a lot of cross-hands arm twirling. Nonetheless, ground effect and late Eighties cars used as little as 1 degree or on occasion nil and even 'positive' caster to try and help the driver turn extremely heavy steering.

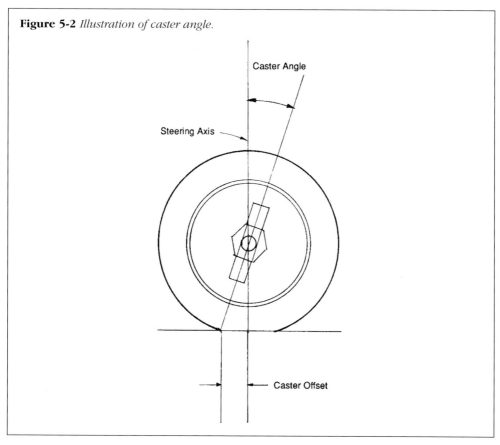

Figure 5-2 *Illustration of caster angle.*

The 'tea trolley' arrangement presents major difficulties in rapid alteration while the angled king pin has similar shortcomings to king pin inclination in that it also applies positive camber and variations in weight transfer at the outer wheel while cornering. It is essential that some form of ready adjustment be incorporated in the basic design, as, unlike in roadcars, the racing version and the drivers who will conduct it will require varying angles for varying types of circuit.

Ackermann angle

Another example where a picture is worth a thousand words: the drawing illustrates what it is. Achieving it is easy with rear mounted racks because the steering arms will point inwards away from the wheel rim.

On various Brabham models, designer Gordon Murray also tilted the arms quite steeply uphill. This was more a convenience in the design and manufacture of the front upright than any alteration in the chosen geometry which was dictated by the final position of the trackrod end.

What Ackermann provides is reduction or avoidance of sideways 'scrub' by one or other of the front tyres when turning by making the inner wheel follow a tighter circle than the outer. A moment of reflection will show that this is exactly what the tyre contact patches want to do, certainly at lower speeds. At higher velocities opinions vary, the opposition school maintaining that as the outer wheel is then carrying the majority of the weight and operating at a higher slip angle than its partner, what the inner wheel is doing or which way it is pointing becomes less and less important, to the point of irrelevance.

My own view, not applying to Ackermann alone, is that any single thing that helps the tyre contact patch to do a better job and enjoy a happier existence has to be worth any trouble to achieve. Being by any standards important, and with some tricky complexities, it has a dedicated chapter (4) covering development, design, incorporation and data on its effects.

Anti-dive and anti-squat

Without any frills, these two effects are self-explanatory in name, and are achieved by simply tilting the lines through either the front or rear wishbone chassis mounting points upwards towards the centre of the car. It is a geometric approach, as opposed to one utilising adjustment and alteration to coil springs and/or dampers, and it seems to drift in and out of fashion as the years pass by. Sometimes only anti-dive will be present, preventing the nose tearing itself to pieces on the ground under heavy braking. Sometimes it will be on just the rear, hopefully helping the rear tyres avoid altering their camber angle and thus enhancing grip under acceleration.

Unfortunately, because they are geometric they are quite capable of working the wrong way when loads are reversed, and introducing very much unwanted nose or tail lift at inopportune moments.

Although illustrations, naturally enough tend to show considerable angles in search of clarity, angles in practice are surprisingly small. In practical terms, we are talking about an inclination of perhaps one inch on a base of 12–15 inches, or an angle of barely more than a couple of degrees. Like many other small subtleties, whether it is being used or not, let alone to what extent, may be impossible to spot by the casual, or not-at-all-casual observer.

The value of building such a facility into a suspension has, in racing terms altered a little in importance away from simply stopping things scraping on the ground to controlling the attitude of the car as closely as possible for aerodynamic reasons. During the ground effect days of the venturi cars, the angle of attack of the side pod became extremely sensitive to alteration, and the current flat-bottom cars are now almost equally sensitive to any variation in ground clearance and the exact nose-down attitude. In a sense, more sensitive as there is more suspension movement.

Both affect downforce, and consequently grip and the function of the tyre according to Sod's Law, generally for the worse. While top drivers are well able to

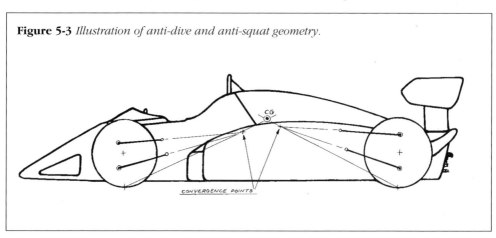

Figure 5-3 *Illustration of anti-dive and anti-squat geometry.*

cope with smaller happenings, they are unsettling, make for less precision and smoothness, and strong complaints upon return to the pits.

Brake Reaction Forces

Brakes are a study on their own but the forces they exert in stopping the car have to travel along the suspension links in any outboard installation – which at the front is just about every current racing vehicle. Views are divided on rear installation with strong arguments involving cooling, unsprung weight, aerodynamics and calliper mountings for both approaches.

Not only must the links or wishbones themselves be strong enough in tension and compression to hold half a ton or more decelerating from over 200 mph, but the loads must be fed into tub or chassis mounting points strong enough to guard against even the tiniest movement, let alone failure.

One example where it can be done to perfection with relative ease is the rear pick-up on the lower rear wishbone. These normally feed the loads either directly into the gearbox, or better still into a transverse plate or casting attached to the gearbox. Such an approach has great rigidity in all planes with a minimum of weight and complication. It can be a very different story, particularly at the front, and the solutions, some most elegant but others very definitely not, are yet another interesting paddock study.

'Stiction'

Having successfully created a near-perfect suspension in all its beauty and perfection of detail, it can be a bit depressing that once loads start feeding into it, it may not work quite as hoped.

One reason very hard to locate precisely is that the ubiquitous multi-directional spherical join, as well as sleeve bearings rub two faces together when working. Unorthodox and unwanted resistance particularly to small movements creeps in.

Big strides in slippery, high strength plastics have allowed the use of thin interlayers (PTFE on a woven base is one example) in such bearings and has improved them vastly in terms of wear but at a certain cost in 'stiction', so that designers still attempt on occasion to use a small needle roller or ball bearing if they can be sure of rotation in only one plane. It removes at least one more unknown, unless something else then flexes a few thou and produces erratically worse effects than a spherical joint could ever manage.

Apart from the suspension, 'stiction' is most likely to show itself somewhere in the steering mechanism. One tight joint, whether supporting the column rotation, in a front upright or on the end of a trackrod, can produce an unpleasant dead or wooden feel that destroys any hope of driving with precision and sensitivity.

A personal test and yardstick is that with the vehicle jacked up at the front you should be able to turn the steering wheel from lock to lock with the end of the little finger bending the joints sideways. If your finger protests at this, the steering is too tight, and will have to be dismantled one joint at a time until the trouble is found. It may be that joints with no interliners (the other type always have some degree of resistance to rotation, however small) will have to be fitted before this can be eradicated. If such stiffness is left uncured, it is capable of masking a load of other problems, virtues or vices as well as any meaningful driver feedback.

Four-wheel steering (4WS)

It could be argued that this recent favourite of the ad-men has no place in this discourse on racing suspension, but such is the sophistication of the two most recent Japanese versions that its adoption by our world is still far from an impossibility.

Nissan Skyline GT-R which features Nissan's Super HICAS four-wheel steering system. (Nissan)

4WS has come a long way from building in roll over or understeer through the geometry of the rear links to persuade the back wheels to toe in or out in a more or less predictable fashion. Porsche devised a clever system that relied on cornering forces to distort rubber bushes in the rear suspension to produce geometric understeer in its road cars – but kept it well away from the 956/962 racers.

However, the latest approaches of Mazda and Honda both put mechanically controlled steering movements into the rear wheels of a road car. The methods are different but the aims are the same; to keep the car stable with mild understeer at high speed while giving considerable oversteer at low speed, sufficient to help parking in tight spots.

Translated into racing terms, if such movement can be inserted with delicacy and accuracy into the behaviour of the rear wheels it might be very worthwhile indeed, and was one of Benetton's experiments. A little reflection will show that it could become an answer to the appallingly difficult problem of power understeer in racing cars with very high power combined with phenomenal rear grip. This partnership can be capable of defeating any known pair of front tyres in the appropriate circumstances, and causes designers and drivers alike endless distress, but it seems likely to come under that sweeping phrase 'drivers' aids' and thus be banned almost before it has started.

Path through the jungle?
It should by now be crystal clear that the only hope is to try and maximise everything in a jungle of conflicting needs and aims. If a computer could give the answer it would have long since done so. Ignoring the engine, as we have done throughout, dare we define the winning formula as 'Reliability, grip and handling'?

We have arrived in the mysterious and puzzling world where one car works just that tiny fraction better than another (McLaren at San Marino 1988, through to Ferrari in 2000–2004, read seriously better) so that it wins, even within the top group of the best-of-the-best. One area too often forgotten still lies within a designer's grasp –

reliability – and the ancient law is that to finish first you must first finish. While you can say that this applies to every part of a racing vehicle because it carries no non-essentials, the suspension is by far the most important from the point of view of driver safety in a dangerous world together with survival of the main fabric if there is trouble in testing, practice or race.

The suspension then has the curious double duty of not falling off under any circumstance other than one – a major off where all has gone beyond the control of the driver. When that happens it hopefully breaks off everywhere without ripping mountings and strong points in the tub. If this delicate balance of strength, weight and materials has been struck with skill, damage is kept within the bounds of immediate repair, rather than demanding a completely new car. We are speaking in terms of practice with a couple of hours or an overnight available to those unsung heroes with the big Snap-On roller chests.

As well as talented design, money is a very great help to reliability. Not only does it make possible the best of materials, parts and skills, but it also permits used bits to go regularly into the scrap bin. Not following damage but on a fixed schedule of the most carefully estimated periods of time. Neglect to 'life' components, or to scrupulously throw away what looks perfect after it has done a precise amount of work is one of the routes to failure or disaster.

Keeping suspension one race too many or even for more than one race, an engine or gearbox beyond its rebuild schedule, are things not done by the serious operators. Crack testing is a way of life, and do as much in house as possible (everything?)

2003 Ferrari 2003GA during the 5-year period of Ferrari dominance. For no very obvious reason, within two years they could not get on the bottom step of the podium. (LAT)

Elio de Angelis driving the controversial Lotus 88. (Phipps/Sutton)

because it permits checks and double checks and triple checks not easily carried out in somebody else's factory (unless you are Marks and Spencer, which does precisely that with every firm that supplies it with merchandise).

Grip – and more so, handling – mean different things to different men and given the power and organisation of the FIA, circuits have become ever smoother reducing the need to deal with bad surfaces and their demands for large wheel movements, lower frequencies and bigger ground clearances. Hence the uproar when distant or street circuits produce ripples, surface changes, even a manhole cover or a drain to upset cars running with barely an inch (25 mm) ground clearance.

In recent years, approaches to grip have tended to by-pass suspension in its dynamic form, reduce its movement to the minimum and ask everything of the tyre. Active, with its hugely sophisticated control systems, became a major contribution more to keeping the car almost motionless in relation to the road surface than permitting any roll or wheel movements. Ground effect achieved an increase in the 'weight' of the cars of 400% and more, increasing tyre grip massively after wings had already transformed lap times, and the ill-fated Brabham fan car did the same thing. Chapman's variation on the theme with the 'twin chassis' Lotus 88 met finally immovable opposition, while hydraulically adjustable suspensions for height went the same way.

It is difficult to avoid the impression that technical breakthroughs and truly innovative approaches whether in suspension or elsewhere too often meet the most violent opposition either from those who never thought of it first, or did not see quickly enough how it was admissible under the regulations. Often these ideas did not cause a ripple until they won – or were revealed by somebody with enough reputation to suggest they might well win, given a little time. Even the great Colin Chapman was not immune, opposing the Fan Car as vehemently as he defended his Twin-chassis. Finally FISA came in in singularly heavyweight fashion with its own sweeping and draconian restrictions.

The end result was yet again a return for a time to at least a little suspension movement, shorter swing axle lengths, more emphasis on wheel angle, modestly reduced frequencies, all spurred on by fixed rim widths carrying control tyres. Commercial pressures far outside motor racing forced Goodyear to re-think its approach in terms of huge numbers of special qualifying tyres with endless variations introduced even between practice and race day.

The freedom of teams to wring small advantage from a different compound or alternative carcass was removed (for a time) the day Goodyear revealed the deal that would give everybody the same tyre, with limits on the numbers available. It met with general approval, while even the critics probably felt a secret relief that the equation had been ever so slightly simplified. And the approach of very little suspension movement, high roll stiffness, cutting the ability of the car to change its attitude to the smallest limits while asking the tyre to take on a lot of the suspension task stayed at the forefront. Nonetheless, when Goodyear decided to call it a day, Bridgestone and Michelin were not slow to take on the challenge.

Nil-droop and monoshock suspension

Despite the rule book which has long required moving suspension (with springs and dampers?), designers moved more and more towards the classic solution for any very awkward problem – get rid of the problem itself. In this case it was suspension movement.

How to lock everything virtually solid without getting caught? One of the answers was to use short dampers that were at full stretch at normal ride height so the wheels

Monoshock suspension on Ian Scott Megapin.

could not go into droop, but only come clean off the ground if roll forces became great enough.

On this stretched damper was installed a coil of such magnitude that almost no anticipated loads would ever be sufficient to compress it. In case they did, solid nylon 'packers' could prevent even that. In practice, it proved very protest-proof, as well as giving virtually the whole of its task to the tyre. It provided a progressive addition to ultimate weight on the front or rear axle lines or the two inner wheels of approaching half the total unsprung weight of the car, combined with a substantial leverage, all opposing nose lift, tail squat, or roll.

This weight would normally follow the road surface under coil/damper control, but instead it becomes an appreciable part of the equations involving weight transfer, centre of gravity and leverage moments. But its effect in a corner other than on a particularly well balanced and extremely stiff car with high roll resistance, is to try and lift one or other of the inner wheels in 'skewed roll'. Worst of all, driver error putting a car astride the kerb could mean The End, stranded with wheels in midair. A further development, sometimes combined with nil-droop is the beam axle, otherwise known as the monoshock. (See Chapter 10 for a study of this unique approach.) Two wheels linked to a single coil/damper can only rise or fall together, UNLESS some flexibility or compliance is inserted in the linkage to permit a little roll. This will be found often as a twin stack of Bellville washers (small version of clutch diaphragm) which flatten if squashed hard enough, or tiny coils or bump stops hidden in a mysterious casing, perhaps on the pushrods. Interestingly the 'solid car' rapidly became a 'solid at the front' car with appreciable rear softness, converting it into a moving aerodynamic device (clearly illegal) as it altered its rake angle depending on speed.

While much went on in teams that were not members of the 'Active circle', Lotus stayed on their own road, and Patrick Head at Williams chose what was at first a self-levelling and ride height control system, hydraulically operated with a computer 'brain' issuing the orders. Initially named Reactive it was simple, light, could not do a lot that Lotus' Active could, and did not need to. It turned out to be the pointer to everybody's future. McLaren and later Benetton followed much the same route, but Williams' record began to speak for itself. In due course 'unbeatable' McLaren were first humbled and then struggling.

Five more years brought massive leaps forward: control of rear wheelspin, press-button clutches, no more leadfoot over-revving of engines, electronic throttles not doing the same thing as the driver's right foot thanks to black box intervention, engine monitoring and telemetry.

Followers of Formula One are still arguing into the 21st century about the wisdom of the demise, in a sweeping FIA banishment of so much technology from a technological sport. It was said this would make it cheaper for poorer teams while removing the gap between winners and losers, be simpler and more interesting to watch, not to mention slower and safer. It sounds unkind to point out that almost every target, save only safety, has been missed. Team brains continue to outwit the rulemakers – a struggle that can on occasion be better than the actual racing.

Without offering comment on such optimism it is worth considering the fate of another solution – proferred by Patrick Head no less – that a more effective and simpler way – would be to reduce downforce and as a consequence tyre grip even to the extent of banning wings. Its fate has been to be totally ignored. One does wonder a little how those with the true power in Formula One see its future.

Even 15 years later, it was still being ignored, as teams poured money into new, bigger and multiple wind tunnels to keep downforce figures hovering around 4 G – even more in braking, however hard the rule makers tried to define new restrictions.

Chapter 6

Active, reactive

... the future that was (for some)

AFTER SOME NINE YEARS of furiously high pressure development of 'Active Suspension', the much disputed decision by motor racing's powers-that-be to ban it totally in no way diminishes its importance in the outside world. It was a mega-leap forward at least of similar magnitude to the SU carburettor compared with a bit of petrol dampened wick dangling in the inlet tract in an earlier era.

Whether it is ever permitted further development or not within Formula One is perhaps now irrelevant when on its unveiling in 1987 it was already capable of vastly

Nigel Mansell in the dominant 1992 Williams FW14 with active suspension – note the 'flat' cornering attitude. (LAT)

improving the ride, roadholding, stability and steering of even the very best of current road – and off road – vehicles. It could alter your average car out of all recognition, like 0.9 G cornering force, still the province of an extremely good competition car from a roll-free large American saloon.

Yet mysteriously, in its most publicly visible form, in 1987 Formula One, 'active' suspension by no means set the world on fire. With measured improvements in cornering speeds on the road of 10% to 15%, and needing a bare 1% superiority in Formula One to be trouncing the opposition, it appeared not immediately able to achieve this.

Why not? Yet again an old adage appears valid: 'The brand new will always be beaten by the last of the old – at first'. A prime reason would appear to be that the contemporary alternative combination of a barely moving suspension utilising a sophisticated tyre to do much of its job, running on near perfect surfaces is able to carry out its task quite superbly. So well, in fact, that a number of the complex and different-to-achieve virtues of the 'active' are either much reduced in value or barely needed at all.

But they are certainly needed, and will transform in the coming years, railway trains, aircraft landing gear, mundane cars, trucks, buses, big earthmovers, farm tractors – virtually anything that employs the wheel.

Like carburettors before electronic fuel injection and engine management arrived, the combination of coil spring, hydraulic damper and a geometrically planned linkage for each wheel has reached an extremely refined point. But as we have seen in earlier chapters, it faces an impossible reconciliation if every aspect is to work perfectly. Wheels assume unsatisfactory angles, the frequencies of sprung and unsprung weights are hopelessly different, springs that give a comfortable ride also permit extreme roll, anti-roll bars helping but imperfectly.

The attractions of a 'brain' that would instruct and operate a vehicle suspension, softening the ride yet stopping roll, keeping it precisely level whether under braking or the influence of a family and luggage, keeping the tyres in ideal attitudes all the time, were very great. Unsurprisingly, Lotus were very early on the scene, and when they first revealed 'Active', their probably conservative guess was that they were two years ahead of any competition. Colin Chapman originally gave the go-ahead to a team of one: Lotus aerodynamicist and ground effect developer Peter Wright. The team grew to 30 and from the very first had the strongest links with the aircraft world in particular David Williams of the Cranfield Institute of Technology, leader of their Flight Instrumentation Group and his team.

Fighter aircraft had already begun to enter the world where, to get the fastest possible aerobatic response, a plane was actually unstable and wanting to fall out of the sky, restrained only by a computer controlled system that balanced it until the pilot asked for action in a hurry. The situation and mechanisms required were not dissimilar to those of a Formula One car and perhaps the most vital part was a 'transducer controlled actuator'.

We now move into a much different vocabulary to that of conventional suspension, and without wishing to insult any reader, there is an appendix glossary for those initially unfamiliar with some of the terms, but the actuator and its operation is so fundamental to 'active' that it will stand some description.

The actuator is a hydraulic ram fitted with miniature lightweight ultra-sensitive valves (made by Moog, the US company that created the music synthesiser used so widely in the pop music world) which is mounted where the coil/spring damper unit normally resides. The valves can alter its resistance to shocks and loads in tiny fractions of a second, and are controlled by the transducer. This a device which can translate movements and their speed into electrical signals, and vice versa. It will all function so fast that the actuator becomes effectively both damper and a spring of infinitely variable rate (and, as will be seen, anti-roll bar as well).

The signals (four sets, of course, one from each wheel and all different in subtle ways) are then directed to an on-board computer and microprocessor for advice on the next move. The computer is also looking after a high pressure (3000 psi) hydraulic pump which is delivering, or accepting back, oil from the actuators as they move.

If this sounds complex, it gets worse. It is not enough merely to know what the road surface, car weight and speed are doing to the wheel and tyre at each corner of the car and translating this data into electric impulses which mean something to the on-board computer. The true secret is electronically instructing those corners what to do next in a bewildering variety of situations, involving ride height, roll angle, frequencies, acceleration (or deceleration) – in fact, The Programme.

Further, human development of The Programme requires a method of recording everything that happens for later analysis and modification. Oh, and a way of altering all the controls and effects while on the move will be needed, at least in any development vehicle.

Unbelievably, the then tiny Lotus team had a crude version of all this not only built and working within months, but a Mark Two version on a Grand Prix grid within three years. The version was heavy and the Lotus 92 ran only in Brazil and Long Beach. And it did not win. But this was a fact which deceived nobody who cared to apply his mind

Nigel Mansell drives the first Formula One car with active suspension, the Lotus 92, at Long Beach in 1983. (LAT)

Ayrton Senna takes the first Grand Prix win for a car with active suspension in the Lotus 99T at Monaco in 1987. (LAT)

to its future possibilities and the quality of the team driving it forward. They had given a whole new meaning to the phrase 'a steep learning curve'.

Consider the remarkable range of things it achieved in – even by Formula One standards – an unbelievably short time:

It put springs, dampers and anti-roll bars in any conventional sense into the museum.

It managed to beat the very best of the established Grand Prix opposition twice on the rougher street circuits of Monte Carlo and Detroit, to pick up a string of Grand Prix placings, to stick tight within the first two rows of the grid almost all year (including one pole position) and post fastest race lap twice, putting up a new record at the quick, demanding and classic home of the Italian Grand Prix – Monza. And without being unkind to the dogged and reliable Nakajima, those results were effectively achieved by one driver, the fabulous Senna, in a single season.

It could maintain a steady ride height with a varying load of fuel which, if it had no other ability at all, would make it worthwhile to any Grand Prix car.

It could abolish nose-dive under braking and squat under acceleration.

It could, though nobody at the time wanted it to do so totally, get rid of roll.

It did not need bump stops, corner weight adjustments, spring changes or damper alterations.

It performed all the tasks of a component that designers have dreamed of – an infinitely adjustable, sensitive and variable anti-roll bar.

It was already able to carry out these delicate tasks despite the endlessly variable baselines of four tyre contact patches, track surfaces, weather and altitude.

Finally, it not only did them, but recorded everything; critical for later analysis.

Given this torrent of proven or imminent virtues, the sane reader will not unnaturally be interested to know why Team Lotus appeared to kick their Active into touch after a most promising first season. Part of the answer is that in reality they did no such thing; and variations on the theme went on being developed and used but very much more discreetly.

The full reasons, like those for Honda saying goodbye to Williams just when all seemed sweetness and laurel wreaths, and FISA's ruthless and total ban on 'electronic gizmos' precisely as several teams were succeeding on their own pioneering paths, are so obscure as to verge on incomprehensibility.

All had superficial, one-line explanations: 'Toughie Frank Williams upset the Japanese by not kowtowing over a Japanese second driver', 'Team Lotus could not afford to pay the bill for Active Ride development', and from FISA, 'It's all too expensive and helps drivers go faster'. It is perhaps not unreasonable to wonder in the latter two cases exactly what motor racing is supposed to be about, and what springs, dampers, roll bars and tyres, not to mention money have been doing all these years.

None of these explanations has much validity in the real world of complex deals and the prime aim of winning at almost any cost. Like the secrets of government shrouded for 25 to 50 years after the event we may have to wait some time before the full pictures get publicly pieced together.

For the time being all that fascinating and challenging technology has joined leaf springs and wooden spokes in the bin of history. Many would say that in the case of

Figure 6-1 *1. Pitot tubes to measure the speed of the air (taking into account car speed); 2. 'Accelerometers' to measure the up and down movement of the suspension; 3. Moog servo valves to control actuator motion; 4. Two accelerometers and an inertia platform which measures the dynamics of the car (placed under the driver's seat); 5. Computer brain of the car (under seat); 6. Springs to support the car when the Active system is not operational and to save power when it is; 7. Accumulators to maintain hydraulic pressure; 8. Radiator to cool hydraulic fluid system; 9. Pump to generate hydraulic pressure; 10. Tank for hydraulic fluid inside gearbox.*

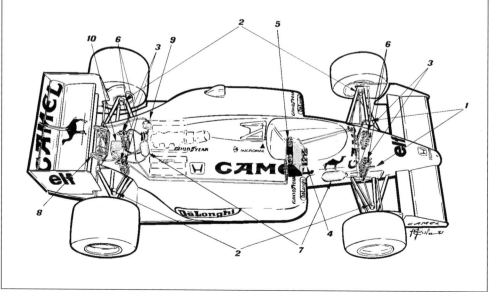

Figure 6-2 *A seriously simplified map of the basic layout of AR – to supply instructions and collect and record data to be downloaded later in the pits for study and analysis.*

USE OF THE GRID IN THE FORMULA 1 LOTUS & GTP CORVETTE ACTIVE RACE SUSPENSION

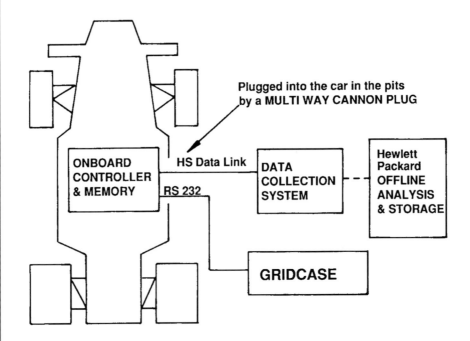

Plugged into the car in the pits
by a **MULTI WAY CANNON PLUG**

ONBOARD CONTROLLER & MEMORY	**HS Data Link** **DATA COLLECTION SYSTEM** **Hewlett Packard OFFLINE ANALYSIS & STORAGE**

RS 232

GRIDCASE

GRIDCASE
1. INITIATE DATA COLLECTION
2. ON LINE TRANSDUCER CHECKS & DIAGNOSTICS
3. CHANGE SETTINGS IN THE CONTROLLER
(FROM KEYBOARD OR MICRO-DISC)
EG.   STIFFNESS
       DAMPING
       HEIGHT
       HANDLING BALANCE

Active Ride, the baby was thrown out with the bath water as FISA grappled with how to outlaw things like traction control 'thinking throttles' that obey a black box rather than the driver's foot, automatic start clutches, and gearboxes that can 'learn' a circuit and decide when, where and into what gear to change, all by themselves.

Despite the ban, it seems inconceivable that a new and future era will – or would wish to – succeed in keeping the ban if Formula One wants to be a true leader in technology rather than – God forbid – simply an interesting and entertaining show for the global TV audience.

As Lotus's Peter Wright observed before the team's demise in F1, that early equipment bolted on the Lotus 99T and Hendrick-run IMSA Chev/Lola 'Corvette' was not hard to see or identify by those whose job it is to understand and develop electronic control and computer software as Williams, McLaren and others rapidly proved.

The heart of the matter remained throughout for all teams: how to programme the 'brain' with precisely what to do and when. Now the mechanisms for Active Ride are banned under that blanket phrase of 'driver aids' the alternative industrial objectives are still hugely important, commercially and financially. The true loss belongs to racing and is a sad one.

AR is likely to be seen in the foreseeable future on every luxury car worthy of the name. It can provide inward lean on the fastest of future railway trains. It can ensure that the weight of a vehicle picking a precarious path over rough or muddy country will stay equally distributed over each of its four – or six, or sixteen – wheels. Big

Senna in action in the Lotus 99T – note the pitot tubes mounted on either side of the nose. (sutton-images.com)

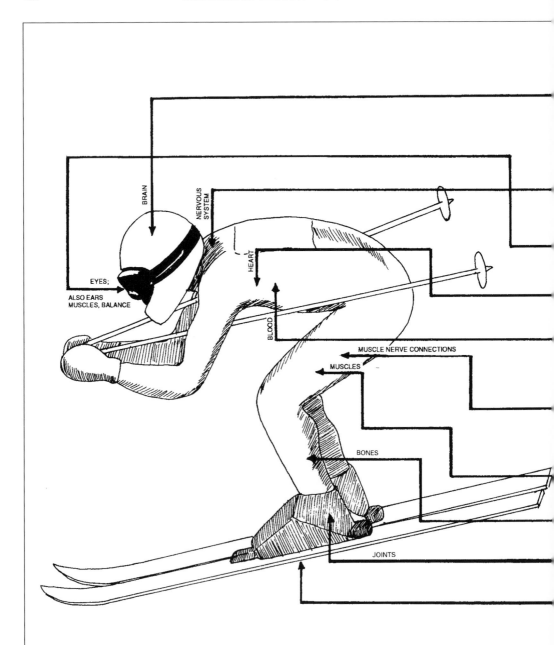

BRAIN

NERVOUS SYSTEM

HEART

EYES;

ALSO EARS
MUSCLES, BALANCE

BLOOD

MUSCLE NERVE CONNECTIONS

MUSCLES

BONES

JOINTS

Figure 6-3 *Peter Wright's favourite analogy for Lotus's Active suspension was that it functioned like a downhill skier. The comparison is an apt one, and exhibits extraordinary similarities, as well as illustrating the prodigiously difficult task that he and his team tackled. The complexity of a skilled human skiing downhill at speed involves perhaps millions of messages and instructions electronically transmitted to and from the brain in ways still barely understood. Active, while 'simple' in terms of the human body, still has the same immense problem of measuring large numbers of widely differing forces, centralising that information,*

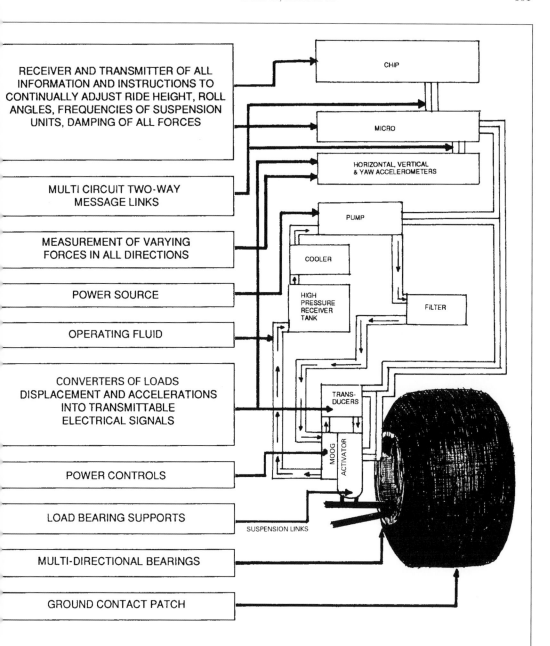

deciding what actions should be taken to deal with it all, and then sending the necessary instructions to the mechanisms involved to successfully control the contact patch with the ground – all in very short periods of time. When the skier first learns to ski, he at least already has a fit, functioning electro-mechanical system complete with the most sophisticated of controls: his body. Lotus had not only to learn how to programme its equipment, but to create that equipment and make it work at all in the first place.

Computer equipment in the Lotus pit used to run telemetry for active suspension. (LAT)

trucks, fire engines, troop carriers, long distance buses and earth moving equipment can all be made to handle, ride and grip the ground in far superior ways.

Imagine the most mundane of family cars that will give a luxury ride up a farm track with the family and luggage on board. On the dash is a switch that will turn the car into a circuit racing saloon. Its general mechanisms may well be identical to a passing mechanical shovel (itself transformed in performance) with only a different master 'chip' in its computer.

Such implications put Formula One in its place as a good place to wave the flag, an admirable arena to force the pace of development against the hardest opposition, but sadly not essential for the survival or success of AR. They also provide a most powerful argument that the controlling powers of Grand Prix racing should not play King Canute with this or any other tide but should support the sometimes rickety contention that it is a pioneering leader in a technological world. One has to ask how future spectators will react to paying to watch racing cars that they know (even if not in technical detail) are basically inferior in a fundamental way to the vehicle they have left in the car park?

AR will not initially appear on every family car for the oldest reason in the car or any other business – cost. The actuator and its valves have to be made in very large quantity, perhaps by production methods not yet devised to bring down the price, likewise the hydraulic pump, as well as the electronic controls. But anyone who doubts this may happen has only to remember that a small calculator capable of solving advanced mathematical formulae came down from around £130 to below £10 in less than 10 years.

In several ways the various approaches in Formula One were all barely halfway houses 'tacked on' to conventional wishbones with geometry that alters wheel angles in the course of any movement. If the car is not going to roll, trailing arms with perfect vertical wheel control could come back into their own. They were not a lot of help on the front of the ill-fated BRM V16, though the VW Beetle and Formula V had survived well on them.

Forty years on one box under the driver's seat and two more in the side pods would accept 28 channels of information, matching them to 80 different parameters, for immediate action, and making around 250 million decisions during an average Grand Prix.

The basic approach to all this was termed by Lotus 'modal control'. Vehicle movement is split into four modes of wheel movement while the body is considered to stay perfectly steady. These are: a) Heave, in which all wheels rise or fall equally in relation to the body total bump/droop; b) Pitch, front wheels falling or rears rising, or vice-versa; c) Warp, a 'diagonal' movement with the front 'axle' tilting one way while the rear tilts the opposite; d) Roll, left wheels rising with right wheels falling or *vice versa*.

Needless to say, there are mixtures of all of these. Each wheel possesses five channels and sends information on all of them to trigger instructions back to itself. These are: load, acceleration to the left or right, and displacement up or down.

Approximately 20% of Red Bull Racing's computer equipment on their pit wall in 2006 – what a contrast! (LAT)

Finally, the chassis has a further eight channels – acceleration and deceleration in three planes, lateral, longitudinal and vertical measured by suitable accelerometers, mechanical speed, and an air pressure pitot head speed crosscheck.

The hydraulic actuator at each wheel is irreversible – which means in practice it is locked solid, and the wheel cannot move until the computer has got the message(s), analysed the situation and then instructed the actuator precisely what to do with the wheel and its tyre. Depending on The Programme, the body can stay absolutely level, at a constant ride height compensating not only for a reducing fuel load, but also for the tiniest momentary tyre deflection, eliminate squat or nose dive, permit precise amounts of roll, or cause a car to roll inwards should that be thought a good idea (and currently it's not).

The function of the anti-roll bar in preventing roll and, more importantly, transferring part of the car's weight from side to side and one end to another during cornering is taken over to the remarkable extent that it becomes not simply adjustable but also infinitely variable all the way through any particular corner in any manner the driver or road might demand.

As the actuator has taken over the tasks of the spring, it might well be asked what a coil is doing visibly in situ around the unit. While it has an emergency function of supporting the car off the ground given total hydraulic failure, its primary job is to hold the car at ride height when the engine is stopped, and save the hydraulic pump the job when it is running.

As the hydraulic system does not have to do any work supporting the sprung weight there is an appreciable saving in power required to drive the 3000 psi pump, and its size. Nonetheless, once the car is on the move the coil is totally under the control of the actuator.

Development had been from the beginning a classically British, semi-informal partnership. In broad (very broad) terms, Lotus did all the physical, mechanical, installation and testing work, defining what they wanted, while Cranfield did the electrics, having built the computer and provided the ways of doing electronically the jobs that Active required.

Said Wright: 'Precisely what it does, and exactly how it does it is what we aren't telling anybody. That is our secret'.

The research and testing that has already gone into it is stupendous even by Formula One terms. Not only every circuit in the world, but every corner on each of them present differing situations, all needing analysis and a corresponding set of instructions to be built into The Programme.

Power curves, wing settings and gearing have always affected handling with conventional suspension, and they did not stop doing so for Active. But there are much improved ways of dealing with them. The 99T had onboard facilities to record precisely what had been happening over a given period and laps. On arrival in the pits, a plug-in extractor removed the information for immediate play-back and study in the pits garage. Alterations equivalent to a complete change of coils, damper settings and roll bar size could be given to the car's Brain virtually instantaneously – no contest when measured against even the fastest, most skilled mechanics in the world.

Said Wright at the time: 'Obtaining very exact measurements was critical. We put a lot of time into this, and then the change of engine (from Renault to Honda) clouded earlier knowledge. We learned that finesse and accuracy were vital. It takes time. In total we ran over 24,000 miles at full Grand Prix speeds. We can talk to the driver on the move. We never changed anything then, but we could change up to 80 parameters at a pit stop'.

On suspension geometry: 'It could be argued that geometry is more important rather than less with Active. The wheels can move a great deal over bumps, be soft in heave yet very stiff in roll. Senna gave us one good example in Rio where there was one bumpy place where he had to lift off to brake in a conventional car. With the Active car he could just drive straight over it.

'It may be that the actual aims of the geometry may alter – for instance, reversing the camber change curve or different linkages that become very good if you have eliminated roll'.

Another firmly entrenched view that low roll centres are imperative to reduce jacking and weight transfer but at the penalty of excessive roll would lose much of its validity if the car did not roll anyway.

Scrub, or varying track under bump/droop conditions disappears if you no longer need the particular geometry that produced it.

So, with weight cut from a starter installation of over 40 kg down to 20 kg, a derisory power drain of 5 bhp or so from the engine, an ability to mix it with the very quickest and win – at times – it has to be asked, 'Why didn't it wipe the floor with everybody?'

Says Wright: 'I think it was because Formula One has been steadily optimised around one fundamental. It is done very much on smooth tracks with tyres, springs, roll bars and aerodynamics that have been very well developed together.

'The package has very little suspension movement and a tyre that allows that to work. We came along with a suspension system that had to work with a tyre that was a suspension system in itself.

'We arrived at a time when all the tyres were the same – supplied by one company to everybody. We needed to change the tyre but could not. Many of the things that Active could do superbly were either not needed or not needed very badly in Formula One in its current form'.

But time does not stand still. Formula One will alter, tyres will alter, company policies will alter – and Lotus' Active Suspension Group will have been toiling and advancing behind the scenes. Sooner or later they may come together again. Be ready to buy a ticket and beg a pits pass.

To be fair, such an investment is already worthwhile on the long chance that the Williams security screen might slip for a moment. Even if it did, Patrick Head's approach to suspension and the computer betrayed little more than Lotus of precisely how it worked.

First versions used an apparently conventional damper with coils, but with centre piston rods of such massive size as to suggest strongly that they contained part of the mechanism. In later modifications this was incorporated into the suspension pushrods on each wheel.

Though Williams politely but firmly refuse any technical data whatever there were two strong pointers to the system. Frank Williams had always had an undisguised loyalty to Britain and British products and brains verging on the fanatic. In 1972, Automotive Products not only produced a design for a highly sensitive, quick acting self-levelling and no-roll system but had a prototype installed in an experimental Rover.

Further, they put it on show in Washington (USA not the UK home of the Japanese) and contemporary photographs show a singular resemblance to the Williams units. It was driven, as is Lotus Active, by a 3000 psi pump and hydraulic system but was basically controlled by a number of pendulums which sensed horizontal and vertical G-forces and issued instructions mechanically to valves for each wheel.

Substitute accelerometers, and microcomputer and the speed of electric signalling, technology still in its infancy in ordinary industry 35 years or so ago, and the requirements of Formula One very soon found a practical answer. The AP system was noisy and cost quite a lot of money, serious handicaps in a vehicle mass market but not in racing.

As Lotus made clear at the time, Active could analyse, control and optimise what the wheels did while the chassis was regarded as static in space. Williams looked to the other side of the coin, seeking to stabilise the body and all its aerodynamic surfaces in relation to the ground and the airflow.

The team's aerodynamicist, Frank Dernie, later to go to Benetton, confirmed the principles, if a little guardedly:

'Our Reactive system was conceived to optimise the aerodynamic performance of the car as opposed to the suspension dynamics of the vehicle.

'In effect, the system is a fast load levelling device, operating in such a way that gross changes in load due to braking, cornering and aerodynamic effects give only relatively small body movements'.

A short sentence covering several thousands or tens of thousands of hours work, but nonetheless illuminating, bearing in mind the current static ground clearance of a F1 car of about one inch (25 mm).

And he was not kidding about those body movements. As it turned out the ever improving on-car cameras meant Williams could not keep all their secrets, in particular

Damon Hill and Alain Prost in the all-conquering Williams FW15s in 1993 – note the 'flat' cornering attitude in a very fast corner, in fact it almost looks as though the cars are leaning into the corner. (LAT)

that the FW15 did not nosedive under braking if they did not wish it to. Even more remarkably it could and did on certain carefully chosen corners, not merely stay level and roll free, but actually rolled inwards like a banking aircraft. It also had nose-lift under heavy braking, presumably compensating for tyre squash. As the on-car cameras look forward from a fixed mounting point, it was and still is, even in a non-move era, quite easy to sight the front top wishbone with the front wing to study what actually happens dynamically. Just about nothing. In case you cannot quite believe what you are seeing, in some old video Damon Hill in one interview uncharacteristically let slip (or perhaps deliberately as a bit of advanced psyching of the opposition?) that inward roll was indeed in use on their cars.

So here we are with the wheel turned apparently full circle, and all those supposedly old-fashioned springs and dampers and anti-roll bars being hastily, if metaphorically, retrieved from everybody's scrapbin.

Shall we see universal monoshocks transforming all to virtual beam axles under those beautifully liveried skins? The 21st century bodywork will hardly conceal the 1920s concept. Certainly Goodyear or any other tyre company entering the fray could almost aim the advertising towards their now total contribution to how Formula One cars handle, go round corners and grip the road.

Will there be complex (but non-electronic) linkages that will adjust the precise application point of downforce, wherever it might have been created? If the driver can mechanically adjust bellcrank leverages from the cockpit – and thus effectively the spring rates and suspension frequencies – in mid-lap, is this a driver aid? If so, does this ban cockpit adjustable anti-roll bars – either a driver aid or a driver liability depending totally on his skill and sensitivity? And what for Heaven's sake is the flat bottom of a single seater but a moving aerodynamic device as it rises and falls in relation to the road – when such things have been banned for years. Not to mention the uses to which compressed air might be put, in both operational and aerodynamic terms.

The scope for new young designers who can apply a new glossy approach to all that old kit looks quite promising. But first they will have to oust those old chaps like Head and Newey, Barnard and Brawn who have been down the road years ago with not inconsiderable success.

One other approach to roll, currently under serious development for the car industry, is inventor Mike Mumford's answer to the question, 'what does a car really need?' Given the answer, 'Better ride and less roll', computer/hydraulic control of an otherwise orthodox tube or bar is a solution if it can be produced simply and cheaply enough.

Dynamic Roll Control uses hydraulic rams (what Lotus call actuators) to pre-load or stiffen the bars in a planned and progressive way as soon as the car tries to roll. The springs are totally relieved of their share of the job, and in consequence can be softer, operating at a lower and more comfortable frequency.

The computer programme needs to be able to distinguish between roll and single wheel bump, and a high pressure hydraulic pump and system operating – like Lotus and Citroën – at around 3000 psi is also needed but prototypes have been up and running very successfully.

It is a vastly simpler concept than Active, and amenable to a two-step introduction to road cars – firstly to existing cars without total redesign, but then into future vehicles where it would provide freedom to use geometries at present unacceptable because of what they do in roll.

Whether it would be worth the weight, complication and power consumption in racing – or would even be acceptable at all under the rules – is still a question mark.

Chapter 7

The pros – a dying breed?

... designer suspension

SO WHAT HAPPENS IN REAL LIFE? Up to now we have been looking at suspension design construction and application, at least partly in a theoretical way.

Much of what has been spelled out is already in print, though you might have to dig energetically both to find it, and then to translate the tendencies of some academics towards florid and obscure language into simpler terms. Lest this sounds critical, it was brought on by once reading the phrase 'Oversteer tendency in the non-linear handling regime.' After some thought it appeared in context to mean 'cornering' but it has to be unnecessary obfuscation on a stratospheric level.

Without being too sure of the relative pay rates, there were – and still are – notable similarities between the racing car designer and the football manager. Both have to bring together a variety of disparate and often unpredictable things, a number of

Gordon Murray's 1988 McLaren MP4/4 won 15 out of 16 races – a dominant performance. (LAT)

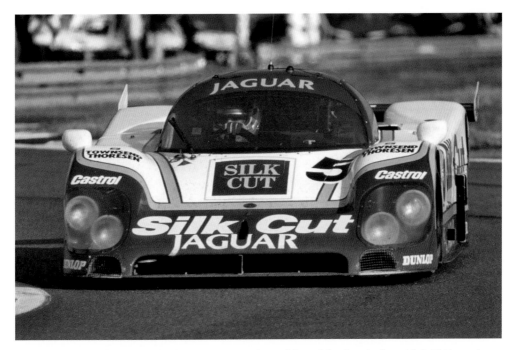

With its ground-effect tunnels, the Jaguar XJR-8/9 could qualify ahead of a mid-field Formula One car. (sutton-images.com)

which they cannot control or forecast, working over a relatively long period. When the moment of truth or action arrives, neither can take any part of immediate consequence. Week after week, and month after month in the season, the plaudits tend to go to the stars – players, drivers – and their undoubtedly glittering talents.

But designers and managers get one front seat for certain – the hot one at the inquest when it all goes wrong. Sometimes the situation can be retrieved in the short term, sometimes it cannot. What then comes into play is the degree of tolerance of the directors, the team managers or the sponsors. Some will accept that non-stop success is a hard act to keep going. Some will not.

Football managers would seem to hold a handsome lead in the numbers fired, payed off, or encouraged to go elsewhere. But quite a number of racing car designers have felt the same merciless pressures exerted by any sport the lifeblood of which is not just money, but money in huge amounts. Succeed or else …

And finally, the supply of the truly gifted in either sphere is strictly limited – perhaps a dozen in cars and two dozen in football, even looking worldwide. Because suspension is only one of their problems, the varying approaches to and thoughts of three of the men (so far as I know, there is no woman yet doing such a job) to the creation of a racing car are naturally complex. Neither Trevor Harris, nor Tony Southgate, nor Gordon Murray got the proverbial clean sheet of paper on which to work. Motor sport has a controlling web of regulations ranging from the clarity of a stated engine capacity (1500 cc seems definite enough?) to 'areas licked by the airstream' and attempts to block avenues of future development almost before they get started.

Both civil and criminal law learned long ago that it is virtually impossible to use words to define all situations. Human ingenuity outwits or circumvents given the slightest chance. And if the law happens to be not only conceived in French, but written in the same language, thus demanding a translation with all the possible nuances that may or may not be read into the new version, it is not hard to see the scope for aggro and misinterpretation. Consequently, the small print of FISA usually takes precedence in first considerations of design. Any idea, however bright, must have at least a fighting chance of not getting your vehicle chucked out without ever reaching the grid.

You do not have to look very far back for excellent examples. Lotus had an epic one with its 'twin chassis', which never got the chance to demonstrate the potential of its suspension; the Brabham 'fan car' managed one race before going into a museum. Unrestrained ground effect tunnels and skirts survived longer, but only at the cost of the bloodiest of battles between constructors and legislators – and the rule makers won in the end.

That is to say, they won in terms of the technical specification of the cars, which had to become flat bottomed, forsaking the infinitely refined aerodynamic tunnels below the cars, but they lost their stated objective of making the cars slower. Inexplicably to the outsider, Sports-Prototypes were left free to continue with full length tunnels, making them so formidable a Jaguar XJR-8 would blow off a mid-field Formula One car.

Substantial increases in the power of 1500 cc turbo engines – 900–1,000 hp at their peak – allowed much more 'wing' to be dragged along by the single seater brigade with little loss of straightline speed. The downforce bonus in corners soon had everybody not only going as fast as before, but yet again slicing lap records down and down. Fairly predictably turbos got the order of the boot, in favour of engines where only Nature is allowed to push air down the inlet tracts. Air valve springs, engine management systems, variable inlet ram pipes and power units with desmodromically operated multi valves capable of altering their opening and closing automatically arrived to retrieve the lost power and speed, as 900 hp came again. Once again, the powers-that-be took violent steps, banning 10-cylinder, 3-litre engines completely, in favour of 2.4-litre V8s. Just for good measure, tyres were to come from one manufacturer in due course and could be freely changed without having to last a complete race, ensuring corner speeds more likely to rise than fall.

What the pressures of international rules and regulations has produced is a whole new breed of designers and constructors – amateurs who turned pro right outside F1 and kindred international levels, creating a mini cottage industry, often having served their apprenticeship by building their own competition car for sheer lack of finance to buy one. They build and sell, sometimes complete, sometimes in kit form, small simple road/sports, GTs or even lacking a hood as well as serious single and two seaters powered by anything from a 6-litre V8 to a range of 'mini F1' motorcycle units, light alloy twin cams, high revving (11–12000 rpm) integral multi-speed gearboxes sometimes singly sometimes a dozen or two. Premises are normally modest and staff tiny or non-existent with the boss sometimes doing something quite different as his 'proper' job to earn the housekeeping money.

Quite a number achieve both commercial and competition success in their targeted field, but all have to be designers of some level of talent or other. While there are approaching 100 without counting 'one-offs' and as many levels of skill and reasons for embarking, three examples spring immediately to mind. For David Gould redundancy in industry put him on a long road to total triumph in the British Hillclimb Championship – currently won twice and his designs occupying nine out of top ten runners: John Corbyn borrowed the tag Jedi from *Star Wars* for his own tiny 500 cc single seater, which expanded to support a flourishing national circuit championship as well as sprints and hillclimbs. Electronics engineer Steve Owen quit a top job when his boss wanted him to move 300 miles, and has now produced a remarkable 140 cars virtually singlehanded (but together with wife Lynn an exceptional driver on her own account who also shares the wheel of their 'works' carbon tub car) to establish their OMS marque very solidly indeed. Although dozens more all over Britain have failed when the years of midnight oil burning have proved too demanding or the standards higher than they can achieve, a number now operate on very high technical levels with carbon composite tubs from their own ovens, aerodynamic knowledge and development of their own wings, TIG welding, automated lathe and milling facilities and export customers across the world.

But we digress. All these are aspects of a technological explosion that has enormously increased the number of variables needing to be balanced in some way if a car has to have any chance of success at all. For obvious reasons, nobody is going to be giving away a lot of trade secrets to the world at large but some are willing to lift the veil a little on how they go about the job, their priorities in the conception of a new car, their preferred solutions to some parts of the puzzle. All have earned the utmost respect for their views the hardest way – by beating everybody else at the same game at one time or another.

Trevor Harris

Trevor Harris is '60-plus' and still freelances from his home in Santa Ana, California. Together with Patrick Head he has a strong claim as the longest-lasting top designer in world racing. He has worked not only in Can Am, Indy Cars, Formula One and IMSA (American) Sports-Prototype racing but also in fabrication, bicycles, motor cycles and

Harris at the drawing board he has used all his life, having never been seduced away by any CAD programme a computer might offer.

off road racers. When we first met him he was doing a major project with a new IMSA car for Nissan.

The Japanese long ago sought out the talents of Harris for a top secret competition design that still lies 'somewhere in Toyota's cellars' some 20 years later. Nissan came to him late in 1987 to do an IMSA GTP car that would face updated Porsche 962s and the Jaguar attack on the US series under Tom Walkinshaw.

Pundits forecasting a Jaguar-Porsche battle were more than a little shaken when Harris's Electramotive Nissan put itself on pole by two seconds at the first race, won the second at the swooping Road Atlanta from pole and the third at the tight, twisty Palm Beach, also from pole.

He had only had time to graft a new 4/5ths, including a complete new tub, onto what had already been a much modified Lola. The opposition could take no heart from his moving on to a complete new car for the season to come.

The Nissan was the latest achievement of a 'great all rounder', a man who has managed to earn a living in design since he was 22 with ideas that include exhaust manifolds, aerodynamics, an infinitely variable gear for a pedal cycle which for a time financed his racing, the tiny wheeled Frisbee Can Am, Indy Cars, Shadow Formula One, making chassis, uprights and wishbones with his own hands.

Harris reflects the immense variety of motorsport in America, compared to a European tendency to focus on single seaters and Formula One. He stopped work on a cross-desert racing truck with 24 inches of suspension movement to talk on how he sees the job at which he has successfully avoided starving for nearly 40 years.

'I built my first special at 15, but I never thought of myself as a designer. I only say that now because I don't actually make the parts with my own hands. I can draw, weld, fabricate, lay up fibreglass. I've worked as a freelance for the Japanese, for Rick

Elio de Angelis driving the 1979 Shadow DN9 – a car which Trevor Harris engineered. (LAT)

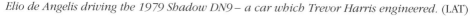

Galles and Dan Gurney, for Don Nichols who founded Shadow, and a lot of racers to keep the money flowing. The job and earnings are always erratic. I designed an up-and-down pedal cycle, and then an infinitely variable gear to earn the money to support my own racing. It earned me 60,000 dollars but finally the options were not taken up though I still hold the valid patents.

'I believe I'm the only American ever to have designed complete cars for both Nissan and Toyota. The secret project for Toyota in 1967 seemed to be some kind of exercise – very curious altogether. It just disappeared into the cellars after completion.

'There are no courses for race car designers. I think the only way to really learn this business is to build the parts with your own hands. If you haven't done this I question how you can design parts that can be made by other people.

'One fundamental is that no matter how good a vehicle is, if it is difficult to work on you will be beaten by one that can be adjusted more quickly. Better to work on it than dream about it. This is a very practical business and simplicity is an extremely high priority. But there is no cast-iron list of priorities, they will vary with the vehicle and what it has to do, and you have to get these right first, whether it be ground clearance, fitting a particular engine, downforce, whatever.

'Looking back at that earlier project, the IMSA for Nissan; it had to be an update on an existing car, followed by a completely new one. I was given four months and a much altered three year old Lola T810 without budget or time for a new car. I made four initial decisions:

1. There was neither money nor time for a new rear suspension, it had to stay.
2. The tub needed to be much stiffer which meant a complete new one from scratch.
3. A complete new front suspension, both geometry and because accessibility was poor; it was difficult even to change coils and space was very limited.
4. Despite 3, I might have to use the original front uprights at least to begin with.

'Assuming you have taken care of fundamental stiffness and geometry, aerodynamics have to be vital. You need the highest downforce with the lowest drag that can be achieved. And you cannot combine a high downforce car with a flexible chassis. Downforce and stiffness go hand in hand, and rigidity includes suspension links, uprights or hub carriers and mounting points. For instance, I much prefer fabricated uprights to cast ones. Castings have too many problems in manufacture for my liking – wall thickness, internal voids and so on.

'Designers like to assume they have done a really good job and will not normally like to subject their product to actual test. But they must remember they can screw up and be willing to admit it and make changes.

'You cannot reduce the unwanted in a design to zero – you can only hope to minimise what is not good. You can draw the position of the Roll Centre in static geometry but the dynamic position is a different matter. The point about which the car rolls can be totally modified by altering the springs, or the weight transfer and the consequent loading on the tyres.

'Tyres are something of an unknown. A race tyre can have, say, a rate of 1500 lbs/inch and rising, but you don't know how that rate will alter. I've asked for data. When Firestone agreed to make special tiny tyres for Don Nichols' Frisbee Can Am car, I asked their top brass exactly those questions at the time. They said they had never been asked them before and never carried out any tests to find answers.

'I don't feel I have ever personally done a definitive step forward. It is technology that forces things forward. I keep asking myself "what is the next technology"? Perhaps my perimeter spoiler – a projecting lip all round the bottom edge of the all-enveloping body was my biggest step at the time. It is appearing on road cars 20 years later, but it has been a bit of a trademark of mine.

'I recall one of the most satisfying things I've ever done was a front suspension package for Shadow that put everything into a tiny space. It was a private satisfaction combining looks with efficiency. If a thing looks bad I cannot do it. Parts for me are alive; they have a character to them. This business is more than engineering. The day a computer is able to do both a real neat looking part, and the whole job as well, I'll get out.'

Happily Bill Gates' Microsoft steamroller had still not put him out of work 20 years later. 'I still use a pencil on my two drawing tables as I did at the very beginning' he admits without embarrassment. 'But there are very, very few of us left now who can still do a whole car design from the tyre contact patch up. And in more and more areas, more and more restrictive rules prevent you doing what you know would be preferable. They have virtually legislated hi-tech out of most areas of the sport. Happily, I think I am in one of the last corners of freedom, where I can do pretty well anything I want to – offroad racers. Vehicles that can do 110 mph over ground you'd find too difficult to even walk over, sometimes for days on end and still stay fast and in one piece.'

He is no stranger to these as his CV already contains winners including the infamous Baja 500 run down the Californian coast into Mexico. Somewhat grudgingly he admits 'I know I do not make all the pieces with my own hands any more. I draw and advise and somebody else puts them together. If you need 24 in of suspension travel at the front and 30 in at the rear – which you often do – you can have it. I am currently on with just such a design for a client in Hawaii, very keen to win the next Baja. He has the money and is already a very good driver. We shall see. We have a very strong and enthusiastic group here – the South California Off Roaders, and I have

1990 Nissan NPTi-90 IMSA car, designed by Trevor Harris. (LAT)

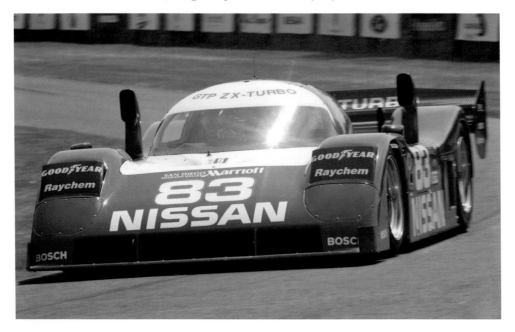

really enjoyed this designing – essentially racing trucks including one for Pikes Peak' (American's famed miles-long desert hillclimb). It is sometime since he penned the Shadow F1 car, but he has never lacked customers to help pay for a home, wife and grown son, and though he prefers to work alone he at one stage found himself doing a Group C car for Nissan, early on the carbon monocoque scene – but with the handicap of finding 249 other people in the design dept. 'It was endless struggle with paperwork and I like to have control. You still make mistakes, but then it is clear they are yours. You cannot blame them on anyone else which suits me'.

As WW2 finished the young Harris, still attending high school, was cutting a horizontal eight inch slice out of a scrapyard saloon to join the street dragracers that in due course pulled 99 mph over the standing ½ mile. He reflects; 'It taught me to weld and a lot more about metal and I raced it while still at school. Then I did engines too – though not now.' His conversation moves effortlessly ahead half a century to remark; 'Off road is so completely different to circuits but at least one priority is just the same – reliability. That old one about to finish first you first have to finish – just as true as it ever was. I depend a lot on spring selection and damper valving, getting a good turn radius and eternal problems with driveshafts and CV joints. The weights involved of solid axles and huge wheels and tyres are considerable. You need it all to stay together.' Bearing in mind he says he had his last 'proper' job at 19 and cannot visualise retiring, his immediate prospect of 'an unbelievably heavy rear axle and 39 inch racing tyres and wheels' he clearly considers light work for a pensioner. 'If 40 hours will get you a win, even 42 hours but still running may achieve second. Even now you cannot get CV joints that will do some of the tasks you would like to ask of them. The Baja 500 demands 10, 12 or 14 hours non-stop with complete reliability – and the computer still cannot beat the human brain's ability to produce original work. To create something that works is deeply satisfying for me.' Not to mention the customers still beating a path to his door.

Tony Southgate

Tony Southgate is a freelance who worked for years from his village home in Northamptonshire. He has been designer or consultant to many major teams over the years, including Lola, BRM, Shadow, Arrows, Chevron and Osella and for more than three years at Jaguar for their highly successful return to the World Sports-Prototype Championship in the late Eighties.

A few years ago, at the height of Porsche's domination of the WSPC, Southgate was bold enough to observe publicly that he felt the 956/962 left a lot to be desired and should be beatable with a more up-to-date approach. In due course, when Jaguar re-entered the fray, he got his chance.

'The 962 had been the car to beat for some time. It was quite obvious the chassis side was a very basic, fairly flimsy construction, which meant that the suspension side was not working as it should and the aerodynamics were very bitty. Stresses gave the engine a hard time and crankcases start to break up. Porsche have the resources but are very slow to respond to racing needs. Their Indy Car was an example – I looked at it and it was a three-year-old car. They work like a big corporation and worry about their reputation. A small team does it now and cannot worry about that. The Jaguar was all about trying to do it right.

'When I left school I did an engineering apprenticeship as a design draughtsman in a contract office. You get everything there, allsorts. Then I went to work for Eric Broadley at Lola for five years. In some ways I thought I was better than Eric – he'd been a quantity surveyor and some of his early drawings were on the back of old quotes, while I knew about heat treatment and things.

A youthful Southgate deep in driver consultation with Ricardo Patrese during his time with Arrows. (sutton-images.com)

Tony Southgate's 1986 Jaguar XJR-6. (sutton-images.com)

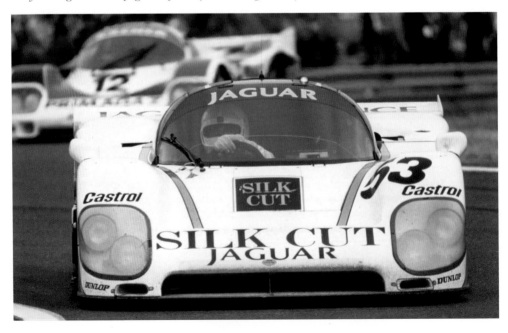

The Jaguar XJR9-LM brought victory at Le Mans in 1988. (LAT)

'But he sent me down to a wind tunnel in London to put small models in it. The experts there had no idea, they couldn't talk car language and all racing cars looked like an E-Type which didn't work. My knowledge on spoilers and lips and things was all self taught and while I wasn't quite sure how or why they worked, they did.

'It was difficult in those days. Now you never plot a suspension – you just press a few buttons – but the first move still has to be by a human being. Electronic gadgets do the plot, but you still have to decide what you want and where your points are going to be. You must still decide that.

'I don't have a single reference book in my office. Well, just one I think, Costin and Phipps from a long time ago. Design is largely evolution. You rarely go completely mad and revolutionary. You might hear its happened, but everything has been done before in 1901 or so. The clever thing is to put it on a racing car and make it go out and win races.

'It's how I think. You look at everything you've done before. You look at other people's work. You feel you can improve and don't give any secrets away. We do still look at roll centre and geometry, but if I gave you positions or camber change details my opposition would think I was mental – or they wouldn't believe them.

'You are under severe pressure in all racing. I wouldn't want to be working at Ligier at the moment (the brand new Judd car had just failed to even qualify at Rio). If it all works you are the big hero but if it doesn't you have very few friends …

'The most interesting of current suspensions has to be the Williams. The Jaguar is almost antique compared to computer control. I tried to buy Lotus Active on behalf of TWR but they wanted a million pounds or something for the principles, let alone buying the hardware.

'The starting point of a design is not always the same. With the Jag I was told, "do what you like, but use this V12". You have to come to grips with that – you very rarely start with nothing.

'Suspension is less important at first, but much more so when the car is up and running. In the design stage it is low among my priorities, for ground effects and the engine size and shape influence the type. You certainly don't say, "I'll have pullrod, or pushrod", but you have the general idea of what you want – ideally it will be like this but you might have to compromise on it a lot.

'Aerodynamics come first, but again you have to be realistic. You might have to throw away some advantage because it is simply not practical, is inaccessible or too heavy. Too much work to do on a car in the time available will defeat you.

'At the end of the day it has to be a practical car. Above all you have to have reliability. You need durability to run 24 hours plus practice at full racing speeds. There is a lot of pushing and hitting each other in sports cars, always scratches and wheel marks on the sides when drivers come in. It is not usually deliberate but they are very close to each other so some things look pretty beefy in a sports car, and you design bodywork to be strong and not to have bits sticking out that can get knocked off.

'The Jag project was very satisfying. It still looks quite good. There have been changes en route but the suspension system in its day was quite interesting because of one thing and another.'

What one thing and another? Southgate moves the conversation immediately to the 1982 Osella …

'Osella was a little team with no money then, but I did a front end with bellcranks and co-axial roll bar which made a very nice compact installation.'

Any disasters? He affects to remember only one – and that by Lotus.

Southgate's dominant Audi R8 design, seen here in its final 2005 guise. (LAT)

'That terrible all-adjustable 77. When they first put it on its wheels it collapsed onto the ground ... The Jag had only two structural failures in three and a half years. One was a wishbone, and personally I think it hit something, but I redesigned it anyway.

'When you are young you believe anything, and then experience seems to disprove the theories so often it makes you wonder what the hell it is makes it work at all. You put a proven suspension on one car and it's fine. You put it on another and it is hopeless. It is so easy to lose track. You have to keep a very open mind, stay flexible and change, if necessary, on the day. If it's wrong, you must bite the bullet and throw it away.'

He carried this sometimes painful and always ruthless purity of approach into a series of projects in the years after his Jaguar triumph, but always with a clear view that it would not go on for ever. His private target was to retire at 60 then some years away, with perhaps his biggest success – a major involvement in the Audi R8 still to come. After the Jaguar, Toyota sought his talents for a 3.5-litre Group C car before they were outlawed, and he made a considerable contribution to the McLaren GTR. 'Then I went off to Ferrari for the 333 which was partly made at Dallara and the rest at Maranello. I'd heard they were doing a sports car and gave di Montezemolo (then Ferrari's racing chief) a ring and he said to come over, and I ended up commuting backwards and forwards for about 2½ years.' Always somewhat diffident about his skills he asserts; 'I didn't really change much. I gave it a new nose and full aero package that was 1994, 5 and 6 and I really enjoyed it. They were racing the car in America and I was going over and doing a million details. They had very big plans but it sort of fizzled out when nobody came up with the cheque. I think Ferrari built about ten but only sold perhaps five.

'We did go to Le Mans with a semi-works car and I did a lot of trick bodywork for it – more slippy. They were first and third in practice but I got the impression Ferrari didn't really want it to win as it would make the F1 team look a bit sick which they considered much more important. We started two cars – on Pirellis which were no good. One went out on the first lap, while the other lasted 18 hours until it crashed. That was the end of the Ferrari job, but I went on to TWR who were doing a team of three cars for Nissan – I think the R3 – for Le Mans. It was a new team and a mad panic, with Brundle quickest in practice but it turned out the gearboxes would only last a couple of hours, obviously a serious problem. But they got that sorted by the next year and placed 3rd, 4th and 5th. I thought that pretty good, but apparently Nissan were not too impressed as they hadn't won – and it all folded.

'Soon after that I went to Audi. Ullrich (one of the world's leading race engineers and team leaders) gave me a two year contract and when I got there I found they were already a long way on with two different cars for Le Mans and I realised I was not there so much as a designer as a consultant to the building teams. They had never tried such a thing before. A lot of the lads there had worked on single seaters and had a tendency to make things as light as possible. Their idea of "massive" for Sebring or Le Mans was simply not strong enough. The two cars already almost built were a coupé and a roadster. The coupé which they were favouring looked terrific, but it was a stylist's car, not a race engineer's car. I felt a closed car has too many handicaps at Le Mans – weight, doors, windows, ventilation and cooling for the driver, time wasting with doors, seat and belts on driver changeover, and general access to all sorts of things that really add up in long races. It was 150 kg overweight, and the whole front suspension and mountings could flex if you tried hard enough.'

When Southgate studied the alternative – the R7, forerunner of the planned R8, destined to be one of the great sports/Le Mans cars in the history of motor racing, he was a happier man. 'I mainly concentrated on lightening and the aero package. It was very flat and low with a flip-up at the back and a rear wing integral with the body. I really wanted it chassis-mounted but for various reasons I went along with it in the end although clips that will not move at 230 mph are not an easy problem. With about 3,500 gearchanges in the race, the gearbox and dogring failure turned out to be the weak link and would only last a couple of hours, and then had to be changed. It was third, but Audi didn't rate this. They had expected to win outright.' What was the sequel? Southgate reveals:

'I had done the aerodynamics in an aircraft tunnel in Switzerland. While I was there I heard that Peugeot had changed their 'box in 17 minutes and then managed to get it down to 9 minutes. I was absolutely gobsmacked. I came back and by the time of Le Mans we had worked out a way of changing everything in one go – not just the box but the clutch, wheels, tyres, driveshafts, brakes – the lot, in 6 minutes. In fact we could manage 4 minutes if really pushed, the time of a normal stop for brakes, fuel, driver and other checks. We used pneumatic tools, dry break couplings, very careful planning, practice and so on. All we had to do was wheel it into the garage, shut the door, where nobody could see what we were doing, do the change and wheel it out and get on with the race. Of course it leaked out and then it was banned and anyway the team cured the gearbox trouble with a redesign.'

He reflects on what was not only the end of his job at Audi, but his planned and pending departure from the job that had been his life. 'The Germans like to go their own route. As the R8 progressed they had a team of 25 blokes, CAD drawings, men who learned quickly and well. All they had needed was a bit of aero guidance.' Others might feel his influence has been very great on one of the greatest sports cars ever, but there were no apparent backward glances from Mr Southgate. Later in 2000 he kept his promise to himself and retired. 'I'd done 40 years at the job and I found I was quite happy to do nothing – bit of club racing, visit friends and have them visit us, read a book, FStudent judging, back to the roots in 750 club.' By any standards a talented and fulfilled man – but will there be many – or any – more quite like him in future motor racing's very/top levels?

Gordon Murray

Gordon Murray took over the design 'hot seat' at McLaren after John Barnard departed to Ferrari. He had never worked full-time professionally for anyone but Brabham, but his first McLaren stupefied the whole of Formula One by qualifying 3.5 seconds faster than any other car in its second race, a degree of superiority almost unique in motor racing.

The road began as a racing obsessed teenager in South Africa, building his own special, working in an engineering factory while doing a sandwich course in mechanical engineering at the local technical college. Barely 20, he sold the special – and everything else he owned – for the fare to Britain and a job in motor racing if he could find one.

'Designing used to be such a solitary thing – all think and talk to yourself, but I don't know if there is such as a racing car designer any more. I was the only one in the drawing office when I started at Brabham. Nowadays I hardly pick up a pencil and have a team of 16 people. It has moved on to being leader of a team.

'Most of Formula One is evolutionary. The apparently new, nearly always happens because of some outside influence – new regulations, different engine, or perhaps the end of the road with no light at the end of the tunnel with the current car. You run out of flexibility with it, and you are very lucky to get three seasons out of a Formula One car.

Nelson Piquet drives Gordon Murray's Brabham BT53. (LAT)

'There are certain parameters you cannot alter, fuel capacity, size and weight of the driver, the wheels and tyres. If we lost Alain (Prost) it would mean a new car. It is tailored to him to half an inch everywhere.

'The first aim is to separate out the good and bad points of the previous car – get the drivers to be absolutely frank about what they liked or didn't like, its vices and its strengths. Then you have to try and eliminate the vices and keep the strong points. You have to sort out what you want to do to make it better. When you've added in a cooling package and a planned weight distribution you have very little elbow room.

'To alter the suspension is easy but if you find you have lost good turn in or something in the process, it becomes a very complex thing. Once you have made the decisions on the basics you go to the wind tunnel – let the aerodynamicist loose. You have to have a good aerodynamic package, what I would call the first level of importance.

'Suspension is still very relevant. You have to decide on the geometry you want and to do the layouts for it, but it does tend to get compromised more than it should because it is one of the few areas in which you can make alterations to some degree. Once you have settled the geometry, fitting it in is one of the last things in many ways.

'You need straight load paths, of course, with light weight and strength and all these can be quite difficult to achieve. There are a lot of very complicated suspension systems these days, but I prefer to keep it as simple as can be achieved. This is what you might call the second level of importance and the third level is all the minor stuff.

'Movement of the suspension has become of less consequence. It has been more and more constrained since 1983 (instigation of flat bottoms) since you have to run cars extremely low with little bump and little droop. This became as small as 1.5 inches in ground effect days, but it crept back up a little, to 2 inches or so at present.

'Weight distribution is veering back to 40f/60r again, although it was about 45/55 in ground effect days with the driver much further forward.

'The biggest long term factor in a car is the engine. You need if at all possible to stay with the same one for a number of years. At Brabham I had to do everything again from scratch with three totally different engines and I'm doing it again with the Honda. You need a new everything and then to go out and try to win …

'Satisfying achievements? Well, I always hated those little tube brackets and frameworks hanging off things, and I moved to special or modified castings feeding suspension loads straight into the gearbox and the Cosworth DFV cylinder heads. I did bulkheads machined from solid rather than fabrications. We had carbon fibre monocoque parts for the Alfa V12 in the late Seventies and I think the first carbon discs and pads. We really struggled with those – every kind of trouble but they were, and are, such a big help with unsprung weight and inertia loads. And they saved 30 lb on a full car set.

'I did a pullrod front suspension on the BT44, but that was actually three years old then. What happened was that soon after I got to England I discovered this magic formula – 750 Racing – incredibly cheap with very few restrictions. I went round the paddock at Silverstone with a camera and black and white film and decided that I had a chance of winning if I built a monocoque, very light with the lowest possible centre of gravity. Given these two and comparable power you will win, although being six foot four inches didn't help.

'To get the lightest possible wishbones, I had to get rid of the bending loads in the bottom front from mounting the coil and damper on it, which was pretty general in 1970. Some of those bottom wishbones would have held the world up, and with restricted room I came up with a linkage with a bellcrank at the bottom so I could lay the suspension units down. I made the suspension and began the monocoque but I was working such long hours trying to get somewhere it was never finished. But when I was doing the BT44, I decided to lift the whole front end from my 750 design. It saved me a month of working and thinking, and had quite an impact and everyone uses pull or pushrods now.'

What promised at first to be one of the biggest steps forward in F1 design history – the ill fated BT46B 'fan car' brought him face to face with the fact that inter team politics, always seething below the surface, can sometimes overwhelm design brilliance, however groundbreaking. His creation of a car that used part of the fan driven airflow through its engine radiator to suck it down onto the ground, providing seriously improved tyre grip was conceived and built in an unbelievable 20 weeks. But it survived only two more, filled with bitter argument about its legitimacy until Bernie Ecclestone, then owner of the Brabham team but also largely the creator of FOCA (F1 Constructors Assn) and deeply sensitive to political unity within it, reached an agreement that it would be allowed to do one GP before being mothballed.

Niki Lauda took it to victory while Murray went on with its non-fan, Alfa powered successor, and a further eight years of pioneering and winning including a World Championship in the BT52, to finally the radical but unsuccessful and undeveloped 'low line' BT55 with its BMW engine lying on its side. It was to be the last car he would do at Brabham.

Murray reflects on the ill-fated, low line BT55 with its heavily canted BMW engine.

'Well, the new McLaren (the 1988 MP4/4) is the same height and has exactly the same driving position as the '55. There were four reasons why it did not win.

'With hindsight, I was much too ambitious in how much we lowered it. The rather tall BMW had to lie down so far it produced a heavily offset crank needing a special gearbox and drivetrain, and what I did wrong was to try to do it in the time available.

'Secondly, the engine never worked properly in the lay-down position. The exhaust and turbo system was a nightmare and it had incurable oil surge and drain problems in corners. One way it was OK, but not the other.

'The weight distribution gave dynamic c. of g. movements that messed up the traction.

'And then Bernie (Ecclestone, owner of the team) who is totally non-technical and had always left that side completely to me, started to get involved in the technical side. We had had 16 years with never a cross word until then, and things were changing with his deeper and deeper involvement in FOCA.

'Then McLaren made approaches to me and I just felt it was the end of the road at Brabham. It was really the only place I could go for a step up and a totally new challenge.'

The results of that new challenge took 16 months to arrive on the grid and left opposition timekeepers staring at stopwatches in stupefied disbelief, so great was the initial superiority in the hands of two of the better drivers of all time – Prost and Senna. Would he – can he – say why?

'Well, it's a very simple car, very low, with a good aerodynamic package. Chapman laid the drivers right back – it's not a new idea, and drivers will never sit right up again. It has a lot of good flow to the rear wing and low frontal area. It has a simple basic design particularly at the front where everyone has got very complicated on suspension. We're quite pleased with how it has gone.'

Even with the perspective of years, this remains one of the more classic understatements on record. It went well enough eventually to rewrite motor racing history.

Gordon Murray with Alain Prost looking pensive during the dominant McLaren season of 1988. (sutton-images.com)

His 1987 move to McLaren was ostensibly 'as part of their management team' for its boss Ron Dennis has never named one of his designers as an individual chief, referring only to his cars being the work of 'his team'. What Murray certainly did do, apart from his unspecified work on the F1 cars was the concept and design of an ultimate supercar – the unique 3-seater, central driver, 230 mph, McLaren F1. Some 20 years on it is still the most dramatic and fastest road car anyone might own given only having £634,500 (including VAT) each at the time of original sale of the 100 made. Six years later a full race version went to Le Mans – and won outright. While the road version may never have had an owner/driver capable of using it anywhere near its limits, this small and exclusive band have the pleasure of possessing a rare jewel and delight amongst automobiles.

For ten more years Murray worked on behind the scenes and then announced he would leave 'to pursue an independent career'. Though he no longer has any visible presence in F1, his achievements make him more than entitled to be counted among the great designers before teams grew into hundreds of experts more in need of a brilliant leader and organiser of men than one with an inspired technical brain. It might be argued that the new solo acts are the aerodynamicists hidden behind their wind tunnel desks virtually unknown (save the extraordinary Adrian Newey) to the outside world. The ones who can be seen are now technical directors and/or the 'strategy men' weaving impossible wins from their pit planning and interpretations of complex tyre, fuel and tanksize calculations as a race unfolds. Together with tyre stops these all tend to produce races that have a first ten lap flurry, a middle section of numerous complicated but essentially meaningless changes of position only resolved in the final laps, it does not make for dramatic or even comprehensible action for the major part of a race. What spectators, whether in a grandstand or in front of the telly, make of this it is difficult to know. Informal discussion whether with aficionado or casual, seem now too often to indicate degrees of incomprehension, even boredom. Without major simplification could F1 be apparently growing its audience worldwide while dying below the surface?

The rewriting never ceases as the list of really top class operators lengthens rather than shortens. Patrick Head, still in the midst of the fray at Williams, his late disciple Adrian Newey at McLaren and Red Bull Racing, Ross Brawn and Rory Byrne at Ferrari, John Barnard ex-Benetton and Ferrari, Gary Anderson, Malcolm Oastler, Neil Oatley, Alan Jenkins and the remarkable Adrian Reynard. Few, if any have talked in real depth perhaps as much from the difficulty of trying to explain the extraordinary complexities of what they are trying to do, as much as professional caution and reticence. The higher the stakes, the stronger the pressures to stay silent. All clearly have some touch that is absent from others however skilled and hardworking. It has to be that mysterious 'something' locked within every world-class operator, whatever his sphere …

But slowly and remorselessly, as money, number of team members and aerodynamics and the wind tunnel have all grown in importance, the 'one-man-band' solo figure has had to add another skill to his armoury – team management. Designers now have to be successful leaders of men as well.

Perhaps time for a brief reflection on the place and job – if any – for the next generation of designers or if they are even going to exist in the future structure of this so called sport. As the 21st century gathers speed, both literally and metaphorically, what it has already become is a huge moneymaking machine with four massive pillars at its heart, four huge edifices with thousands of experts on their direct payrolls and tens of thousands more peripherally involved in its success.

Currently called Ferrari, McLaren, Renault and Williams, each run for many a long year by one highly motivated and talented man, this quartet have used a multitude of different approaches to create virtually 'identical cars' in terms of performance, capable of lapping within hundredths of seconds of each other – closer still when finishing within one second after two hours of racing, and created by different engineers in different countries, speaking and thinking in different languages, and working in different technical centres and wind tunnels. Planning to disrupt this status quo are, among others, the seriously financed Red Bull Racing, Toyota and Honda with looming overall, China and possibly the Middle East. The designer/architect par excellence of this extraordinary structure within which they all operate is still for the time being, one Bernard Ecclestone, but he despite his power, does not appear to be the reason for these remarkable similarities.

If not, who or what is? Well, two major forces stand out. One, the ever increasing numbers of highly experienced and talented brains of men moving from team to team in a small field of choice, with another being a rules strait-jacket largely imposed draconically from outside the teams by an iron administration. Speaking only in suspension design terms, many aspects of the racing car, not least aerodynamics, have now come to be considered of greater importance in F1 if not elsewhere. Nonetheless, none have displaced the fundamental target, however it might be achieved, of getting the utmost limit of performance from each of four similar tyre contact patches sitting on the road.

In view of this, perhaps any hopeful future designer wishing this wealthy elite to come knocking at the door bearing wads of pound notes, dollars or riyals, should consider obtaining a decent degree in design and manufacture of rubber goods to be a good start.

Gordon Murray also designed the superb McLaren F1 road car and its racing sibling the GTR, which won Le Mans at its first attempt in 1995. (sutton-images.com)

Chapter 8

The amateur at work
... a long-standing tradition

BY NO MEANS ALL readers will be necessarily enthralled with the idea of showing the rest of the world just how it should be done. But for those who feel that more exact details of the approach, some simple maths, finalising geometry and coils and roll bars and so on, have been a bit sparse up to now, there follows one man's approach – mine.

To be more exact and more honest, a distillation of much I have heard, read, discussed, theorised upon and taken to practical experiment in a number of cars, together with friends of like mind and obsession. In case you should find the following in any way unsatisfactory, unsuitable to your needs, or dubious from start to finish, blame me rather than the friends. Risking such verdicts, we will consider how the general design of a racing car, and the specific aspects of a suspension that has a decent chance of working without a fundamental redesign, may be tackled by somebody outside professional circles.

Bear in mind that just about everyone of current fame and success was 'outside professional circles' when first starting.

David Gould was building hillclimb specials in his wooden garage and ran a specialised electrical contracting team before redundancy forced him to attempt to go professional.

Colin Chapman was 'moonlighting' in a North London lock up building his 750 Austin Seven before he was a world figure. Eric Broadley's Lola was a side-valved Ford club racer before it was an Indycar or a Grand Prix car. John Barnard designed model boats long years previous to McLaren and Ferrari. Adrian Reynard was constructing his own special and addressing local motor club meetings on the finer points of the art on his way up the ladder. Gordon Murray built not only his own racing car but much of its Ford-based engine including pistons before ever leaving South Africa for unknown Britain.

None of them seem to have followed a formal route into motor racing design, even if there has ever been one. Some have a high level of technological education or experience (though aimed at other targets) and some do not. As the Greek shipping tycoon Aristotle Onassis is said to have observed: 'The only rule is that there are no rules', and for a small select group this seems to be true as they take unorthodox ways to the top with talents somewhat hard to define.

They utilise those talents in a sport with high technological content, in which there is undoubtedly a 'Great Divide' between those with virtually unlimited money and resources, and those who have less, a lot less or are very pushed indeed. In reality all share almost every difficulty with each other, but will have to solve those difficulties in different ways, with a different sequence to their priorities.

For instance: it is difficult to refute the point of view that all suspension design must begin with the tyre, while spring frequencies, geometry, weight transfer and a dozen

The author in his Terrapin Mk7 at Harewood in 1978. This car featured suspension by Pirelli seat webbing in tension with top rocking arms and a supercharged Mini engine. (Author)

Quarter of a century later – same man, different car. No blower, but 50 more injected BHP, 140 lb less weight and new slicks! (www.whatnonegatives)

Simon Durling making effective use of David Gould's Gould GR55 – David started as an amateur designer/builder, but his cars now dominate the British Hillclimb Championship. (Gould)

other parameters are tailored to the rate and characteristics of the carcass and compound. The flaws in the practical application of this standpoint are two-fold. Tyres are still a very difficult manufactured object in which to forecast precisely how they will perform in a variety of situations. And should such forecasts be available – and they verge on the impossible to extract from any tyre firm – the amateur cannot influence or alter them in any way.

In truth he can, just a little, by altering pressures (and hence the rate) and fitting them onto varying widths of rim (which will alter the carcass stability and performance under cornering forces). And this is barely less than the professionals can manage with a control tyre enforced on every entrant.

'Beyond here lie dragons' the old mapmakers inscribed when reliable information dried up completely. Such ignorance does not obliterate the need to give the tyre contact patch, the single most important thing on a racing car, the very best chance to perform to its maximum. This might be loosely defined as keeping it flat on the road, distorting it as little as practicable, not grossly over – or under – loading it at front or rear, and keeping it as near a proper running temperature as climate or speeds allow.

It may come as some surprise to know the precise detailing of the chassis/tub will not be near the top of our list. Only its stiffness is vital. Its function is that of a large, complex bracket, with the sole job in life of locating accurately and rigidly, in space, the various components ranging from suspension pivots to the driver's backside. It must fit them, not the other way round.

We have already considered to some degree how important are the current regulations in force and how they have to come first. A never ending war, Rulemakers versus The Rest, ensures that the fabric of those rules is forever bending, creaking and sometimes giving way completely under the unrelenting pressures of the determined, the devious and the frankly dubious, fuelled by immense sums of money at the top levels of the sport.

'Reading the regs' is step one. It is no use to arrive in the first scrutineering bay with a world beater that is just slightly the wrong size. Sounds very basic? It is, but it has still happened painfully publicly to some of the most experienced; McLaren for one, concerning a little matter of overall width, and Osella losing to Italian scrutineers in a 'new car or modified one' argument. Other requirements can include safety standards, materials, wheel travel, wheelbase and track, tyre and rim sizes, body dimensions, overhang sideways, forward and back, cockpit size and access – the list seems never ending.

Once the small print has been digested, the first move is to do side and plan views to scale of the items that must be part of the finished car and permit no variation. These will include the human being that will drive it, engine/gearbox unit, fuel tank whether 2 or 42 gallons, oil tank if dry sumped, the steering wheel and gear lever, and the line on which the pedals and thus the driver's feet will lie.

We could go into a lot of detail on these aspects, and the various and graceful solutions that have been found to them over the years, but they will have to give way to the prime objective here – suspension.

Once you are embarked, the sequence often appears to work backwards. Firstly one decides what is wanted and then one moves on to try and achieve it.

The Priority List:

1. Regulations.
2. Tyres.
3. Wheels.
4. Hubs and uprights.
5. Geometry.
6. Roll centre.
7. Instantaneous roll centre/swing axle length.
8. Chassis/tub (The 'Big bracket').
9. Springs.
10. Dampers.
11. Anti-roll bars.
12. Steering.

Regulations

The importance of these has already been discussed. For UK competitors, the main source will be the RACMSA's 'Blue Book' which comes free with the competition licence.

Tyres

The enormous availability and variety of the 13 inch diameter tyre, whether new or 'slightly scuffed' makes it highly likely to be the first choice. Any larger diameter is usually employed only because vehicle size or power forces the option. The smaller 12 inch is a rare bird, and the desirable (from a weight and inertia point of view) 10 inch Mini size suffers from a marked lack of choice in width, construction and tread compounds.

Wheels

These will be totally dictated by tyre size and the type of centre fixing or stud pattern of the hub flange. Do not invest any of your funding into wheels, however attractive and low priced, until you know exactly how and to what they will be attached. It is far easier to obtain a wheel with the centre you require than to alter a hub and flange to suit the wrong wheel.

Hubs and uprights

Although technically two items, together with their bearings, spacers and seals, they are so closely interrelated as to be a single component. In one swoop, it dictates wheels, offsets (or insets, if you prefer), method of attachment, and the vital positions of the upper and lower outboard suspension pick-ups. The professional would have these made to his own dimensions, whether cast or fabricated, but the amateur can often alter pick-ups, especially up or down, by designing his own bushes, spacer plates or inserted pins to modify the upright. This is a valid example of first deciding what you need, and only then setting about achieving it.

Happily it may not be necessary because, as we shall see fairly soon, the aims of the final suspension geometry can very often be achieved utilising outboard points already chosen by somebody else for a different situation.

Geometry

Any decision on springs, anti-roll bars, weight transfer or wheel frequencies cannot be made until the lengths, angles and pick up positions of the wishbones have been finalised. But the basic injunction to 'stay low' where centre of gravity and roll centre are concerned is a vital one to keep to the fore.

The front end of the author's own suspension design on his hillclimb Megapin. Note the far forward mounted R & P (see Chapter 4) and the central anti-dive mechanism with rubbers in compression. (Author)

We are now at the heart of things, and that heart – in my view at least – is The Roll Centre.

You have to have at least one firm base on which to begin creating your suspension design, and nothing I have been involved with over some years has shaken my conviction that the best, and possibly the only, reliable starting point is the Roll Centre. You have to cling on to something.

Where the roll centre is located statically in various designs of suspension can most clearly be seen in drawings rather than attempting any explanation in words. What it is, at least theoretically, is the point in space about which the vehicle will rotate when it leans over in a corner. As this point will dictate how the chassis suspension pick-up points move, and hence what the wheel and tyre will then do, the importance of controlling its position in space, should this be possible, will be clear.

The trouble with all theoretical suspension concepts is that they alter once real life cornering and other forces come into play, because the static data on which they are based alters. The Dynamic Roll Centre (as opposed to the static one) can and does move up, down, and sideways. How far and which way are two of several questions not easy to answer.

Roll being itself a function of another equally invisible point, the Centre of Gravity (which though fixed can appear to exert itself dynamically as if it had moved), it can be seen how the variations and uncertainties are rapidly multiplying. Leverages alter, the car's attitude alters, weight transfer from inner to outer wheels alters, and at the end of the line, the tyre contact patches start distorting under a complex and varying series of loads.

Such uncertainties do not invalidate careful pre-planning and design, otherwise one car, however laid out or badly unbalanced would work as well as any other. Clearly this is not the case, so how to make a start?

Currently there are four options:

1. Copy exactly, through friendship or purchase, a successful design already running. The obvious hurdle in this is that every point in it that moves must be reproduced precisely in space, and a suitable identical upright may not exist. And once your copy begins to diverge from the original, potential roadholding shortcomings creep in. You must anyway make your own analysis of it or any future modifications will be fumbling in the dark.
2. Draw your proposed layout, then re-draw and re-draw with gradual movements of wheel and chassis in bump, roll and droop. You will soon be into scores and then hundreds of drawings while researching variations of variations. Barely practical even for the drawing office of a major manufacturer.
3. Use a computer to vary a mathematical model of your brainchild. The prime virtue of the computer – its ability to do a million or 100 million repetitive calculations at high speed in search of a solution – is perfectly suited to the task. What is difficult is creating a suitable programme (a set of instructions which it can follow), though several are now on the commercial market, together with an analysis and design services. Even more difficult is deciding the targets to seek for your chosen objectives.

    The major teams and big manufacturers have been into computer technology now for decades, but apparently still without producing the perfect answer. One reason for this may well be deciding the questions that need to be asked in the first place, as well as interpreting the answers. The human brain is still paramount in interpolating what the computer will spew out.

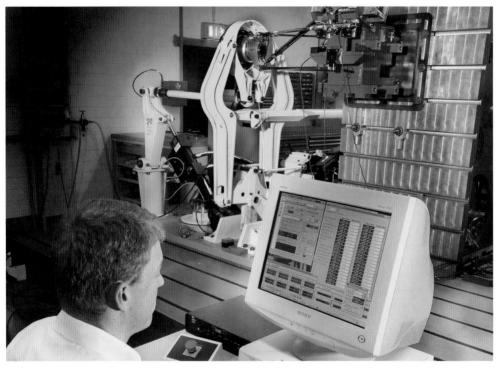

The resources available to the top Formula One teams are awe-inspiring. Here (above) a Toyota F1 car front suspension is being tested on a single-post rig, whilst below the complete car is undergoing a full race simulation to gather suspension data on a seven-post test rig. (Toyota)

4. The String Computer. Born of desperate necessity when Richard Blackmore and I were designing the first Terrapin (Mini rear-engined, single seater with spaceframe chassis) at a time when computers were room sized and cost a million pounds or so. The approach was to make a working model of an unequal length wishbone suspension to scale and to give it freedom to move not only the wheel and upright but also to rotate the chassis and wishbones about a variable roll centre. Finally the string supplied a way of indicating in small increments what the roll centre might be doing. Do not laugh. It was easy and cheap to make, and proved such a good basic, if apparently crude tool that later cross-checks when computers had made the downward mega-leap into every high street electrical shop showed that results it gave correlated quite closely with the electronic versions. It was not able by its construction to work to much closer than 0.060 inch (1.5 mm), while a computer operates to a 'thou' or less if you ask it.

This is not a really major handicap as the critical thing is achieving the right objectives within reasonable limits rather than getting the wrong ones with total accuracy. Its worst shortcoming is that very long Swing Axle Lengths, when the wishbones approach nearer and nearer to parallel, make manipulation of the string impossible by one person. However, half scale and a friend operating at the far end of a long room will overcome all but the most extreme situations. Details of its construction and use are given in Appendix 1.

First experiments indicated that roll centres do indeed move sideways under some circumstances, as well as up and down. This can be shown by using the computer to plot first an outer wheel, then an inner wheel (left roll, then right roll). Unless you have hit the jackpot first go, and the roll centre stays at an unaltered height it will

The String Computer in action! (Author)

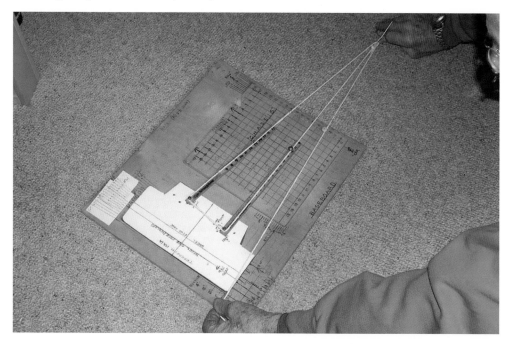

normally rise for one wheel and fall for the other. Clearly it cannot be in two places at once, and it has in fact moved sideways to the intersection of the two lines joining the instantaneous roll centres to the tyre contact patches. Careful experimentation can reduce this to almost negligible proportions.

While roll centre and geometry in general have been publicly rubbished as unimportant by some designers, it is clear from analysing various competition cars that the close control of the roll centre (sometimes within .015–.020 over the total wheel travel) is beyond luck and has demanded a good deal of private attention.

We can now get down to more detail, attempting to quantify and define a few aims, and then consider how to achieve them – should they be achievable.

Roll centre
The roll centre lies in the bracket between an inch below ground to (at worst) some 12 inches above, in the case of the centre of a solid axle. All racing cars are probably now located within one inch below to two inches above ground. Low centres give less weight transfer to the outer wheel, smaller or nil jacking effect but high potential roll angles. Suitable and variable anti-roll bars must handle this. Front and rear centres are conventionally at different heights to give a tilted Roll Axis with the lower centre at the lowest and/or lightest end of the vehicle but this is by no means universal.

Instantaneous roll centre/Swing Axle Length (SAL)
These are another couple of invisible variables in less than precise ways. IRC is the intersection point of lines drawn along the wishbones, and SAL is the distance from this point back to the wheel.

Short SAL (20–40 inches) gives very good roll centre location, keeps the outer wheel vertical in corners, but going badly to positive camber in droop and negative in bump (acceleration squat and braking).

Long SAL (70–180 inches) provides lower roll centres but less control over their sideways movement, minimal scrub (track variation), poor outer wheel control going into positive camber, but only small camber change in bump/droop.

Medium SAL (40–70 inches) is the transition area between long and short with, as you might expect, a bit of this and a bit of that.

Ultra-long SAL (near parallel: one example had 14,000 inches) provides excellent vertical control of very low roll centres but possible sideways movement, wheel angles virtually unaltered in bump/droop but very poor control of wheels in roll, with near equivalency to body roll angle.

It will be evident from all this that, as in life, you cannot have everything. Roll effects, wheel angle, scrub and roll centre location have to be balanced against each other and different situations (circuit, hillclimb; free or restricted tyre width; tolerable roll angle or ground clearance) may demand different priorities.

Having discussed an approach that costs literally nothing, the use of a computer is so much faster it permits vastly more experiment in the limited time any of us has available. A commercial programme will provide an analysis of given data, refining it as you feed in altered dimensions. But beware – some are difficult to use rapidly and (or) display results in far from crystal clear ways. Try to use your choice at least once before laying out any cash. And remember they never tell you what you want, only what you will get from a specific layout. You still have to make the decisions on what you are seeking. That screen supplies the figures but none of the secrets why.

Doing it on your own home computer demands a programme of some complexity, but certainly not beyond a reasonable maths student with tenacity. I know at least three who have done it in various forms so there have to be many others.

To grossly oversimplify, you have to reduce the suspension dimensions to a number of triangles that will vary in a sequential as well as interrelated way in the length of their sides and their angles. Not all small computers can cope with the demands, so research is needed, but having seen and used the David Gould-written programme (Gould as in Chapter Eight) its attractions are considerable.

But even with such a facility, comprehension of the principles and specific aims are still needed as you have to feed data in before you get answers out.

Remembering that we began with the tyre, the String Computer is literally as well as metaphorically a 'wooden wheel' model. It cannot really insert deflection under load of the tyre carcass, although a rough attempt can be made by mis-setting the bottom of the wheel on the 'road' to reproduce your estimate of how much the carcass has deflected. As this has to be the most difficult to quantify variable by a considerable margin, you will have to decide whether to do totally without it, or take the gamble of an attempted inclusion. Either way, never forget that the wider the tyre, the less happy and efficient it will be as it leans away from the vertical. Keeping the tread area flat on the ground so far as humanly possible is of the highest priority.

Springs
Taken for sake of simplicity to be coils, and another example where we work backwards to find what is required. The key to the decision is a formula that combines the coil rate, the leverage on it, and the sprung weight that will rest on it. These permit a direct comparison of 'softness' or ride quality between a Formula One car, a road saloon car and a loaded 30 ton tanker if you should so wish. It is known as the natural frequency of the suspension, quoted either in Cycles per minute (CPM) or per second (Hertz or Hz).

Coil springs are available in a vast range of sizes and rates. (AVO)

Figure 8-1 *Table comparing suspension frequencies for a variety of cars including early 1600cc Gould, a Len Terry Formula 5000, a typical ground-effect F1 car and a 1600cc rally car.*

Suspension frequency examples and calculation method.

Data	1 Wheel frequency (CPM) F	2 Sprung weight (net corner wt. in lbs) SW	3 Susp. leverage SL	4 Susp. leverage squared SL²	5 Effective Coil Rate lbs/ins ECR	6 Coil crush (inches Static) Crush	7 Wheel Rate (lbs/ins) WR	8 Static Deflection (inches) SD	9 Coil Rate (lbs/in) CR	Remarks CR is actual spring fitted to vehicle
How obtained	Designer's choice or $187.8\sqrt{\frac{WR}{SW}}$	Gross corner wt. less unsprung wt.	Designer's Calc. choice or Measure		Calc. $\frac{CR}{SL}$	Calc. $\frac{SWXSL}{CR}$	Calc. $\frac{SW}{ECR}$ or $\frac{CR}{SL^2}$	Calc. $\frac{SW}{WR}$	Designer's choice or WRXSL² or ECRX SL	
Gould Terrapin	Front: 102	138	2.0:1	4.0:1	80	1.31	40	3.45	160	First experiment
1600 cc	Front: 107.3	138	2.0:1	4.0:1	90	1.17	45	3.1	180	Better
(1980 to 1983)	Front: 113	138	2.0:1	4.0:1	100	1.05	50	2.76	200	Better
Data: Gross Wt. with	Front: 120	138	2.0:1	4.0:1	112.5	0.93	56.5	2.44	225	Less improvement
drive 1060 lbs.	Front: 126.5	138	2.0:1	4.0:1	125	0.84	62.5	2.21	250	"Over the edge" but retained
Front: 384 lbs.	Front: 132.7	138	2.0:1	4.0:1	137.5	0.76	68.75	2.00	275	Too hard
Rear: 676 lbs.	Front: 96.3	238	2.0:1	4.0:1	125	1.64	62.5	3.81	250	Ground effect of 0.55G (400 lb split equally to each wheel)
Sprung Wts.										
$\frac{384}{2}-54=138$ lbs. Front	Rear: 113.5	280	1.565:1	2.45:1	159.7	1.59	102	2.74	250	First experiment
	Rear: 120	280	1.565:1	2.45:1	178.9	1.42	114	2.46	280	Better
	Rear: 124.3	280	1.565:1	2.45:1	191.7	1.33	122.5	2.28	300	Better
	Rear: 129.4	280	1.565:1	2.45:1	207.7	1.23	133	2.10	325	Final choice
$\frac{676}{2}-58=280$ lbs. Rear	Rear: 111.2	380	1.565:1	2.45:1	207.7	1.58	133	2.86	325	Ground effect of 0.550 (400 lb split equally to each wheel)
	Rear: 134.3	280	1.565:1	2.45:1	236.6	2.14	143	1.96	350	Future plan
LT25: F5000	Front: 118	230	1.87:1	3.49:1	167.9	1.37	89	2.58	314	From "Racing Car Design
(Len Terry design)	Rear: 125	440	1.36:1	1.85:1	269.8	1.63	195	2.26	367	and Development"
March 763	Front: 104	190	1.75:1	3.06:1	102.8	1.85	58.8	3.23	180	Pre-ground effect circuit car
(1976 F3)	Rear: 119.5	310	1.27:1	1.61:1	159	1.95	125.5	2.47	202	
Typical F1	Front: 410	315	2.0:1	4.0:1	3000	0.1	1500	0.21	6000	Note on weight calcs:
ground	Rear: 504	385	1.2:1	1.44:1	3.333	0.16	2.777	0.14	4000	Formula Minimum
effect car		very low								580 kg = 1276 lb
showing		speed								Driver = 164 lb
results of										½ fuel = 160 lb / 1600 lb
varying	Front: 290	630	2.0:1	4.0:1	3000	0.2	1500	0.42	6000	45%F = 720 lb
downforce	Rear: 357	770	1.2:1	1.44:1	3.333	0.23	2.777	0.28	4000	55R = 880 lb
(pre-'83)		Medium								Est sprung wt.
		speed								per corner:
	Front: 237	945	2.0:1	4.0:1	3000	0.31	1500	0.63	6000	F: 315 lbs
	Rear: 291	1155	1.2:1	1.44:1	3.333	0.35	2.777	0.42	4000	R: 385 lbs
		High								
		speed								
Rally	Front: 78	495	1:1	1:1	85	5.8	85	5.8	85	Standard
Sunbeam	Rear: 95	310	1.24:1	1.54:1	97	3.2	80	3.875	120	Standard
1600	Front: 102	495	1:1	1:1	145	3.4	145	3.4	145	First experiment
(5 link rear	Rear: 133	310	1.24:1	1.54:1	194	1.6	156	1.98	240	loose
axle and	Front: 118	495	1:1	1:1	195	2.54	195	2.54	195	Final choice
MacPherson	Rear: 120	310	1.24:1	1.54:1	157	1.97	127	2.44	195	for loose
Strut front)	Front: 128	495	1:1	1:1	230	2.15	230	2.15	2.30	Final choice
	Rear: 133	310	1.24:1	1.54:1	194	1.60	156	1.98	240	for tarmac
	Front: 118	495	1:1	1:1	195	2.54	195	2.54	195	Tarmac experiment
	Rear: 133	310	1.24:1	1.54:1	194	1.60	156	1.98	240	skewed roll onto front with bad U/steer
	Front: 146	495	1:1	1:1	300	1.65	300	1.65	300	Future tarmac
	Rear: 161	310	1.24:1	1.54:1	282	1.75	227	1.36	350	"possible" for even less roll

Note: Calculations *from* frequency required:

$$WR = \left(\frac{Freq.}{187.8}\right)^2 \times SW. \quad CR = WR \times SL^2 \text{ (then apply inclination correction if necessary (see page 200).}$$

Before coming to the formulae themselves, we need to have an idea of what is in or out of the ballpark. Although it has been said that an ideal frequency is that of a man walking normally – some 120 CPM – riding in a wheeled vehicle turns out to be a different matter, and experience of millions of road and sports cars has produced a reasonable guide to the practical frequencies. These lie in the 60–80 CPM bracket for comfortable road cars, 80–100 for firmer and more sporting machinery, 100–125 for racing cars without wings or ground effect.

Beyond this, downforce which effectively increases the sprung weight and tiny ground clearances will mean that even higher frequencies – or even smaller movements of the car on its suspension – will be essential, however hard the ride, with the tyre taking over more and more of the spring's job. Figures of 200–350 CPM are nearer current trends, and at the peak of the ground effect era, cars left the grid at up to 500 CPM. Even when 3 G and 4 G downforce had pressed its iron hand down onto the cars, the wheel frequencies still lay between 200 and 300 which gave drivers a brutally harsh environment in which to work as well as an imperative need for good track surfaces.

A reasonable starting point is suggested as 130 CPM for a circuit car, plus or minus 15, and road, though not race, experience has shown that the front frequency needs to be about 10% lower than the rear. This is to avoid pitch, a nose up/down oscillation caused by the front wheels rising over a bump first, followed shortly afterwards by the rears. Once started, it is at best unpleasant and at worst is capable of sending a yumping rally car into a complete somersault.

However, practical experience on the track shows that on good surfaces with high frequency suspensions this 'rule' is no longer necessarily valid, and front frequencies may well be higher than the rear when a search for better balance is going on. It is as well to remember that the deeper you go into the whole business, the less valid seem to be so many hitherto firm and reliable 'rules'. Do not feel that you have to abide by them, including any in these all-too-human pages.

There are also effectively three rates to any spring fitted to most vehicles. First is the Coil Rate, or the amount it compresses under a given load (in lbs/in or N/mm) usually etched or painted on it by the manufacturer. Second is the Fitted Rate (or Effective Rate), or how strong the spring appears to be on the car, taking into account its mounted angle relative to the leverage on it. A steeply inclined coil will be 'softer' than one at 90°.

The third rate is Wheel Rate, or how strong the spring appears to be to the wheel bouncing up and down at the end of its links and the calculation involves squaring the leverage. For those readers possessing modest mathematical talents, the reason for this is illustrated, together with a number of examples of data for differing cars and the sequence for any calculations of your own.

The four formulae you will need are:

$$\text{Wheel Frequency (CPM)} = 187.8 \sqrt{\frac{\text{Wheel Rate lbs/in}}{\text{Sprung Weight lbs}}}$$

$$\text{Fitted Rate (lb/in)} = \frac{\text{Coil Rate lbs/in}}{\text{(corrected for mounting angle)}}$$

$$\text{Wheel Rate (lb/in)} = \frac{\text{Fitted Rate lbs/in}}{\text{Susp. leverage}^2}$$

Figure 8-2 *The varying leverages provided by different suspension layouts. All must normally be squared for final frequency calculation. Note that Point C will also be the mounting for pull or pushrod outer ends.*

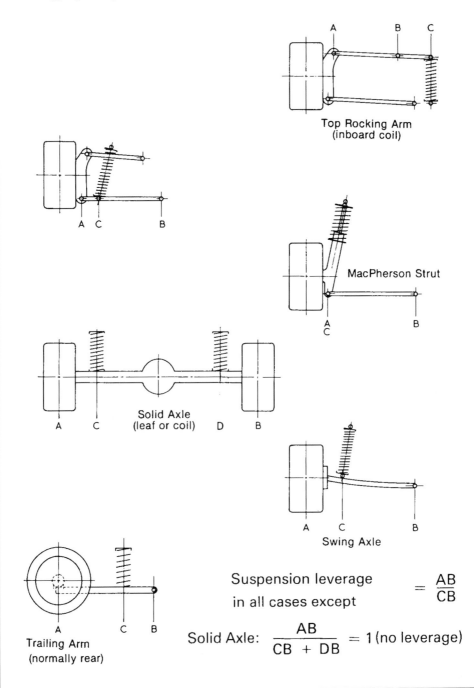

Top Rocking Arm
(inboard coil)

MacPherson Strut

Solid Axle
(leaf or coil)

Swing Axle

Trailing Arm
(normally rear)

Suspension leverage in all cases except $= \dfrac{AB}{CB}$

Solid Axle: $\dfrac{AB}{CB + DB} = 1$ (no leverage)

Figure 8-3 *This diagram hopefully makes clear why the simple leverage on a coil or pushrod must be squared for final frequency calculations.* (Darell Staniforth)

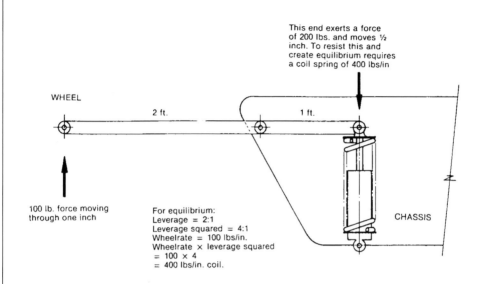

This end exerts a force of 200 lbs. and moves ½ inch. To resist this and create equilibrium requires a coil spring of 400 lbs/in

WHEEL

2 ft.   1 ft.

100 lb. force moving through one inch

For equilibrium:
Leverage = 2:1
Leverage squared = 4:1
Wheelrate = 100 lbs/in.
Wheelrate × leverage squared
= 100 × 4
= 400 lbs/in. coil.

CHASSIS

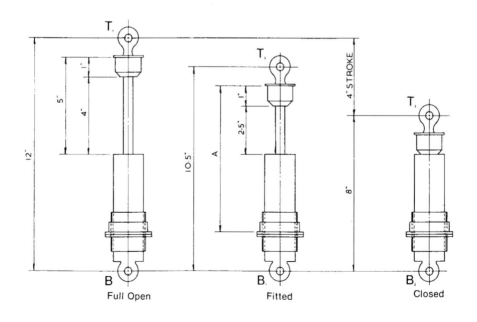

Full Open   Fitted   Closed

$$\text{or} \quad \left(\frac{\text{Wheel Frequ.}}{187.8}\right)^{2} \times \text{Sprung Wt. (lb)}$$

$$\text{Coil Rate} = \text{Wheel Rate} \times \text{Susp. Leverage}^{2}$$

These will allow you to go forwards or backwards depending what information you already have or need to find out.

A final point is that having decided on the rate of coil needed to do the job, a spring maker can produce the same thing in differing physical sizes by altering the wire diameter and number of coils, a great help if you are trying to get a particular spring into limited space.

Dampers

The precise relationship between a damper, the coil surrounding it and the rest of the car is an extremely subtle and sensitive one, even in this day and age often being fine tuned by testing and 'seat of the pants' feel once the car is running. Lotus for one earned substantial sums of money providing exactly this expertise to major manufacturers but as in so many areas, one needs at least a basic approach so that completely impossible units are avoided.

So long as leverages are the same (ie a concentric coil/damper unit) the damper sees the coil – and deals with its attempts to oscillate – in terms of the actual rate or

Dampers come in various configurations, sizes and end mountings to suit many applications. Those shown here are classic single-adjust dampers with screwed spring platforms and integral fluid reservoir from AVO. (AVO)

strength of that coil, ignoring inclinations, wheel rate, etc. The bump resistance of a damper is (almost) always less than the rebound – by a ratio of about 3–1 on an average road car, a relationship that has been distilled over many long years in the motor industry.

Racing brings the need for much tighter control. The increase in damper research, knowledge and development in recent years, including the development of double, triple and quadruple adjusters, has been so great that they now demand a section of their own (see Chapter 10). Gentle damping of a soft road coil demands considerable movement during which the forces have time to decay. The 10 inches total on a rally or off-road car may only be 1 inch or less on a circuit vehicle, with instantaneous loads from bumps or 'kerbing' many, many times higher. Comfort is a non-starter compared to grip and this sacrifice has brought the racing figure down to 2 or 1.5:1. As both bump and rebound can be made stronger while keeping the same proportional relationship, both spring rates and varying car weights will alter the value of 'strength'.

Anti-roll bars

Although there have been several successful, if complicated attempts to prevent a car rolling, or even rolling inwards like a banking aircraft, both geometric and electronic as in the Williams FW14 and 15, roll made a comeback in the aftermath of the sweeping FISA ban on 'Active'.

The initial and sometimes only resistance to roll comes from the springs but there is a limit even on a racing car to which the springs can be made stronger and stronger simply to resist roll. They may also be resisting more at one end of the car than the other leading to a condition of 'skewed roll' or 'falling over' in which the car is visibly down on an outer front or rear wheel – a far from uncommon sight in races for saloons or older sports cars.

Bars appeared on the scene fairly early on, as a piece of non-adjustable bent steel rod, sometimes doing duty as an actual suspension link, and we have already had quite a detailed look at what they do and how in Chapter 2. It is now appropriate to try and quantify their power and plan how the bar can be used in a forecastable manner to strive for perfect balance for at least part of the time.

A truly sensitive and adjustable bar did not properly arrive until inboard suspension made a whole new design approach possible. Once there was a convenient, strong and geometrically pure point at the inboard end of a top rocking arm from which to twist a suitable bar, they became shorter and lighter, strong, needle-roller mounted for efficiency, and finely adjustable. Blades instead of bent ends also permitted remote alterations that allowed the driver a piece of the action in mid-race.

As we embark on design and installation of our bars, one aspect that may at first be difficult to get clear in the mind (it was in my case) is the exact strength of a given bar and precisely how you compare it to the coils. It is a matter which is complicated by bars having effectively two rates, one normally quoted in a pure engineering context and the other one that will relate it directly to the car's suspension.

The first is its Angular Rate in lb/in/degree, or in radians. Without wishing to insult the mathematicians, a radian is actually 57.29578 degrees, or half a circle (180 degrees) divided by pi (3.142). We will not go into why this figure may be more convenient in an academic situation but it is certainly far too large a deflection to work happily on a racing car and the degree is used from hereon.

To begin to correlate bar and coils, we have first to know or calculate its Angular Rate and the load in lb/in needed to twist it one degree along its length. We immediately discover that one degree can mean any linear distance depending on how far from the bar axis we are measuring, ie how long is the lever arm? If our lever arm (the bent bit or blade at the end of the bar) is, say, four inches long, the tip will move a certain distance for one degree. Double the lever arm to eight inches and you double the distance moved by its tip, with the same load in lbs/in – actually with half the force in pounds, over double the distance (see Figure 8-4).

So we have a variable Linear Rate, dependent solely on the length of the lever arm, while the Angular Rate stays constant. The car's interpretation of being able to move the lever arm twice as far with half the effort is, needless to say, that the bar has become very much weaker or softer.

But how much in terms of the coils? And what was it in the first place?

Once again we shall have to work backwards by first finding the roll moment of the whole car. We then assess how much the springs contribute to roll stiffness (remembering they have been chosen only in terms of wheel frequency and available suspension movement). From these two figures it will be possible to decide what further roll stiffness is required to limit roll with the target of around 2.5 degrees for a saloon and 1.5 degrees in a single seater at 1 G cornering force as a maximum and preferably less.

These are somewhat arbitrary figures based partly on weights and leverages exerted within a typical saloon or single seater, and partly on the demands of certain geometries with which any increase in this amount of roll will produce wheel angles that are unacceptable.

But this is getting ahead of ourselves. We must forget, temporarily, any calculations to do with the bars and decide how and where they may best be fitted. Criteria are

Figure 8-4 *Anti-roll bar twist and stiffness. Drawing shows that 5 degrees of twist on a bar (including a suspension torsion bar) means different amounts of actual linear movement of the lever arm depending on its length and force applied (400 lbs/in both cases). See pages 35 and 36 for illustrations of different anti-roll bar types.*

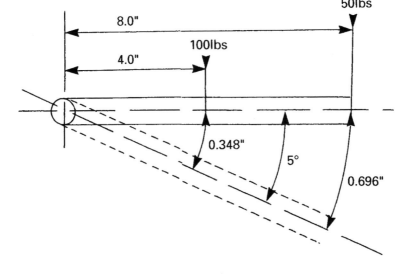

that they dodge the driver's legs, gearbox, etc, and sit on rigid, low friction mounting points convenient to the suspension, accessible for change or adjustment, with freedom for the lever arms/blades to move full travel without fouling.

The normal link from bar to suspension has small spherical joints at each end with left/right threads to allow accurate setting of length without dismantling. The mountings will decide the length of bar, suitably designed to permit different diameters to be rapidly installed, and the maximum/minimum space for any adjustable lever arm. Blades show one of their many advantages here, needing no extra space for adjustment in length as they need only to be rotated from vertical to horizontal within their own width.

An elegant way of fitting a bar very strongly yet permitting complete and rapid change to a different diameter is used on Van Diemen cars. The bar has a projecting spigot at each end which fits a small ball bearing itself held in a rigidly located split alloy housing. Any alternative with the same spigots, irrespective of diameter or whether tubed or solid will go straight into the same mounts.

We now have our length and lever arm dimensions, and given a stiffness requirement can at last calculate the bar dimensions in diameter and wall thickness to get what we want. It is taken that the bar in serious racing machinery will be of tube because it always has a weight/stiffness ratio advantage over solid metal. Complete details of this approach, together with all the formulae and example figures for a typical single seater, will be found in Chapter 9.

There are varied opinions on what constitutes the balance required but a reasonable first target is that there will be no weight transfer from front to back or vice versa in a steady state corner. Knowing what bar alterations can then provide in modifying front or rear roll stiffness (or both), track testing will be the basis of final refinements.

Yet again, as in the notable case of the roll centre, this is a static situation on paper, or at best in a steady state with our mount hurtling round a corner of constant radius at a fixed speed. We all know this never happens. Racing cars are always having the accelerator or brake pedal pressed firmly downwards upsetting the centre of gravity, weight transfer or roll forces at one end or the other, often in very quick succession, trying to skew roll all those neatly predicted forces and points in space.

Only practice, driver and development engineer talent and a responsive vehicle will contrive to put the finishing touches. Like charm, some have a large measure to start with, some acquire and polish it, while some unfortunates never ever manage to understand what it is they lack.

Steering

Already considered in Chapter 4 – especially the need for lightness (massive physical effort at anything rarely makes for delicacy of touch) – but we must now decide how and where to locate the rack and pinion. There are two major considerations: avoiding and protecting the driver's legs, whether in normal racing or in an accident, and avoidance of bump steer.

Bump steer, a well-known phrase but not always clearly understood, is the phenomena in which either or both front wheels will start pointing themselves in varying directions as they rise and fall without the driver turning the steering wheel. This can be every bit as bad as it sounds, and at its worst will introduce straight line 'darting' instability, and highly unwanted uncertainty in cornering feel. Only after the location of all the front suspension pivots has been finalised can the rack position and its required length be determined.

Figure 8-5 *Methods of determining the correct position for the rack and pinion.*
(Darell Staniforth)

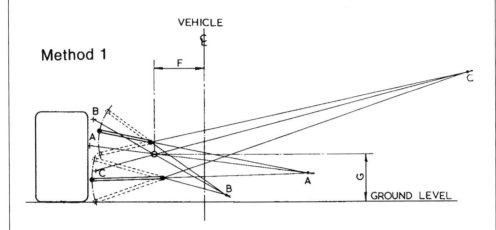

Correct R & P Length = F × 2

Correct R & P Height = G

Method 3

R & P ball ends coincide
exactly with top link
inboard pick-ups with
track rods lying
parallel to top link.

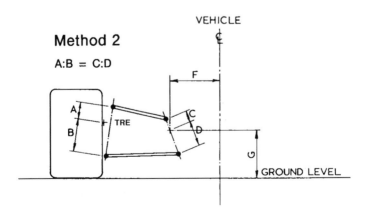

Every bit as important is rack-and-pinion position in plan. Rack bar and trackrods should lie on a straight line across the car between the two trackrod ends. See Chapter 4 on Ackermann for a full examination of this most vital aspect.

Yet again words fall short of pictures in explaining how this is achieved and two different approaches are illustrated. In practice, methods 1 and 2 can give slightly different results and clearly both cannot be right. However, in practice, there are two further fine adjustment methods that remove the small errors that will almost inevitably be found when the car is finally assembled.

Figure 8-6 *Bump/steer gauge, as mentioned in the text. As upright rises/falls (using jack under suspension after removal of spring/damper unit) plate will indicate on dial gauge whether toe in/toe out is occurring and magnitude of change in series of steps from maximum bump to maximum droop.* (Author)

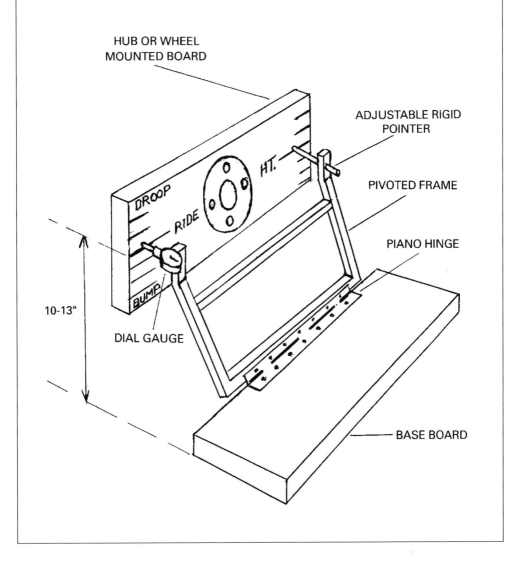

The suspension pushrod has been disconnected at the lower end to permit free bump/droop movement with the screw jack shown. (Author)

The first is altering the height of the rack. It is important if at all possible to provide some vertical adjustment in its position, usually with slotted holes for the mounting clamp bolts and horizontally mounted support blocks that can be spaced up or down. These are usually only needed for really serious trouble or a radical change in the height of the steering arm. All being well, adjustment at the trackrod end alone by varying shims above and below it can be capable of bringing bump/steer into the region of plus/minus .005. Best is a rack with end pivots coinciding exactly with the top wishbone pivot points, though with this the trackrod end must also match the vertical height of the upright top pivot. (See most of Formula One or Porsche 962 for how to do this with minimum work.)

The common approaches to checking bump/steer – a long bar fixed to the wheel and aligned by eye with a floor chalk line, or optical tracking gauges while lifting and lowering the whole car – are either inaccurate, very laborious or both. On page 145 is illustrated and explained a gauge with three virtues; fairly easy to make, simple to use and above all highly accurate.

Support the car on blocks precisely dimensioned to ride height plus 2 or 3 inches. Remove spring or complete suspension unit, or disconnect any pull or pushrod. Fit hub plate (hooked elastics work fine) and lock both wheel and R & P against movement. Rest the fixed pointer against the plate, zero dial gauge on its mid-range point. Use scissor jack to move the wheel up and down, noting toe variations for each quarter inch of movement in bump or droop. Depending on the figures you are, of course, writing down, adjustment to the rack height or bar length will be:

Bump	Droop	Rack adjustment
Toe-in	Toe-out	Raise forward R & P
		Lower rearward R & P
Toe-out	Toe-in	Lower forward R & P
		Lower rearward R & P
Toe-out	Toe-out	Lengthen rack bar (fwd)
		Shorten rack bar (rwd)
Toe-in	Toe-in	Shorten rack bar (fwd)
		Lengthen rack bar (rwd)

In every case of alteration whether in the height of the rack or the length of the bar, the trackrods should be re-adjusted to reset toe-in/out to zero.

Corrections in the height of the trackrod end itself are not nearly so clear-cut, and for reasons of interrelation between the sometimes complex arcs of the top and bottom wishbones (sometimes set on skewed axes, relative to the car centre-line) do somewhat unexpected things. However, tenacious experiment with shims will succeed if you keep at it. Just in case you thought that had dealt with bump steer for good, remember that any increase in caster angle effectively lowers a rear mounted steering arm or raises a forward mounted one, and thus the trackrod end.

If caster angle alterations are planned in the field do the experiments on your flat floor in the workshop, making a note of the shims or alterations that must be made to keep bump-steer well out of the picture. You can then make the needed modifications rapidly without any need for checking at the track.

All the foregoing will perhaps give a small hint of why cars in some teams appear to have some miraculous edge over the opposition. In this area and others they not only know what they are doing, but how and why.

Chapter 9

Weight transfer

... a tricky balancing act

DAVID GOULD WAS INITIALLY one of the most successful of Britain's amateur racing car designers, who then went on to become fully professional and even more successful. Each of his cars has followed three maxima – highest possible rigidity, careful suspension design and some major step forward in concept. His first full honeycomb monocoque, built in the wooden garage beside his semi, took the British Hillclimb Championship in its first season. Thirteen long, hardworking years later he repeated the feat with his own massively modified Ralt carbon tub – and went professional! Twelve more years were needed to reach the situation where his carbon-tub, highly developed car swept to the British Hillclimb Championship with not only a win but 9 of the top ten places.

David Gould's cars – the GR55 design, seen here in the hands of 2003 and 2004 British Hillclimb Champion Adam Fleetwood – have won the British Hillclimb Championship for eight years in succession at the time of writing. (Gould)

Some idea of the effort and thought that goes into Gould's design approach, as well as a wealth of practical guidance, is reflected in the following paper.

Lateral weight transfer and roll resistance, by David Gould

I am sure many of us have stood about in assorted paddocks, beer tents and bars discussing with our fellow competitors the relative merits of 'soft' or 'hard' roll bars, transferring weight to or from the front or rear suspension, etc., our dialogue being liberally peppered with impressive phrases such as roll couple, roll moments, fractional lever arms and the like. I am equally sure that almost as many of us would have difficulty putting our hands on our hearts and swearing that they were fully aware of the major factors involved, or that we could quantify their individual and total magnitudes with any hope of the results standing even the most informal scrutiny.

One of the reasons for this situation prevailing is the lack of comprehensible text books covering the subject. Almost all the written matter available appears to fall into one of two categories, either the author is a professional engineer writing in mechanical engineering terms, thus making assumptions regarding the readers' knowledge that leave us, as amateurs, more confused after reading such articles than before; or the subject is so broadly discussed that scarcely a clue is given which is of use to us.

In an attempt to clear away some of the mystique surrounding the subject an effort will be made to explain the basic principles at work and to introduce a fairly painless method of arriving at figures which will reveal some of the more important forces at work and their relationship with one another.

Weight transfer

We all know that roll bars influence weight transfer and that weight transfer is somehow connected with roll centres. It would therefore seem appropriate to start at the common denominator. To understand how weight is transferred we must first apportion the various components which make up the total weight according to their position in the vehicle.

We will give codes to the terms which will be used in various formulae and these are listed in the appendix. In addition a set of data, not completely dissimilar to that of a medium sized hillclimb single seater will be used to provide examples, and these basic values also appear as sample data at the end of the paper.

A cornering force of 1g is assumed throughout.

Before we begin we need to know the weights involved and their positions relative to one another. These can be calculated or measured as follows:

WF or WR =	Total weight on front or rear axle line.	
UWF or UWR =	The weight of the unsprung components, e.g., wheels, tyres, brakes, wishbones, uprights, etc. at the front or rear of the car.	
UGF or UGR =	The height agl of the CoG of the front or rear unsprung mass. This is usually similar to the radius of the tyre.	
TF or TR =	The distance between the centre lines of the front or rear wheels. (ie, track)	

WF - UWF = SWF
400 - 100 = 300 lbs (Front Sprung Weight)

Figure 9-1 *The final readout sheet for set up – example car data fed into Gould's own programme.*

	Client :	**Mr. Sole**
	Car Type :	**Squire Mk1**
	Date :	**1994-2006**

ROLL BARS, ROLL RESISTANCE AND WEIGHT TRANSFER

	Front	Rear			Front	Rear	Total	
Total Corner Weight :	200.0	360.0		Total Weight :	400.0	720.0	1,120.0	lbs
Unsprung -"- Weight :	50.0	60.0		Weight Distribution :	0.36	0.64	100	%
Axle Height :	10.000	12.000		Unsprung Weight :	100.0	120.0	220.0	lbs
Sprung Cnr Weight :	150	300		Sprung Weight :	300.0	600.0	900.0	lbs
				Sprung Weight Distribution :	0.33	0.67	100	%
CG Height (agl) :	13.000	16.000		Mean CG Height :			15.000	in
RC Height (agl) :	1.500	3.000		Mean RC Height :			2.500	in
Track :	58.000	55.000		Mean Track :			56.000	in
				Roll Couple :			12.500	in
				Roll Moment (1g) :			11,250.0	lbs/in

Roll Bar Dimensions

	Front	Rear			Front	Rear		
Diameter :	0.750	0.750						
Bore :	0.650	0.650						
Length :	36.000	14.000		Angular Rate :	75.5	194.0		lbs/in/deg
Lever Length :	7.000	7.000		Linear Rate :	88.2	226.9		lbs/in

Roll Resistance, Bars

	Front	Rear			Front	Rear		
Wheel Movement :	1.000	1.000		Effective Fract. LA :	0.903	0.360		
Bar PU Movement :	0.950	0.600		Bar Roll Resistance :	4,675.6	4,312.6		lbs/in/deg

Roll Resistance, Springs

	Front	Rear			Front	Rear		
Coil :	200.0	475.0						
Effective Spring Rate :	175.0	400.0		Effective LA Ratio :	1.769	2.789		: 1
Wheel Movement :	1.330	1.670		Wheel Rate :	98.932	143.426		lbs/in
Damper Movement :	1.000	1.000		Spring Roll Resistance :	2,904.3	3,786.2		lbs/in/deg

Overall Roll Resistance

	Front	Rear	Total	
Total :	7,579.9	8,098.7	15,678.6	lbs/in/deg
Distribution :	0.48	0.52	100	%

Dynamic Weight Transfer at 1g

WHEEL FREQUENCY (CPM)

	Front	Rear	Total	
Unsprung Weight :	17.241	26.182	43.423	lbs
Via Role Axis :	7.759	32.727	40.486	lbs
Sprung Weight :	97.122	103.771	200.893	lbs
Total Transferred :	122.122	162.680	284.802	lbs

Front : 152
Rear : 130

Dynamic Weight Distribution at 1g

	Front	Rear	Total	
F < > R Weight Change :	30.158	-30.158	0.000	lbs
Revised Weights :	430.158	689.842	1,120.0	lbs
Wt Distribution :	0.38	0.62	0.05	
Roll Angle at 1g :			0.718	degrees

Notes: Using the same data from the same example vehicle giving similar results to calculation, but with a different way of final presentation will be found on page 201.

$$WR - UWR = SWR$$
$$720 - 120 = 600 \text{ lbs (Rear Sprung Weight)}$$

$$SWF + SWR = SW$$
$$300 + 600 = 900 \text{ lbs (Total Sprung Weight)}$$

Armed with the above we can now commence calculating the first of the three types of weight transfer.

Unsprung weight transfer

The following formulae will calculate the unsprung weight transfers at the front and rear respectively.

$$UWF \times UGF + TF = UtF$$
$$100 \times 10 \div 58 = 17.24 \text{ lbs (Front Unsprung Wt Transfer)}$$

$$UWR \times UGR \div TR = UtR$$
$$120 \times 12 \div 55 = 26.18 \text{ lbs (Rear Unsprung Wt Transfer)}$$

Obviously, the greater the weight and height the more weight transfer there will be, and conversely the greater the track the less weight transfer. Equally obviously, short of chopping the car about or drilling holes all over the place there is nothing we can do to modify this constituent of total weight transfer without major redesign.

Weight transfer via the roll centres

This is the element of the sprung mass which is reacted into the outer tyres directly through the roll centres, and is calculated thus:

$$SWF \times CF \div TF = CtF$$
$$300 \times 1.50 \div 58 = 7.76 \text{ lbs (Front Wt Transfer via the Roll Centres)}$$

$$SWR \times CR \div TR = CtR$$
$$600 \times 3.00 \div 55 = 32.73 \text{ lbs (Rear Wt Transfer via the Roll Centres)}$$

As can be seen from the above, this element of weight transfer can be increased or decreased simply by raising or lowering the height of the roll centre at one end of the car without having any direct effect on the other end. In practical racing terms, it is usually a small proportion of the total transferable weight. However, of interest is the effect when the roll centre is below ground level. In this situation weight transfer is negative, i.e., from outer wheel to inner wheel, a genuine geometric anti-jacking device.

Weight transfer via the sprung mass

This is the mass of the car which rolls around the axis between the front and rear roll centres, and as such is the part of the vehicle whose roll is resisted by the springs and roll bars. It is therefore the area of weight transfer offering the greatest reward for our attention. In typical fashion, however, it is the most difficult to understand and calculate.

For proper comprehension we need to introduce the concept of The Mass Centroid. When visualising the sprung mass, we must never think in terms of front and rear axles, front and rear weights, front and rear heights or front and rear roll centres if we are ever to grasp a full understanding.

Sitting somewhere near the middle of the car is a mass whose centre is the CoG of the entire sprung weight of the car. It knows nothing about front and rear tracks, front and rear roll centres or front and rear CoGs. What it does know all about is its own track, its own roll centre and its own CoG. We will call these the mean track, the mean roll centre and the mean CoG.

Before we can calculate them we need to find the proportion of the total sprung weight resting on one of the axles. The rear axle is calculated as follows:

SWR ÷ SW = WDR
600 ÷ 900 = 0.66 recurring

This indicates that the sprung mass CoG is located at the point 66% (or about 2/3rds) of the distance from the front to the rear axle, i.e., somewhere just in front of the engine.

Having obtained the above we now know the whereabouts of the centre of the sprung mass along the wheelbase of the car, and can thus calculate its mean track, mean roll centre and mean CoG, using the same proportion and based on the known front and rear measurements at each end of the car.

((TR - TF) x WDR) + TF = TM
((55 - 58) x 0.66r) + 58 = 56 ins (Mean Track)

((CR - CF) x WDR) + CF = CM
((3.00 - 1.50) x 0.66r) + 1.50 = 2.50 ins (Mean Roll Centre)

Before we can complete the exercise and calculate the mean CoG we need to know the height of the CoG of the sprung mass at the front and rear axle lines. These can be extremely difficult to measure and a process of deduction from the known location of the major items which compromise the sprung weight is often the preferred method of assessing this information.

((SGR - SGF) x WDR) + SGF = GM
((116 - 13) x 0.66r) + 13 = 15 ins (Mean CoG Height)

All that is required now is the length of the lever arm (or moment) between the mean roll centre about which our sprung mass will rotate and the mean CoG. This is calculated as follows:

GM - CM = LM
15 - 2.50 = 12.50 ins (Mean Roll Moment)

We now have all the information we need to calculate the sprung weight transfer, and the formula is:

SW x LM ÷ TM = St
900 x 12.50 ÷ 56 = 200.89 lbs (Total Sprung Weight Transfer)

It can be seen that the length of LM is dependent on the height and slope of the roll axis; the higher the roll axis the more weight transferred via the roll centres and, consequently, the less weight transferred through the springs.

A little research with a calculator will convince you that these two methods of transferring weight (via the roll centres or via the springs) precisely counterbalance each other and the total amount of weight transferred, no matter which route it follows, always remains the same, i.e., high roll centres leave less weight available to transfer via the springs and vice versa.

Total weight transfer

This is now obtainable by adding all the above together thus:

$$UtF + UtR + CtF + CtR + St = Wt$$
$$17.24 + 26.18 + 7.76 + 32.73 + 200.89 = \quad 284.80 \text{ lbs (Total Weight Transfer)}$$

One might at this point wonder why anyone would bother going to all the trouble of calculating weight transfer in such a complex manner when it is now obvious that the total amount of weight transferable in a given situation is completely predetermined by the vehicle dimensions.

Now look again at the formula for total weight transfer given above. If you have been paying attention, you will have noticed that the term 'St' in the equation (sprung weight transfer), unlike all the preceding terms, was not calculated separately for the front and rear suspensions. This is because whilst its share of the total weight transferred is inversely proportional to the amount of weight transferred via the roll centres, its front to rear distribution is not controlled by any of the factors we have considered so far. The golden rule is: The ratio of front to rear sprung weight transfer is directly proportional to the ratio of front to rear roll resistance. In other words, the end of the car which is stiffest will receive the major part of sprung transferred weight and its exact share will be governed by its stiffness relative to the stiffness of the other end of the car.

Roll resistance

Once again, nothing in life is simple, and if we are to take advantage of our new found ability to apply sprung weight transfer to either end of the car at will, we need to be able to determine how stiff our front and rear suspension really is.

We will now deliberate on the factors which contribute to roll stiffness, i.e., springs, rolls, bars, their strengths and the leverages with which they are applied. Let us begin with one of the oldest roll resisting devices of all.

Springs

In addition to the spring rate, we need to know the ratio of wheel movement to spring movement. This needs to be measured with as much accuracy as possible as this value will be squared in our calculation and obviously any error will also be squared.

The ratio is found by measuring the exact amount of movement of the spring for a given amount of wheel movement. One inch is often a convenient dimension and is used in our example. One practical method to obtain this is as follows. Block up the chassis at its normal ride height and, with the springs removed, measure the distance between the upper and lower spring location collars. Then without disturbing anything else, place a spacer of known thickness between the tyre and the ground and remeasure the distance between the spring collars. The thickness of the spacer (wheel movement) divided by the difference between the two measurements of spring collar distance (spring movement) is the ratio we are seeking.

We can now proceed to calculate the roll resistance of the suspension springs as follows:

$$(\text{SF} \div (\text{WmF} \div \text{SmF})^2 \times \text{TF}^2 \times 2 \times \text{pi} \div 180 = \text{ArF}$$
$$(175 \div (1.00 \div 0.75)^2 \times 582 \div 2 \times \text{pi} \div 180 = 2{,}889.77 \text{ in lbs per degree}$$
$$\text{(Roll Resistance of Front Springs)}$$

$$(\text{SR} \div (\text{WmR} \div \text{SmR})^2) \times \text{TR}^2 \div 2 \times \text{pi} \div 180 = \text{ArR}$$
$$(400 \div (1.00 \div 0.60)^2) \times 55^2 \div 2 \times \text{pi} \div 180 = 3{,}801.33 \text{ in lbs per degree}$$
$$\text{(Roll Resistance of Rear Springs)}$$

The term 'pi ÷ 180' in the above formulae was included to convert the result to units of in lbs per degree. Omitting this produces an answer in units of lb in lbs per radian. As a radian is about 57.3 degrees it is far too large a unit to be convenient or practical in suspension calculations.

Roll bars

Unlike springs, roll bars are not usually marked with their rate and it is therefore necessary to calculate this value before we can begin to find their effect on roll resistance. Again very careful measurement is required for the outside and inside (if the bar is tubular) diameters, as these values are multiplied to the fourth power in the equation. To begin, let us find the angular rate of our bars, i.e., the force necessary to twist them a given amount.

Angular rate

Both the bars used in our example are manufactured from 0.75 in dia x 0.050 in wall tubes. The front and rear lengths are 36 in and 14 in respectively.

$$19{,}700 \times (\text{OD}^4 - \text{ID}^4) \div \text{Bar Length} = \text{Angular Rate in in lbs per degree}$$
$$19{,}700 \times (0.75^4 - 0.65^4) \div 36 = 75.46 \text{ in lbs per degree (Front Bar)}$$
$$19{,}700 \times (0.75^4 - 0.65^4) \div 14 = 194.05 \text{ in lbs per degree (Rear Bar)}$$

The '19,700' is a constant derived from the average modulus of shear for steel. For solid bars, omit the internal dimension '-ID^4' term and simply use OD^4.

Note that the angular rate is exactly inversely proportional to length, i.e., double the length = half the strength.

Linear rate

We must now find the effect of the length of the roll bar lever arms. This dimension is measured at right angles to the axis of the bar and is the distance from the roll bar pushrod pick up point to the centre line of the roll bar. In our example we will assume that both front and rear bars have 7 in levers.

$$\text{Angular Rate} \div (\text{Lever Length}^2 \times \text{pi} \div 180) = \text{Roll Bar Rate in in lbs}$$
$$\text{BF} = 75.46 \div (7^2 \times \text{pi} \div 180) = 88.24 \text{ in lbs (Front Roll Bar Rate)}$$
$$\text{BR} = 194.05 \div (7^2 \times \text{pi} \div 180) = 226.90 \text{ in lbs (Rear Roll Bar Rate)}$$

Now that we know the roll bar rates we can proceed to find their effect on roll resistance. Again we need to measure the proportion of wheel movement to roll bar pick up movement and this can be achieved using similar procedures to those outlined in the section on springs above. We can now calculate as follows:

$$BF \times (WmF \times BmF)^2 \times TF^2 \times pi \div 180 = BrF$$
$$88.24 \times (1.00 \times 0.95)^2 \times 58^2 \times pi \div 180 = 4,675.69 \text{ in lbs per degree}$$
$$\text{(Roll Resistance of Front Bar)}$$

$$BR \times (WmR \times BmR)^2 \times TR^2 \times pi \div 180 = BrR$$
$$226.90 \times (1.00 \times 0.60)^2 \times 55^2 \times pi \div 180 = 4,312.61 \text{ in lbs per degree}$$
$$\text{(Roll Resistance of Rear Bar)}$$

Distribution

Having now calculated all the elements contributing to the total roll resistance of the car, we can now proceed to split our sprung weight transfer between front and rear suspensions. First we will add the spring and bar resistances together.

$$ArF + BrF = Fr$$
$$2,889.77 + 4,675.69 = 7,565.46 \text{ in lbs per degree (Front Roll Resistance)}$$

$$ArR + BrR = Rr$$
$$3,801.33 + 4,312.61 = 8,113.94 \text{ in lbs per degree (Rear Roll Resistance)}$$

You will recall the distribution of sprung weight transfer is proportional to the ratio of front to rear roll resistance. Therefore:

$$FR \div (Fr + Rr) = DrF$$
$$7,565.46 \div (7,565.46 + 8,113.94) = 0.483$$

Thus, the roll resistance of the front suspension is 48.3% of the total roll resistance of the vehicle. The remainder must be at the rear and is therefore:

$$1 - DrF = DrR$$
$$1 - 0.483 = 0.517 \text{ (or 51.7\%)}$$

The dynamic weight transfer applicable to each end of the vehicle can now be found by using these proportions in the following formulae:

$$(St \times DrF) + CtF + UtF = WtF$$
$$(200.89 \times 0.483) + 7.76 + 17.24 = 122 \text{ lbs}$$
$$\text{(Total Wt Transferred to the Outer Front Wheel)}$$

$$(St \times DrR) + CtR + UtR = WtR$$
$$(200.89 \times 0.517) + 32.73 + 26.18 = 163 \text{ lbs}$$
$$\text{(Total Wt Transferred to the Outer Rear Wheel)}$$

Clearly when in a corner the outer tyres are the ones doing the lion's share of the work. Therefore it is to these we should look to influence car behaviour. As a result of our roll bars, springs, leverages and roll centre positions, the amount of weight

Figure 9-2 *Fairly typical layout of rear-engined single seater, identifying locations of all the key points named in Gould's description of the methods for weight transfer calculation, including push/pullrod and rocking arm.*

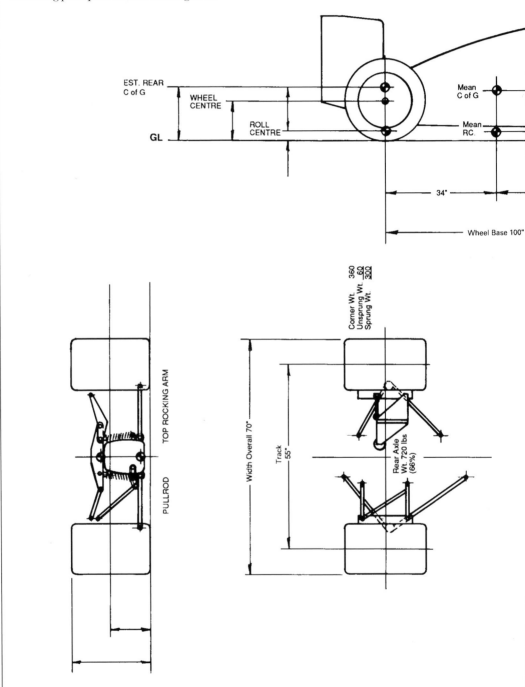

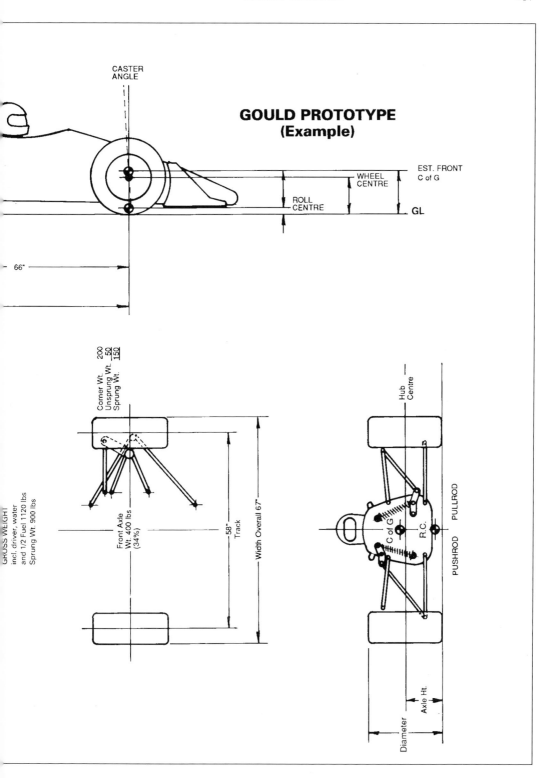

GOULD PROTOTYPE
(Example)

CASTER ANGLE

EST. FRONT C of G

WHEEL CENTRE

ROLL CENTRE

GL

66"

Corner Wt. 200
Unsprung Wt. 50
Sprung Wt. 150

GROSS WEIGHT
incl. driver, water
and 1/2 Fuel 1120 lbs
Sprung Wt. 900 lbs

Front Axle
Wt. 400 lbs
(34%)

58" Track

Width Overall 67"

Hub Centre

PUSHROD   PULLROD

C of G   R.C.

Diameter

Axle Ht.

transferred from one end of the car to the other, as far as the outer wheels are concerned, can be found by calculating as follows:

$$WtF - (Wt \times (WF \div W)) = \text{Wt to or from Front}$$
$$122 - (284.84 \times (400 \div 1120)) = +20 \text{ lbs}$$

$$WrR - (Wt \times (WR \div W)) = \text{Wt to or from Rear}$$
$$163 - (284.84 \times (720 \div 1120)) = -20 \text{ lbs}$$

In other words, as far as the important outer tyres are concerned, when the car is cornering at 1g we have made the rear of the car 20 lbs lighter and the front 20 lbs heavier, a change in the outer wheel weight distribution of about 3.6% towards the front. It is clear that far larger changes can be achieved by using softer or stiffer bars at either end to modify the proportion of roll resistance and consequent sprung weight transfer.

We have now calculated the weight transfers to the outer wheels. These have to be added to the original static corner weights to obtain the total loads on the outer tyres and, as the transferred weight has to come from somewhere, subtracted from the original static corner weights at their respective ends to find the inner wheel load for each end of the car. All still at 1g.

$$(WF \div 2) + WtF = \text{Total Outer Front Tyre Load}$$
$$(400 \div 2) + 122 = 322 \text{ lbs}$$

$$(WF \div 2) - WtF = \text{Total Inner Front Tyre Load}$$
$$(400 \div 2) - 122 = 78 \text{ lbs}$$

$$(WR \div 2) + WtR = \text{Total Outer Rear Tyre Load}$$
$$(720 \div 2) + 163 = 543 \text{ lbs}$$

$$(WR \div 2) - WtR = \text{Total Inner Rear Tyre Load}$$
$$(400 \div 2) - 163 = 197 \text{ lbs}$$

At this point the reader may be wondering why he has ploughed through pages of confusing calculations, only to find at the conclusion that all we have achieved is the transfer of a few pounds between the two outer wheels. The heart of the matter, and the basis of this, easily the most significant element of non-aerodynamic chassis tuning, is the relationship between a tyre's ability to provide grip and the vertical load imposed on it. This relationship is not linear but is a complex curve. The aim of this whole discussion is to provide the reader with the tools to optimise this relationship and, thus, to maximise grip while still maintaining balance.

Roll angles

The sprung mass is, by definition, the only part of the car which is suspended on springs, and is therefore the only part of the car which can roll. The mount of roll at a given cornering force is therefore determined by the total weight of the sprung mass, its height above the roll axis (mean roll moment) and the total roll resistance of the car (the sum of the front and rear roll resistances). To find the roll angle of the chassis in a 1g corner we can therefore calculate as follows:

$$(SW \times LM) \div (Fr + Rr) = Roll\ Angle$$
$$(900 \times 12.50) \div (7{,}565.46 + 8{,}113.94) = 0.72\ degrees$$

Notice that as the roll axis height – which can be adjusted by raising or lowering the roll centres at either end of the car – controls the value of LM, we can reduce the amount of roll by raising the roll centre heights and vice versa.

Summary

A final sobering thought. All the above calculations assume a totally rigid chassis which does not actually exist. They also assume friction-free mountings, geometric perfection in any linkages, non-flex pick-up points and rigid lever arms, all of which are either rare or impossible in current practical terms.

This should not deter you because everybody else faces the same difficulties, but may have even less idea of what they are doing or in which direction they are proceeding. That can only be to your advantage.

Schedule of Terms		Measured Example Data
W	= Total weight of car and driver	1,120 lbs
WF	= Total weight, front	400 lbs
WR	= Total weight, rear	720 lbs
UWF	= Total unsprung weight, front	100 lbs
UWR	= Total unsprung weight, rear	120 lbs
UGF	= Unsprung CoG height, front	10 inches
UGR	= Unsprung CoG height, rear	12 inches
TF	= Track, front	58 inches
TR	= Track, rear	55 inches
CF	= Height of front roll centre	1.50 inches
CR	= Height of rear roll centre	3.00 inches
SGF	= Sprung CoG height, front	13 inches
SGR	= Sprung CoG height, rear	16 inches
SF	= Front spring rate	175 lbs
SR	= Rear spring rate	400 lbs
WmF	= Front wheel movement	1.00 inches
WmR	= Rear wheel movement	1.00 inches
SmF	= Relative front spring movement	0.75 inches
SmR	= Relative rear spring movement	0.60 inches
BmF	= Relative front roll bar pick up movement	0.95 inches
BmR	= Relative rear roll bar pick up movement	0.60 inches

Schedule of terms	Calculated Example Data
SWF = Total sprung weight, front	300 lbs
SWR = Total sprung weight, rear	600 lbs
SW = Total sprung weight	900 lbs
UtF = Unsprung weight transfer, front	17.24 lbs
UtR = Unsprung weight transfer, rear	26.18 lbs
CtF = Weight transferred via front roll centre	7.76 lbs
CtR = Weight transferred via rear roll centre	32.73 lbs
WDR = Proportion of sprung weight on rear axle	66%
TM = Mean track of sprung weight	56 inches
CM = Mean roll centre of sprung weight	2.5 inches
GM = Mean CoG of sprung weight	15 inches
LM = Mean roll moment of sprung weight	12.5 inches
St = Weight transferred due to the sprung mass	200.89 lbs
Wt = Total weight transfer	284.84 lbs
ArF = Front roll resistance due to springs	2,889.77 inch lbs per deg.
ArR = Rear roll resistance due to springs	3,801.33 inch lbs per deg.
BF = Front roll bar rate	88.24 inch lbs
BR = Rear roll bar rate	226.9 inch lbs
BrF = Front roll resistance due to bars	4,675.69 inch lbs per deg.
BrR = Rear roll resistance due to bars	4,312.61 inch lbs per deg.
Fr = Total front roll resistance	7,565.46 inch lbs per deg.
Rr = Total rear roll resistance	8,113.94 inch lbs per deg.
DrF = Front roll stiffness, proportional to total roll stiffness	48.3%
DrR = Rear roll stiffness, proportional to total roll stiffness	51.7%
WtF = Total front weight transfer	122 lbs
WtR = Total rear weight transfer	163 lbs

Chapter 10

Dampers and monoshocks

...the final frontier?

IF ONE COULD FIND a single redeeming feature about the banning of active suspension from motor-racing, it might be that it put a violent spur into the flanks of damper design. With unequal length wishbones, coil springs and anti-roll bars virtual standard wear for everybody, though with a myriad detail variations on the theme, the possibilities of persuading a damper to provide a new level of sophistication in wheel control was more or less the only way to go.

To the extent that one top designer has stated 'Assuming the best tyres obtainable are used, there are only four things left: more power, less weight, more downforce. Dampers will do nearly everything else. The rest is b******s'. Very sweeping but far from hyperbole. We are not of course talking road comfort here, only tyre contact patch grip and handling balance.

Rear dampers on the author's current Megapin. (Author)

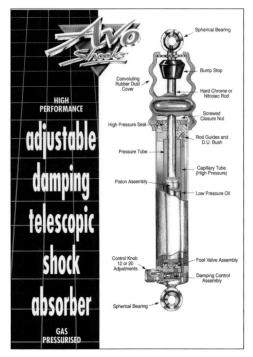

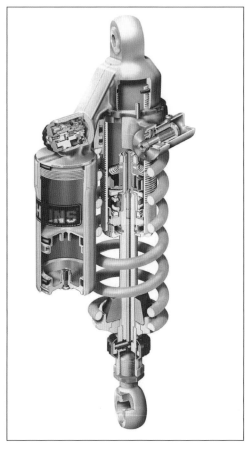

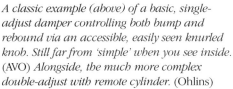

A classic example (above) of a basic, single-adjust damper controlling both bump and rebound via an accessible, easily seen knurled knob. Still far from 'simple' when you see inside. (AVO) Alongside, the much more complex double-adjust with remote cylinder. (Ohlins)

Quickly backtracking 100 years, another very short historical/technical survey might be in order to appreciate both the difficulties and ingenuity shown in that century. It was recognised almost from Day One that any spring, then almost universally a single or laminated leaf type, used on a vehicle moving over a bumpy surface could produce horrendous leaping and bounding of the sprung weight (carriage or bodywork). The spring then, and now, absorbs energy in being flexed under load and wishes to let it go with similar violence. Trying to control or minimise this shock to driver or passengers gave birth to the label 'shock absorber' which, strictly speaking, is incorrect and only now slowly giving way to the more accurate name of 'damper'. Its job is the controlled damping or steady reduction in the oscillation of the spring to bring it speedily back to a steady state.

The first attempts, some of which were to survive for at least the first 40 years of the automobile, tended to be based on friction between the rotating faces of discs of wood, leather, linoleum floor covering, brake/clutch lining materials, and even heavy cardboard for the truly penniless owner. These were normally trapped between a pair of steel arms, one attached to the axle and the other to the body. The best-known was probably the Andre Hartford, using a central nut, bolt and star washer to vary the clamping pressure on the discs until they could ultimately lock solid. Naturally this last stage removed the suspension completely, but stiffness approaching this point had been far from uncommon. An alternative was needed urgently.

Hefty damper fitted to 2003 Citroën Xsara WRC rally car. (sutton-images.com)

There were of course, plenty of one-offs and false starts in hydraulic applications, and it may well be that Lancia was the first production car maker to build a piston damper which they put into their 1924 Aurelia front suspension. Although the UK company of Woodhead (later a massive presence in post Second World War top-class European competition) had a patent in 1930, the American aero industry-linked company of Monroe took a variation of an aircraft landing gear strut into the American car industry in 1934. It was so good in concept that current versions by a number of manufacturers are still, 70 years on, fundamentally similar, even if hugely refined and developed, not least in the low-priced industrial production of very accurate components and high pressure seals.

All attacked the problem in generally similar ways – the now classic telescopic, oil-filled, piston damper, transferring suspension movement to a steel piston going up and down within an oil-filled body. The piston could only be moved by forcing the oil to pass through very small holes that could be tailored to vary the force needed for a given movement. In no time at all the holes became valves, the body and piston rod were given rubber bushes top and bottom to bolt on to the axle and vehicle body, and suspension engineers were discovering a whole new world. Since then, remarkably, nothing much has altered, at least in principle. Refinements, yes. Probably thousands have improved the reliability, production methods and costs to quite remarkable levels.

A popular variation of this damper, that ran in parallel for some time, used the same principle of forcing oil through restrictor valves, but with movement via an outside lever arm that could be used as an integral part of the suspension linkage. These were certainly employed well into the 1980s by British Leyland (as was) on the Marina,

Figure 10-1 *Adjustments with separate bump and rebound facility. Note that these figures would relate to a specific set of control valves or shims. By changing these the damper could be adjusted for a range of coils and vehicle weights.* (AVO)

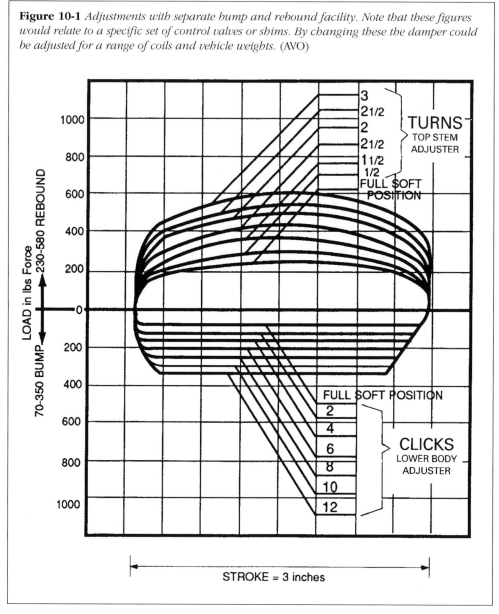

Midget and MG, and thanks to vintage veteran and historic demand for such units, they still keep a cottage industry going with overhaul expertise and spares. However, the elegant combination of a telescopic damper and a coiled steel spring is now perilously near universal.

Study any current Formula One or Indycar, and apart from the exquisite detail finish and installation, you may detect only a couple of easy-to-spot differences to peering under a 1935 Dodge or Chevrolet – an external screw collar to alter the coil spring mounting and thus ride height, and button, knob or screwdriver slot to adjust the internal valving to offer more or less resistance to movement.

Figure 10-2 *Dyno-plots of what a single-adjuster does to increase/decrease bump and rebound forces at the same time. While both alter, their relationship stays very roughly the same.* (AVO)

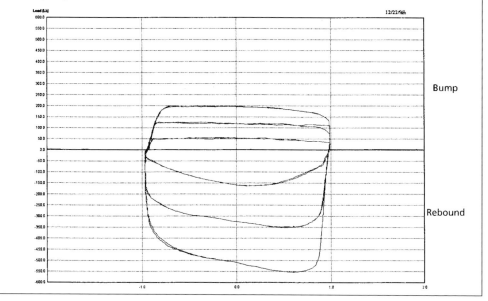

Figure 10-3 *Map of typical internal valving for the deservedly well-known double-adjustable Koni damper. There are at least eight different sets of valves available tailored to coil springs ranging from 150 to 1500 lb/in. Single adjust patterns usually have a fixed bump resistance with any variations confined to rebound.* (Koni)

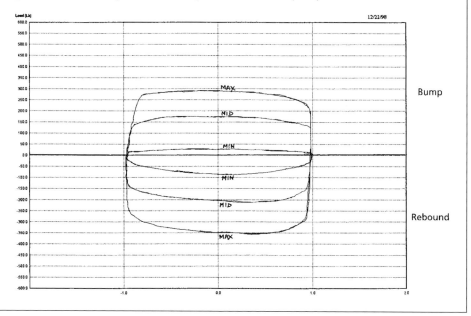

Figure 10-4 *Latest 'shimline' design by Koni. Fitted with a 2 in rather than 2¼/ID coil, alloy body, detachable top eye, (with variable lengths available) and a variety of bump stops, valving is pre-assembled into cartridges which are changed as units – simple, clean and highly damage-resistant.* (Koni)

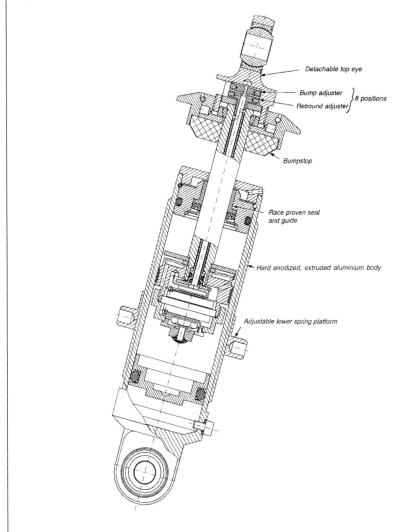

Although the slogan 'racing improves the breed' is by no means universally or even now and again true, competition was to be responsible for huge steps in barely a decade from the late 1980s on, both in the equipment and a new understanding of what damping could do and why. This progression is still going on apace. Such knowledge is usually expensively and lengthily hard-won, so it does not come cheap to those who wish to enjoy its benefits at some later stage.

To the amateur racer this equipment not only costs very serious money, but also then demands a high level of technical approach to get any proper value and results for the investment putting it well out of reach of the majority. But for what it will do at the highest professional level, it is relatively cheap, and that is even with a requirement for several sets per team car: two damper dynos (one in the truck, another in the workshop), computer software, colour printer to classify and file every experiment, nitrogen cylinders with piping and pressure reducing valves plus a range of special tools, shimpacks, and basic spares, not to mention the services of a full-time expert with the experience to weigh and balance the mass of data that will result from test sessions and racing.

Top English racing team engineer John Bright (doing precisely this job with the Indycar championship Ganassi team in the US), built up a stacked shelf above his bench with a fat ringback folder for every racetrack in America on which they ran. In each one was a wad of test and race data, sometimes with differential settings even between one wheel and another. In his head was the skill and knowledge not only to strip, reset, rebuild, repressurize and dyno-test a pair of units in 30 minutes, but also to know the routes that might be followed for a particular effect on the car's performance, or the driver's preference – which are not always the same thing.

Figure 10-5 *Chart defining not only the various valve cartridges available for the Koni 2817, but also how they can be combined for very sophisticated bump-rebound characteristics.* (Koni)

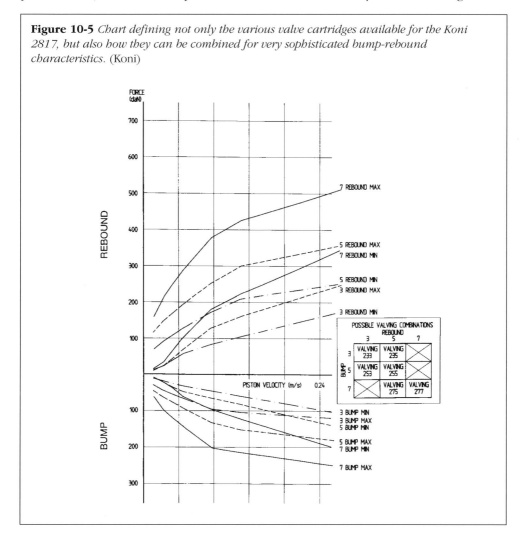

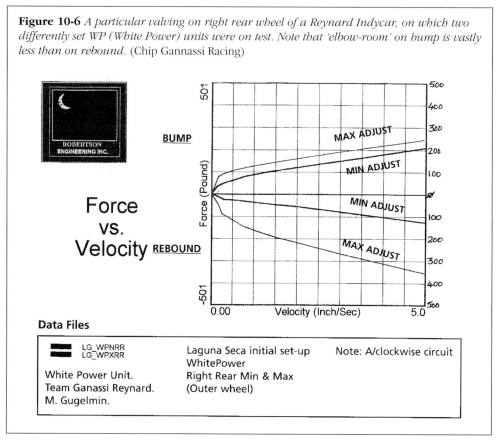

Figure 10-6 *A particular valving on right rear wheel of a Reynard Indycar, on which two differently set WP (White Power) units were on test. Note that 'elbow-room' on bump is vastly less than on rebound.* (Chip Gannassi Racing)

Very early in its life, the telescopic damper split along two internal design paths, essential to deal with an awkward yet vital aspect of the oil it contained – effectively incompressible or solid. Because the piston rod was required to slide in and out of the body, the space in which a fixed quantity of oil would be stored had itself to be variable in some way or something was not going to work. There were two answers which came to be tagged 'twin tube' and 'monotube'. In the first the body had an inner and outer wall leaving a space into which the oil could move as the damper closed up. The alternative was to introduce nitrogen under pressure which turned the contents into a compressible emulsion capable of expanding or contracting with piston movement while modified valving dealt with the mix and its differing flow rates and behaviour. While this proved short-lived, development on both these themes included trapping the nitrogen in a flexible bag, or moving the required 'spare space' to a remote cylinder with its own valve assemblies and fully floating piston to isolate the gas cushion. There was in fact a lengthy time interval before the separate reservoir appeared, during which designers battled primarily with heat and valving problems. Work done by the wheel compressing the suspension spring is effectively turned into heat, which is more than enough to affect oil viscosity and in some situations to burn the paint off a damper body, to varying bleed hole sizes, shapes of entry and exit, location, and in due course, to variable spring steel washer stacks over the oil passages that could be made to flex progressively to provide further ranges of resistance.

Designers were not looking to stop a spring oscillation dead without any overshoot. What came to be known as the Critical Camping Coefficient (CDC) was based on the coil spring rate involved and the weight bouncing on it. It was soon realised that this amounted to almost no suspension at all and ballpark figures appeared in the order of 10%–25% of a calculated CDC. The whole business turned out to be so difficult that Lotus Engineering in particular, was able to use their know-how to offer damper consultancy to some of the biggest car makers in the world, who had discovered it could be very difficult indeed to get it quite right themselves.

Not unexpectedly there proved to be many subtleties in persuading a road suspension to provide acceptable ride quality for anything from a lone driver to a full family of five with their holiday luggage, or a race version to cope with differing

Figure 10-7 *Penske Force vs Displacement Graphs*

For the really serious student, the full version of Penske's remarkable 8100 Technical Manual is perhaps the best readily available – and comprehensible – treatise in both words and drawings on dampers and how they work. Some idea of the complex possibilities available are shown in this combined graph of two of their dyno computer readouts illustrating the relationship between the softest (AA) and stiffest (EE) shimsets that can be built into one of these units. Both use a frequency of around 0.82 Hz (50 CPM) and a 2-inch stroke – not a million miles from the average vehicle on the average road. When you realise that (AA) bump could be combined with (E) rebound, should you so wish, that there is also an (F) shimset too strong to fit on the graph, and that there are 19 sets of shims off the shelf for this unit alone, you begin to appreciate why the number of people who can think their way into what a modern damper may be doing is small and very select. Note that while the (AA) valving shows generally conventional rebound/bump ratio of 3:1 (209–69 lb force) the (EE) shims can provide a weaker rebound than bump (662–712 lb force) if required (see also a clearer diagnostic version on page 179). (Penske Racing Shocks)

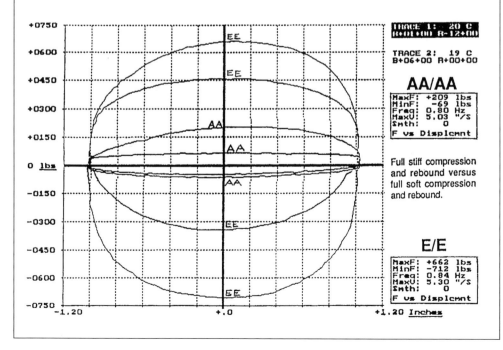

speeds, surfaces and suspension frequencies, not to mention aerodynamic downforce. As ever, it was not so much finding the answers (which needed no more than tenacity, time, money and genius) as defining the objectives and deciding the questions to try to answer. One rule that has stood the test of time – more or less – is that rebound is not only the most important part of the equation but will tend to be about two to four times the strength of the bump. Having said that, it may be 1:1 in some competition settings …

It was also rapidly clear that what was right at one speed or on one quality of road surface could well be wrong – a little or a lot – at different speeds in different places. Certainly the required variations for a full range of solutions appeared infinite. Two aspects turned out to ease the situation a great deal. It was found that internal valving could be made to provide a modest 'spread' covering situations on either side of the ideal, solving a number of road car difficulties. Further, a relatively simple 'single adjust' with an external knob could vary the strength to a reasonable degree, usually on both bump and rebound, but sometimes on rebound only.

Armstrong for one produced a competition version seen in the 1950s and '60s on large numbers of racing and sports cars and fitted with a robust adjuster knob on the bottom of the body. But the unit which was perhaps destined to have the greatest affect on the situation came initially from Koning in Holland – the rightly famed and still widely used oil Koni 'double adjust' originally with a bottom knob for bump, and a top slotted ring for rebound (Type 8211/12). In reality it had a third, invisible, adjustment internally as the valving could be tailored to six different coil strength ranges. This has a simplified and very logical approach giving a driver or engineer exactly what he wants to know, and being concentric the coil and damper see each other for exactly what they are, ignoring the effects of leverages, mounting points, etc. It is also highly effective. Coils are still changed, but more rarely when the designer has got his chosen suspension frequency right, or can refine it as he wishes through bellcrank modifications in a push or pullrod system.

Although it now has serious competitors, Koni has kept its pre-eminence for over 30 years save for a short period when it chose to alter the superbly accessible bump adjustment to a button hidden within the coil which necessitated removal from the car, dismantling the coil and hoping you had got the new bump setting right first time. Happily this was discarded, a well deserved fate, in favour of twin slotted ring adjusters at the top for both bump and rebound (Type 2812).

To bring us right up to date, along with Ohlins, JRZ, Dynamic et al we have the Penske, which is more likely to perpetuate the name of the American arch enthusiast and tycoon, Roger, than many other parts of his huge self-built empire. It was, and is, very complex with a huge amount of adjustment, both internal and external, mechanically and with variable gas pressure, is expensive and needs highly skilled backup. In racing it has proved one of the better ways to go, and it draws the ultimate racer's tribute. Other teams besides Penske now choose to fit them.

They also devised their own answer to a problem that race engineers had become more and more aware of as the whole concept of racing suspension went towards harder and harder with less and less movement. This is that competition (primarily) produced two utterly different situations that had become ever more difficult to reconcile. Valving for low-speed bump and droop (meaning velocity of the piston rod, not speed of the vehicle) characteristic of most speeds on good surfaces, could not cope with high-speed bump and rebound, best exampled by using the kerbs in circuit racing, and hitting potholes, verges and bits of rock on unsurfaced rally sections. If bump settings were softened for the big impacts, they were too soft for most other conditions. This latter also compromised the urgent need for aerodynamic

Figure 10-8 *The rebound adjuster on the 8100 Series shock absorber is located in the eyelet at the base of the main shaft. Inside the window is an adjustment screw which serves as the control point for rebound adjustments. The rebound adjuster has two full turns of adjustment or (12) flats. From the full hard setting, count out (12) flats to the full soft setting. Note: the external rebound adjustment is only a fine device for the main valving located inside the shock absorber.* (Penske Racing Shocks)

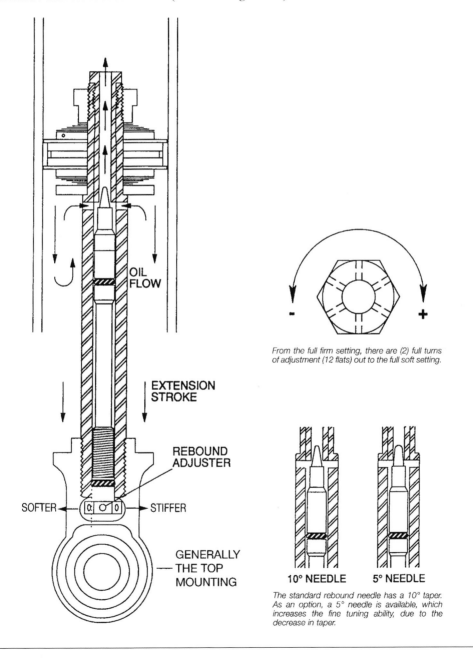

OIL FLOW

From the full firm setting, there are (2) full turns of adjustment (12 flats) out to the full soft setting.

EXTENSION STROKE

REBOUND ADJUSTER

SOFTER ← → STIFFER

GENERALLY THE TOP MOUNTING

10° NEEDLE   5° NEEDLE

The standard rebound needle has a 10° taper. As an option, a 5° needle is available, which increases the fine tuning ability, due to the decrease in taper.

Figure 10-9 *The 8100 compression adjuster is located in the remote reservoir. This allows for the use of increased volumes of oil and nitrogen, essential for consistent damping forces throughout a long race and in extreme conditions. The floating piston is designed to separate the fluid and the nitrogen, eliminating any chance of aeration. In the event of high shaft velocities, the fluid forces open the blow-off valve (figures 2 and 3). The incorporation of the new blow-off valve makes for a more linear damping curve.* (Penske Racing Shocks)

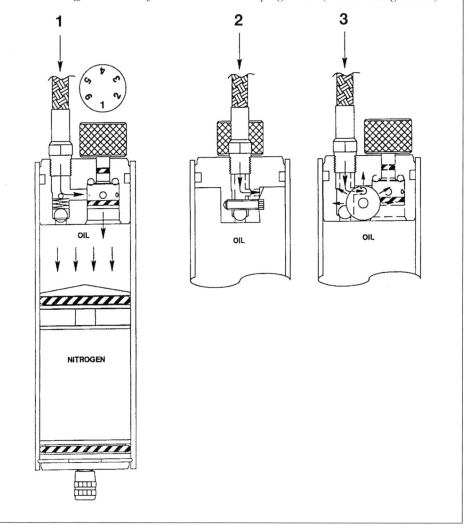

reasons to keep the vehicle as close to the ground with stability as could be achieved.

Initial experiments involved a 'blow-off' valve, to bypass a lot of fluid when the pressure internally rose above a certain point, but this proved less than satisfactory in real life because, for a brief period, the suspension lacked any bump control at all.

Penske's version provided a fully settable high-speed bump control, and for those who wanted to try it, rebound to match. Not everybody jumped at four-way adjustment, although works rally teams were more than happy to experiment, while

Figure 10-10 *Graphs showing how bump stops increase a coil rate both rapidly and significantly once they are in contact with the damper body. A powerful effect that may be difficult to predict dynamically.*

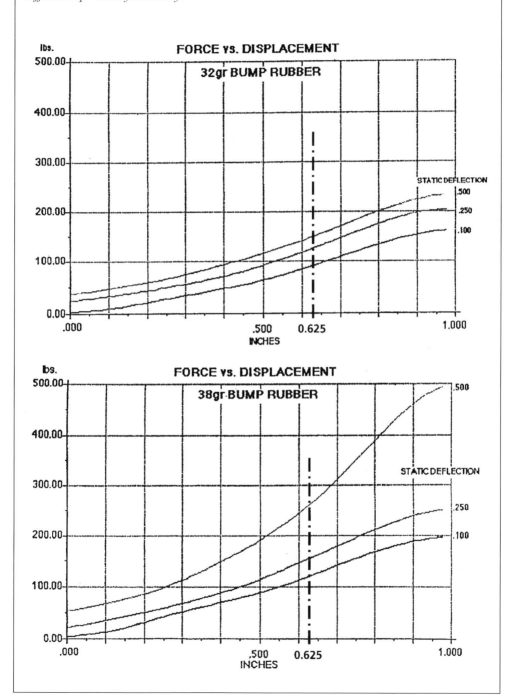

Formula One, at least from a TV armchair, still appear to be spending appreciable time fully airborne without suspension movement at all whether in bump or droop. The initial moves to minimal suspension movement revealed new problems. The time intervals in which valves and fluid had to make physical movements, started to become so impossibly short that it forced a design reversal in bellcrank leverages to unity or more in favour of the coil and damper to obtain more realistic intervals in which the mechanisms could work. Had outboard suspension not been totally displaced by pushrod, even this variation would not have been possible.

It can be seen ever more clearly how far ahead of its time was the much lamented (by me if nobody else outside Lotus and Williams) but outlawed Lotus 'Active'. The system software even then could deal with exactly the difficulties now being encountered, with a polished sophistication all its own. Alas and alack …

So what do you actually have to do with these dampers in which you have so heavily invested, to transform handling and performance? Well, if they should be sealed gas-filled on a production car or in a controlled spec. formula, the answer has to be 'nothing', other than perhaps buy a different one. Any degree of adjustability is a different story, and perhaps more than in any other area of the racing car you get no more than what you pay for.

As the roughest of guides to cost, taking 'A' (£, $ or roubles, say) for the simplest, non-adjustable basic high production roadcar unit, you should expect:

- Basic single-adjust, probably bump/rebound combined rubber bushes – 3A
- High quality single-adjust, alloy collars, Rose joints (also used early Koni Type 8211, plus revalving) – 6A–7A
- Decent quality double-adjust – 12A
- Top quality, rebuildable double adjust – 15A–20A
- Top quality with remote reservoir (rebuildable) – 23A
- Best of best, remote, triple adjust etc, etc – up to 40A

Four-way adjust units do exist, but still seem to be in the area of works development, particularly in rallying, at the time of writing. You only have to watch a gravel rally or desert raid car with a crew of two and big fuel tankage and see how they land from huge jumps to squat instantly like spiders back on the road, to appreciate the remarkable degree of control in suspension that has been achieved.

You have to accept that even if your lottery win has finally come up, buying the ultimate is not going to give you any proper value without a high level of skill and the technical backup of serious testing to make any decent use of them. A good quality single-adjust, and reasonable double adjust do excellent jobs for nearly all of us outside the higher echelons.

Some years ago, Koni as well befitted them, composed and made freely available, an excellent basic approach to setting their double-adjust units, as did Penske some time later. Both are generally applicable to dampers in general, though should you be contemplating a season in NASCAR (the American 200 mph big saloons) Penske produce booklets with precise valving front and rear, and sometimes left and right as well for every major track, road, short oval or banked, in the country.

Something you need to understand and have clearly in mind to even think about dampers – setting them, or using them properly – is how they are quantified, ie roughly what might constitute soft, medium, hard or rock solid, and how these are generally illustrated graphically. Because they are 'velocity sensitive', it means that at low speed (damper not car) with the piston moving in and out slowly as with pushing and pulling by hand, a damper may feel quite soft and easy to move. This is very deceptive. Try to double the speed of travel of the piston and you discover that even moving it at all may be impossible. You have altered nothing in its mechanism. What has happened is that the internal valving permits only so much oil at a given moment and speed to pass through the metering holes. It will take more load at the higher speed to make it move a similar distance. Got it? (If not, it is more likely my failure rather than yours.)

There are at least two ways in general use of illustrating all this for any particular unit, one graphed as load (lb or newtons) v velocity (in or metres/second) or load v displacement (in or mm) and both the 'climbing line' and 'squashed grapefruit' or 'potato' plots illustrate better than words how and when a damper is exerting what force. What it will not tell you unfortunately is what you want, as they will behave differently in different situations, or with changed springs, or varying speed, or with extra passengers, a full tank or aerodynamic downforce increasing the weight. 'Active' could eat this lot for breakfast, but they give current designers a hard time, let alone you or I trying to fathom out our next move.

To give some idea of figures – shaft speeds, loads etc – and the bands in which they lie on the accompanying graphs, the following data should assist. It is an amalgamation of much help and advice for which I am indebted to Avo, Koni, Penske and Spax, who are by no means standardised either in the units they employ or how they are presented graphically. Suffice that this is all aimed at slightly clarifying some basics. The examples are all in Imperial units of pounds and inches. Metric versions will be found by direct conversion into kg, newtons and metres. Seconds normally provide the timebase.

Piston velocities	
low –	0–2 in/second
medium –	2–5 in/second
high –	5–8 in/second
v. high –	9–12 in/second
'mega' –	13+ in/second

Some dyno readouts take the test figures up to 20 in/sec and some quote maximum, virtually instantaneous figures into 40 in/sec under violent kerbing, so the difficulties facing the valving engineer are not hard to see.

Example damper stiffness ranges (Resistance to movement with specific valving installed in the same unit: ie, Penske shim packs AA or FF)

AA (weakest)		
	Bump	*Rebound*
Max.	50 lb	210 lb
Min.	15 lb	65 lb

FF (strongest)		
	Bump	*Rebound*
Max.	1,000 lb	1,150 lb
Min.	750 lb	400 lb

When you consider that shims are available in, for example, A-, A, and A+ steps, all interchangeable with each other right through more than a dozen sets, half a lifetime may be on the short side to sort out an ideal solution. And it may only then give you perfection for that afternoon, on that track …

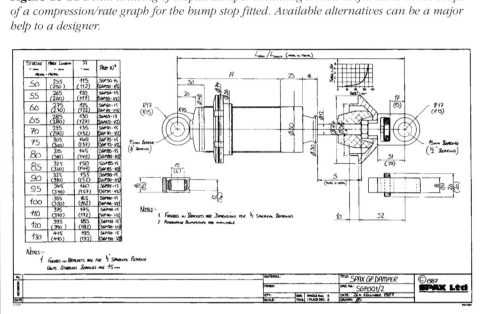

Figure 10-11 *Detail drawing of a Spax damper including a most useful extra in the shape of a compression/rate graph for the bump stop fitted. Available alternatives can be a major help to a designer.*

The racing objective of keeping the tyre on the road for as much of the time as possible with the driver forced to accept whatever comfort level this implies may well be somewhat simpler than keeping a variable number of human passengers not merely free of motion sickness, but relaxed and happy as well. The drawings on page 177 attempt to present a somewhat simplistic view of how the most basic calculation of frequency in a sprung body multiplies up and up again. Supposedly known or fixed data becomes variable in possibly unpredictable ways en route from textbook to track seeking answers to the question 'What are we looking for?'. There are powerful arguments for the view that the tyre contact patch – what it is doing, what is happening to it and how its grip is being affected is not just of major importance, but is the ultimate and only thing that matters. Every other act of designer, builder and driver must finally operate through those four bits of rubber roughly the sole area of two pairs of rubber boots. 'Riding the Welly boot quartet' you might well observe of racing any car.

If the variables and implied compromises on page 177 look frightening, remember that they ignore tyre temperature, weather, mechanical distortion of the tyre under 3 G cornering and 4 G braking loads, and the great sensitivity of wide slicks to camber angles. Is it too much to suggest that McLaren's late 1990s renaissance in Formula One owed more than a little to in-house damper development on their own units as part of their 'secret weapon' in dealing with circuit kerbing that tiny bit better than the opposition? And a 'tiny bit' is just that – half a per cent in a 1 m 20 sec lap is 0.4 second – not infrequently the difference between the triumph of pole and 6th row disaster.

Before investing more than a stamp or a telephone call on new dampers you need to ask certain questions and make a few measurements. What do the adjusters adjust? Can they be rebuilt? Is the valving variable or suitable for your coils? What sort of bearings are in the mounting eyes? Can you get the size you want? Correct length is vital; too long and you will be riding the bump stops, too short and you will be lifting

Figure 10-12 *Somewhat simplistic illustration of how the difficulties and unknowns multiply between textbook and racetrack when seeking answers to the question: 'what damper valving is needed for a given suspension frequency?'*

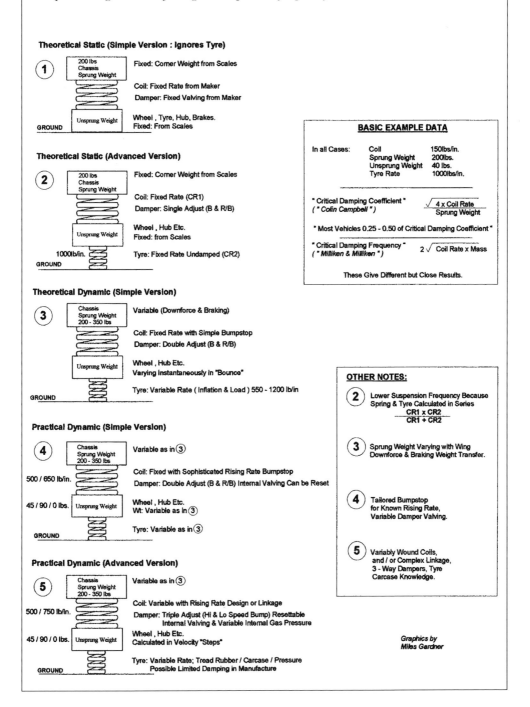

Theoretical Static (Simple Version : Ignores Tyre)

1
200 lbs Chassis Sprung Weight — Fixed: Corner Weight from Scales

Coil: Fixed Rate from Maker
Damper: Fixed Valving from Maker

Unsprung Weight — Wheel , Tyre, Hub, Brakes. Fixed: From Scales
GROUND

Theoretical Static (Advanced Version)

2
200 lbs Chassis Sprung Weight — Fixed: Corner Weight from Scales

Coil: Fixed Rate (CR1)
Damper: Single Adjust (B & R/B)

Unsprung Weight — Wheel , Hub Etc. Fixed: from Scales
1000lb/in. — Tyre: Fixed Rate Undamped (CR2)
GROUND

Theoretical Dynamic (Simple Version)

3
Chassis Sprung Weight 200 - 350 lbs — Variable (Downforce & Braking)

Coil: Fixed Rate with Simple Bumpstop
Damper: Double Adjust (B & R/B)

Unsprung Weight — Wheel , Hub Etc. Varying Instantaneously in "Bounce"
GROUND — Tyre: Variable Rate (Inflation & Load) 550 - 1200 lb/in

Practical Dynamic (Simple Version)

4
Chassis Sprung Weight 200 - 350 lbs — Variable as in (3)

500 / 650 lb/in. — Coil: Fixed with Sophisticated Rising Rate Bumpstop
Damper: Double Adjust (B & R/B) Internal Valving Can be Reset

45 / 90 / 0 lbs. Unsprung Weight — Wheel , Hub Etc. Wt: Variable as in (3)

Tyre: Variable as in (3)
GROUND

Practical Dynamic (Advanced Version)

5
Chassis Sprung Weight 200 - 350 lbs — Variable as in (3)

500 / 750 lb/in. — Coil: Variable with Rising Rate Design or Linkage
Damper: Triple Adjust (Hi & Lo Speed Bump) Resettable Internal Valving & Variable Internal Gas Pressure

45 / 90 / 0 lbs. Unsprung Weight — Wheel , Hub Etc. Calculated in Velocity "Steps"

Tyre: Variable Rate; Tread Rubber / Carcase / Pressure Possible Limited Damping in Manufacture
GROUND

BASIC EXAMPLE DATA

In all Cases:
Coil Sprung Weight — 150lbs/in.
Sprung Weight — 200lbs.
Unsprung Weight — 40 lbs.
Tyre Rate — 1000lbs/in.

" Critical Damping Coefficient "
(" Colin Campbell ")

$$\sqrt{\frac{4 \times \text{Coil Rate}}{\text{Sprung Weight}}}$$

" Most Vehicles 0.25 - 0.50 of Critical Damping Coefficient "

" Critical Damping Frequency "
(" Milliken & Milliken ")

$$2\sqrt{\text{Coil Rate} \times \text{Mass}}$$

These Give Different but Close Results.

OTHER NOTES:

2 Lower Suspension Frequency Because Spring & Tyre Calculated in Series
$$\frac{\text{CR1} \times \text{CR2}}{\text{CR1} + \text{CR2}}$$

3 Sprung Weight Varying with Wing Downforce & Braking Weight Transfer.

4 Tailored Bumpstop for Known Rising Rate, Variable Damper Valving.

5 Variably Wound Coils, and / or Complex Linkage, 3 - Way Dampers, Tyre Carcase Knowledge.

Graphics by Miles Gardner

an inner wheel in your first energetic corner.

Both faults are serious bad news and simply copying the units you already have may be wrong for a variety of reasons. Either acquire a copy of *Race and Rally Car Source Book* and turn to page 70, or take the following steps.

1. Remove the existing coils/dampers and support the vehicle on wooden blocks at its correct ride height.
2. Measure the distance between top and bottom mounting brackets. This will be the fitted length you require.
3. Add 1.25–2.5 in to fitted length to obtain a maximum length.
4. Subtract 2.0–3.5 in from the fitted length to obtain minimum length ignoring any bump stop.
5. Check the rates of the coils and decide if you will stick with them or make a change, and if so what will be the new rate.
6. Measure and calculate the corner sprung weights loaded.

You now have enough information to talk sensibly to the maker or supplier of a damper, or study their catalogue. The figures given will cover a wide range of strokes (the critical bit) from 3.25 in (1.25 plus 2.0 in) for many single seaters, small sports and kit cars, up to 6 in (2.0 plus 4.00 in) for most remaining sports cars and many saloons. Beware that if you are rallying or going off-road, you may need considerably more stroke than this. Note that total stroke is usually split 65% for bump, 35% for rebound. Two final points. If you cannot get an appropriate damper into the space available, you must alter the design/bracket positions to suit one you can fit. Secondly, avoid if you possibly can, the rubber bush end bearings normally supplied on many units, in favour of the small spherical version. These generally have the same bore (0.5 in) but need spacer bushes each side to fit original mounting brackets. The rubber type inject an unknown rising rate into any calculations with both radial compression and rotational shear when the bolts are tightened, as well as making really accurate cornerweight settings well-nigh impossible.

Now to settings. Anyone reading this far will probably be so horrified at the potential complications and cost that they have decided not to do anything at all. Do not despair. A basic unit with single-adjust capability is still capable of very worthwhile improvements, given only that you are willing to take the time for some modest but methodic fiddling about and experiment.

Both Koni and Penske suggest as a start, once the new units are in place, by driving the car with any adjusters on full soft, whether on a road or test track. This will give a feel for minimal damping probably varying from imprecise and mushy to abysmal.

Single-adjuster: You have no option but to simply go stiffer and stiffer a click at a time until things start to feel hard and jolty which may also cause tyre-hop at either end under hard cornering or heavy braking. At that point come back one or two clicks. Note that most very basic dampers stiffen in a major way on the first four or five clicks with a steadily reducing effect up to perhaps ten or eleven clicks when they reach their effective maximum. They will often appear to adjust further but with negligible effect. It makes them an imprecise but most certainly not ineffective instrument. Some can adjust only the rebound while others do both bump and rebound in unison.

Double adjusters: Koni's basic guidelines have been quite widely used, and the redoubtable Carroll Smith called them 'the best information for adjusting shock

Figure 10-13 *Penske Force vs Displacement Graph*
Because of the way damper dynos often print out a force vs displacement graph (see a real-life version opposite) it may not be obvious that the axis of movement in the graph is horizontal, not vertical, the normal mounting position for very many units other than F1. Like an engine piston in its bore, the damper shaft has each time to stop dead in bump or rebound and reverse its direction, as have the controlling valve shim stacks. Add in velocity sensitivity and an unknown varying road surface and the only clear thing about damper design and operation seems to be its lack of clarity. Data from Neil Barnett – Spa Design/Penske

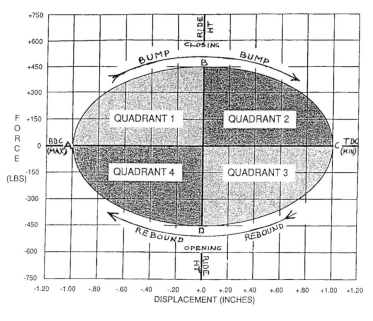

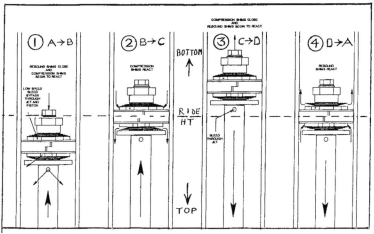

Figure 10-14 *Trouble-shooting Flowchart*

Not too many real experts are willing to go out on a public limb with a simplified approach to helping others with a very complex situation. These flow diagrams are rare examples. The steps progress right through from 'do you have a jammed suspension link' to cover downforce variations, and coilspring geometry and roll bar changes. It assumes not unreasonably a car

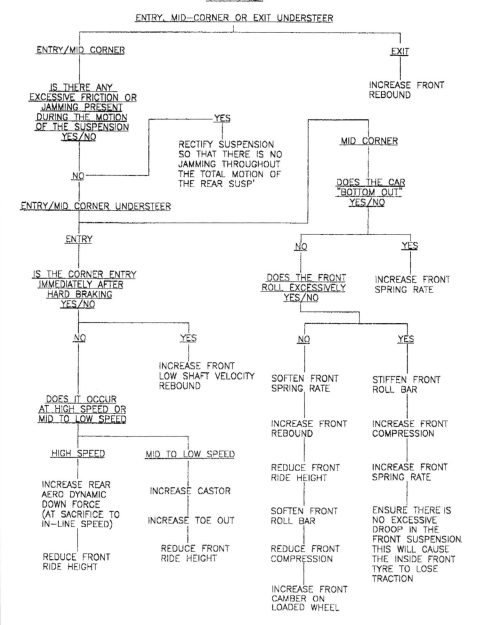

equipped with double adjust dampers, together with variable roll bars and the facility and skills to make spring changes. And its coverage encompasses not only under- and oversteer, but also a variety of racing situations, entering or exiting both fast and slow corners. Charts courtesy of Greg Simmons – Spa Design/Penske

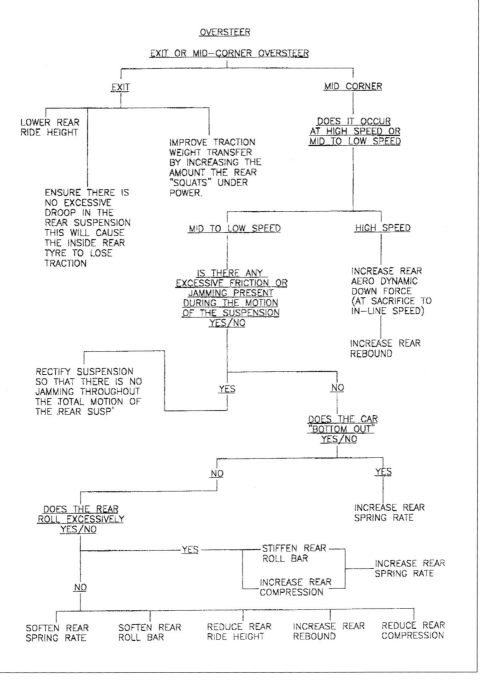

absorbers that I have seen in writing'. This has to be quite a recommendation and seems an excellent reason why their example might be followed here. Note that front and rear settings may well be different.

Bump damping: The ideal setting may be anywhere in the adjustment range and will be reached when 'side hop' or 'walking' in bumpy turns is minimal and the ride not unduly harsh. Either side of this ideal setting, one or other will be more pronounced.

Adjusting the bump control: Early Type 8211 Bottom knob: anti/clock is softer, clockwise stiffer. Late Type 2812, clockwise to left is softer. Upper disc in window below top mounting.

> *Step 1.* Set all four dampers at minimum on both bump and rebound.
> *Step 2* Drive a few laps to get the feel of the car. Disregard body lean or roll and concentrate only on how the car feels over bumps.
> *Step 3.* Increase bump adjuster by three clicks on all four dampers. Drive a few laps. Again increase bump settings a further three clicks. Keep repeating until things start to feel hard and jolty over bumps.
> *Step 4.* Back off (reduce) bump adjust by two clicks. Note: it is very unlikely that both front and rear will match. Get one right and continue the same at the other until they are similar. Make a note of these figures in writing.

Rebound damping: This controls the transition of the car's attitude into roll as it enters a corner. It cannot alter the total roll angle, but only increase the time it takes to reach that point. Roll angle is governed by a variety of other factors including spring rates and anti-roll bar settings. Too much rebound will cause an initial loss of lateral adhesion (ie understeer at the front or oversteer at the rear). It can also cause 'jacking down' when the car slowly loses ground clearance because the coil is too weak to return to its proper length before being hit by the next bump.

Adjusting rebound control: (a slot below the top eye containing a collar with adjustment holes; 3 holes = 1/4 turn. To left: softer, to right: harder): Early Type 8211: lower of 2 discs in late Type 2812)

> *Step 1.* Leave the newly chosen bump settings untouched. Rebound to full soft, and do some laps noting particularly how the car rolls entering a corner.
> *Step 2.* Increase rebound by three sweeps (3/4 of turn) in adjuster slot. Drive it again noting how it enters a corner. You are looking for smoothness without a drastic attitude change or excessive sudden roll.
> *Step 3.* Increase stiffness three more sweeps if necessary until smoothness is achieved. Too much will be indicated as above, so back off two sweeps at the appropriate end of the car.

As with bump adjust it is unlikely you will get both front and rear right at the same time. Continue until you do. Note the figures down in writing.

There are one or two tricky bits that this advice does not address. One is that strictly speaking these settings will apply only to the venue where you are testing. They may well need repeating at every other place at which you compete. Another is how you sense or estimate what is happening is described in words. Without reasonable driving experience in the car you may at first have very little idea of what is going on. Only more car time will deal with this, but you can hurry things up a bit by studiously keeping speeds within your comfortable limit. They will increase steadily without conscious effort as confidence grows (honestly!).

It is also not impossible you will find that going up at all from full soft will cause immediate trouble, (springs too weak) or that final maximum stiffness will not produce the results (coils too strong). If the springs are an integrated part of the design which they certainly should be, the dampers will require internal revalving. Almost certainly this will need somebody with the right equipment and the know-how. Koni provides a guide by means of code-numbers stamped on the body (model 8211) and the spring ranges for which they are suitable. Always be aware that what is stamped on the body may well not indicate the valving actually within if the units are not new and may have had several owners. Get them checked over anyway.

Penske as well as Koni offer basic setting guidelines which are similar in approach. First, obtain driver familiarity with the sensations of minimal damping with everything on full-soft. Then progress stiffening of bump to an acceptable limit, retaining these settings while increasing rebound control. At least both sets of advice share a common basis – seeking the strongest control of suspension movement and spring forces that can be achieved without some unacceptable penalty.

Monoshock suspension
One of the initially unorthodox developments of recent years that has not only survived the rulemakers but is now very firmly entrenched, though still viewed with suspicion or incomprehension in other areas is the 'monoshock'. This is a front suspension design that approximates to a beam axle in bump and rebound and a mega-stiff anti-roll bar in roll within a robust and finely adjustable single mechanism.

Monoshock front suspension on a Gould GR55 hillclimb single seater. (Gould)

Two views of the monoshock front suspension on a Dallara F3 car. (Author)

Separating, so far as might prove possible, the two different functions of suspension – springs and roll bars – and their control had been one of the most difficult problems to surface with independent front suspension. It had been borne of primarily the change from leaf springs to the much lower frequencies, greater comfort, and potentially better use of the tyre of the coil spring. Alas, hand-in-hand with these came much increased roll angles unknown in the leafspring era. Control of this proved not only relatively easy, but also as it happened a very helpful influence on stable vehicle behaviour for the ordinary driver – the anti-roll bar. This was (and still very often is) a simple length of steel rod or bar linked into the front suspension in twist. The more a car tried to roll, the more it had to twist the bar. Furthermore, this introduced fundamental understeer into the handling, a virtue when combining the average road driver's need for something not tailhappy, and that would always let go at the front first, accepted wisdom in virtually all road-car design.

For the next 60 or 70 years it stayed fundamentally unaltered, while being in many cases integrated to do a second job as one of the suspension links themselves. But

Figure 10-15 *Coil spring/damper unit controls bump and droop. Belleville washer stacks control roll in both right and left corners. See also page 186 washer stock data.*

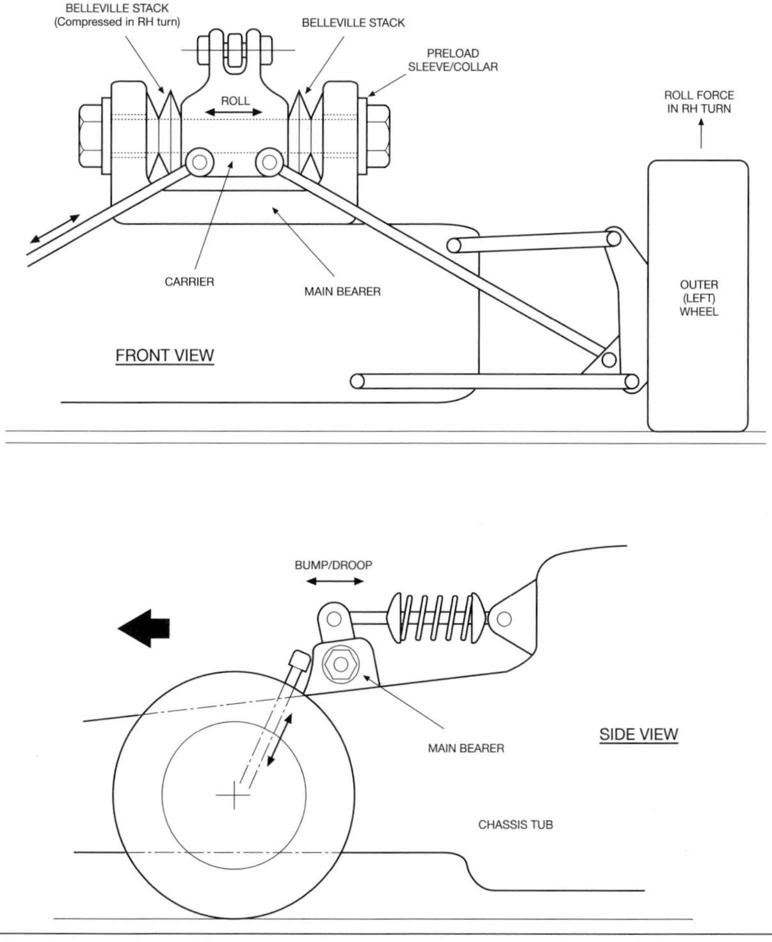

Figure 10-16 *An idea of the complexity possible when running a monoshock car. Dallara's original data sheet with an anonymous race team's notes, partly translated from metric to Imperial and equivalent to ten different anti-roll bars, plus virtually infinite fine adjustment with every change.*

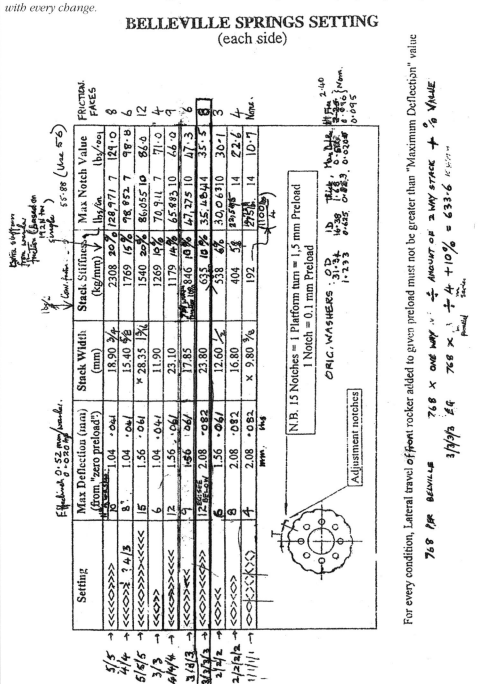

however installed, it always has the same effect. As the outer wheel in a corner rose, it attempted to lift the inner, thus reducing grip on the road. From the moment it became clear that the differing requirements of vertical road surface movements and sideload forces from cornering often interfered with each other in unpredictable and unwanted ways the search was on to separate control of these two functions. It proved far from easy. As hints and tips on a possible solution floated around behind the scenes, in the late '80s some experiments were visible, if not in F1, certainly in F/Ford, but a suitable massively strong yet tiny spring able to deal with the forces involved and a method of utilising it proved hard to find. Among the more adventurous that failed to do the required job, were tennis and golf balls, or a solid rubber stop trapped within sliding sleeve tubes, mini adjustable dampers and air struts inside pushrods. Surprisingly a relatively ancient article in engineering, the dished or 'Belleville' washer emerged as the front-runner.

A large diameter one had already been employed as an 8 in steel ring inside clutches to provide high force with very small movements within limited space. They had another virtue in that varying the numbers, thicknesses and placements face to face or back to back of different numbers could then be shimmed to a pre-fixed length stack capable of rapidly accepting a variable preload with a vast and accurate range of adjustment for any load capacity that might be required. The first really public view of such an installation on a serious scale appears to have been on the Dallara F3 car of 1993. Simple alterations to a set of up to 15 identical washers a side, with a sophisticated and super-sensitive pre-load screw adjuster combined to provide compressive loads ranging from 2000 lb to 120,000 lb from the same washers. The forces of bump and droop had been successfully separated from roll, and with independent adjustment on either. What has occurred before with the arrival of a new development where no rule book initially exists, a small group of crew chiefs and other team bright boys grasp and use what it is all about more quickly than their opposition. Further, the factory boffins had not only done all the preliminary calculations, but provided them in a simple table to any team running one of their cars (Figure 10-17). The only thing they did not – and could not – do was to tell every customer exactly which settings they would need.

Figure 10-17 *If Dallara's own settings chart – based on a single washer – seems a bit on the simple side, there is a wide selection with which you can experiment. This is just a section (less than half a page) of ten in spring steels, plus another four in stainless.* (Belleville Springs Ltd)

Disc Springs to DIN 2093								15% Defl. Defl. mm / Force N		30% Defl. Defl. mm / Force N		45% Defl. Defl. mm / Force N		60% Defl. Defl. mm / Force N		75% Defl. Defl. mm / Force N		90% Defl. Defl. mm / Force N	
Code No.	Outer Dia. (De) mm	Inner Dia. (Di) mm	Thick. (t) mm	Cone Ht. (ho) mm	Overall Ht. (lo) mm	Cone Ht. Thick. Ratio	Weight per 1000 pcs.	Stress σ_{II} N/mm²	σ_{III} N/mm²	Stress σ_{II} N/mm²	σ_{III} N/mm²	Stress σ_{II} N/mm²	σ_{III} N/mm²	Stress σ_{II} N/mm²	σ_{III} N/mm²	Stress σ_{II} N/mm²	σ_{III} N/mm²	Stress σ_{II} N/mm²	σ_{III} N/mm²
D315122125	31.5	12.2	1.25	.95	2.20	.76	6.5	.14 / 481		.29 / 890		.43 / 1,238		.57 / 1,539		.71 / 1,805		.86 / 2,050	
								137	237	307	457	509	659	744	844	1,011	1,012	1,310	1,163
D31512215	31.5	12.2	1.50	.85	2.35	.57	7.8	.13 / 641		.26 / 1,219		.38 / 1,746		.51 / 2,232		.64 / 2,688		.77 / 3,126	
								202	225	430	437	684	635	964	819	1,270	989	1,602	1,145
D31516308	31.5	16.3	.80	1.05	1.85	1.31	3.6	.16 / 255		.32 / 438		.47 / 563		.63 / 642		.79 / 687		.95 / 711	
								-19	278	3	529	64	755	166	955	308	1,130	489	1,278
D315163125	31.5	16.3	1.25	.90	2.15	.72	5.6	.14 / 498		.27 / 926		.41 / 1,296		.54 / 1,621		.68 / 1,913		.81 / 2,184	
								124	275	278	532	462	769	675	988	917	1,187	1,189	1,368

This was more advantage than problem to teams with enquiring minds and the resources for extensive testing time in a search for the tenths of a second that so often separated F3 grid slots. There were some who chose one set of washers and stuck to them through thick and thin – but did not win.

Nor did those who reverted to twin coil/dampers, either creating their own bracketry or with remaining factory parts available for a time from earlier years of experiment. Dallara's arrival was unusual by any standards. Initially largely ignored in the UK where Reynard, Ralt et al held sway, this changed very rapidly once it was seen to be doing the business in Europe. Listed drivers went from two to sixty two in three years, and it seems a not unreasonable assumption that their understanding of the monoshock, together with a full use of Ackermann steering angle in a difficult situation (see Chapter 4) was one of the key reasons for the car's explosive and overwhelming arrival on the F3 scene.

However, it should be understood the first essential to incorporate it successfully into any vehicle is that it be mounted on a structure of superlative rigidity and strength – which means a carbon tub, and a first class one at that. Dallara himself was later to observe that rigidity, not to mention 1200 hours in a wind tunnel were also key elements. Designed to be very stiff with little ground clearance and minimal droop it was at first thought such a car could be run only on the exceptionally smooth surfaces of modern racing circuits, and so would not be a practical proposition on rougher tarmac and cambered corners with one front wheel in mid-air. For the critic or doubter it seems to go against a number of accepted givens, not least that keeping the inner front wheel on the ground at all costs for some grip, however marginal has to be better than having it floating about in thin air. But in fact there is certainly an area where quick drivers confirm that the more they stiffen the car (ie the more the strength of the stacks are increased without going solid) the better the grip becomes …

This was emphatically proved by – among others – designer/driver David Gould who decided to put his own interpretation onto his own carbon hillclimb single-seater

Monoshock front suspension on Ian Scott's Megapin. (Ian Scott)

Author into Shelsley's daunting Bottom Ess at the venue's 100th Anniversary meeting. (Derek Hibbert)

despite strong opinions from some that it would not cope with the notably variable or frankly bad tarmac and cambered corners of some British hillclimbs with speeds topping 160 mph (256 kph). Another nail went in the coffin of those ideas with every new record set by driver Martin Groves on his way to becoming 2005 British Hillclimb Champion in a monoshock Gould GR 55D with a string of new records. His record-breaking form continued in 2006.

So precisely what is it, what does it do, and how? Words yet again fall a little short of a decent picture or drawing. The mechanism from which it draws its catchy (if pedantically incorrect) name, is the easy part. A single conventional coil spring/damper unit tuned to the full sprung weight on the front axle is operated by a fore/aft swinging arm mounted solidly on a carrier (itself free to slide transversely) dealing solely with bump and droop of the front suspension. Two conventional pushrods can force the carrier back and forth across the car but only against the resistance of its own Belleville stacks ie in roll. Thus the roll forces upward from the outer wheel in a corner initially try to push the inner wheel downwards onto the ground (the reverse of a conventional ARB in twist). At the same time the input point of the forces has moved across the car some 75% to alter the leverage in a major way. As in any 'conventional' bar, the inner wheel finally lifts off the ground but in the period before that happens the effects at the tyre contact patch have been radically altering.

An educated guess might be that weight transfer on turn-in from the inner contact patch onto the outer is altered in some way, perhaps being delayed or changed to affect the total distribution in a manner that benefits total front grip prior to the moment the inner leaves the ground. Experienced and longtime racer Allan Warburton, creator of DTA electronic management ran an F3 Dallara in hillclimbs for some time. Asked to describe what the car was like and how it behaved he was terse in the extreme – but emphatic 'It turned in – always.'

Although incidental, it later became very apparent that secrecy of any team's chosen count or arrangement of the Bellevilles was completely assured against opposition or paddock prowler as each stack was buried inside the housing of the slider mechanism. Also, the original design concept has included an incremental and extremely sensitive screw adjust for preloading the stacks. Such repeatable accuracy was well ahead of droplink sliders or rotatable blades, with their angles, joints and twisting forces. All that remained was testing …

Once again we are into the area of 'driver feel'. This has to mean that if it feels good to you or your driver, or shows the best result on the stopwatch, (not necessarily exactly the same thing) you have got it right whatever any critical adviser or expert thinks it ought to be.

It is essential to realise we are now well into the area where there are no more fixed rules and even fewer firm answers. Relatively few of us will have the skills, experience or equipment, including driver sensitivity, to make full (or any) use of the most advanced hardware available. But the one-eyed man has always been one step ahead in the kingdom of the blind, and it has to be worth the effort of trying to see a little further than the opposition.

As Mr Smith also observed sagely after a lifetime of experience in the game; 'This is still only a starting point. You have to experiment and learn in detail how to use shocks. It is not easy.'

Never a truer word, but you never thought it would be, did you?

List of some damper manufacturers and suppliers

AVO Avo (UK) Unit 10B, Laurence Leyland Industrial Estate, Irthlingborough Road, Wellingborough, Northamptonshire NN8 1RN, 01933 270504 (Nigel Killerby)

BILSTEIN Bilstein Distribution (ECP) Ltd, Fulton Road, Wembley Industrial Estate, Wembley, Middlesex, also; Prodrive Ltd, Acorn Way, Banbury, Oxfordshire OX16 7XS, 01295 754221 (Paul Adams)

BOGE Boge (UK) Ltd, Britannia House, Long March Industrial Estate, Daventry, Northamptonshire NN1 4NR, 01327 300353 (Jerry Banks)

DYNAMIC Dynamic Suspensions Ltd, 20 Fison Way, Thetford, Norfolk, IP24 1HJ, 01842 755754 (Dr Rob Williamson)

EIBACH Eibach Suspension Technology, Unit 5, Swannington Road, Cottage Lane Industrial Estate, Broughton Astley, Leicestershire LE9 6TU, 01455 286524 (Julian Gill)

JRZ Suspension Engineering BV, Hunnenpad 176, Oss5349 G, Netherlands, 31-412-625944 (Rob de Rijk, Jan Zuijduik)

KONI JWE Banks Ltd, St Guthlac's Lodge, Crowland, Peterborough PE6 0JB, 01733 210316 (Shaun Pickering)

LEDA Leda Suspension, Unit 33, Hanningfield Industrial Estate, East Hanningfield, Chelmsford, Essex CM3 8AB, 01245 400668 (Len Dixon)

OHLINS (in UK) Ohlins Racing AB, Roebusk House, Cox Lane, Chessington, Surrey KT9 1DG, 0180 9741615 (Dave Phillips, Bengt Ohlsson)

PENSKE (in UK) SPA Design Ltd, The Boat House, Lichfield Street, Fazeley, Tamworth, Staffordshire B78 3QN, 01827 288328 (Ian Maple)

PROFLEX GDB, Old Coach House, Clitheroe, Lancashire, 01200 442345 (Gordon Birtwhistle)

QUANTUM Q Racing Services Ltd., South Unit, Downlands Farm, Drayton Lane, Chichester, West Sussex PO20 6EL, 01243 788812

ROCKSHOX (US) UK: advanced mountain bike suppliers; rear suspension units/coils

SACHS Sachs Auto Components Ltd, Meridian Business Park, Leicester LE3 2WY, 01162 630888 (Herr Strobl)

SHOWA Japan (UK agent pending)

SPAX Spax Ltd, Telford Road, Bicester, Oxfordshire OW6 0UU, 01869 244771 (Jeremy Rossiter, Tim Aust)

WP (née White Power) WP Competition Suspension UK Ltd, Unit 1 Lincoln Court, Borough Road, Brackley, Northamptonshire, 01280 705888 (Peter Babbage)

Appendix 1

The string computer

NOT EVERYONE, even in these days of Apple Mac or IBM checking the laundry list and pantry stock levels of baked beans, will have the resources or expertise to use computer techniques to design a wishbone suspension that has a fighting chance of working reasonably well and in a known manner. Do not despair, and do not burst into uncontrollable laughter either.

When friend and fellow designer Richard Blackmore and I were first struggling to bring the Terrapin from an idea to racing reality, we desperately needed some way in which to analyse what an existing suspension might be doing and/or create our own with known objectives. Bill Gates's Microsoft, the Net and spreadsheets were some way in the future. Our answer was an analogue computer, generally known as a working model. It was, and is, a deceptively simple device for such a complex subject, but you have to start somewhere and even the mathematical model approach through current computers will only give you answers – hundreds of thousands of them if you require it. You still have to ask the right questions, and then sort the wheat from the chaff in the answers.

Eschewing the electronic approach, the String Computer does not demand either mathematical or drawing office skills. A full scale version might be ideal but half-scale (my own) is rather more practical, especially for the longer Swing Axle Lengths. The photographs show its component parts and how it is actually operated. Cut the composite parts from hardboard or thin plywood. These are:

a. **Baseboard** with ground level, bump/droop markings, car centre line with angles of roll from the vertical axis, wheel centre line with angles of negative/positive camber and ground level line, also with angles of roll from the horizontal.
b. **Two calibrated strips** which will represent the wishbones (A-arms).
c. **The 'chassis'** board marked with a vertical and horizontal lattice from car centre line and ground level. The significance of this item is that it will be free to rotate about the roll centre, once this has been identified, and thus permit roll to be inserted into the action of the model.
d. **An outline of the wheel and tyre/upright/pick-up points** for the vehicle you are designing or analysing.
e. **Ball of string**, sundry pins and screws and a wire hook with a handle.

The method of operation is as follows:

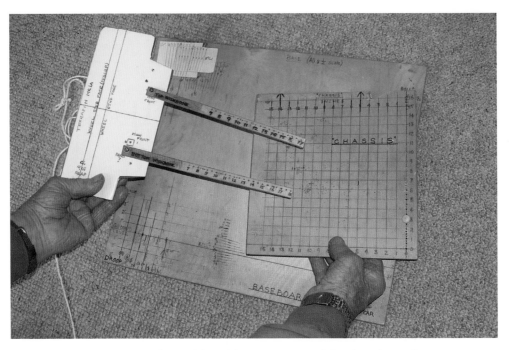

String computer components for double wishbone suspension (above) and MacPherson strut suspension (below). (Author)

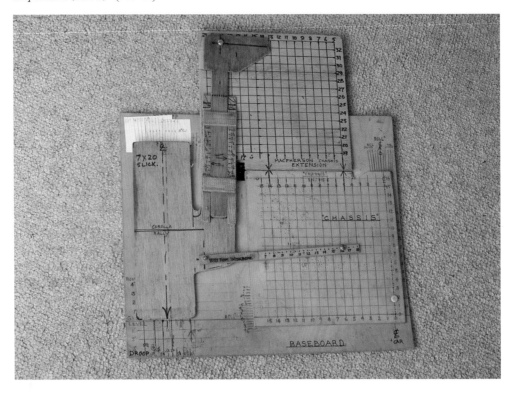

i. With wheel vertical and set on its centre line, pin the wishbones into their chosen positions, then align the string along the top and bottom links, and finally bring it back from their intersection point to the contact point of the wheel with the ground.
ii. Insert the Roll Centre pin where the string cuts the centre line of the car.
iii. Rotate the 'chassis' board through one degree while keeping the wheel at ground level.
iv. Note all the results.
v. Reset the string to follow the new angles of the wishbone links, and Roll Centre pin if necessary, and increase roll to two degrees.

The effect of the model is to reproduce much more realistically what actually happens to a wheel and tyre and the roll centre in a corner rather than the simpler and more conventional movement of it simply rising and falling. This last can, of course, be checked quite simply by raising and lowering the wheel while keeping the chassis board horizontal (ie parallel to the ground).

You now commence a series of experiments, varying the dimensions and locations of the top and bottom links in search of your chosen movements and inclinations of the wheel, together with, so far as possible a fixed roll centre.

Work within practical limits of bump and droop, which will be considerably less on a single seater than on a saloon or some sports cars. Don't forget that you do not want to end up with ideal suspension points that are either unsupportable in thin air or lie in the middle of the driver's calf muscle.

Some examples of variously sized upright/wheel/tyre combination cut from hardboard or plywood. (Author)

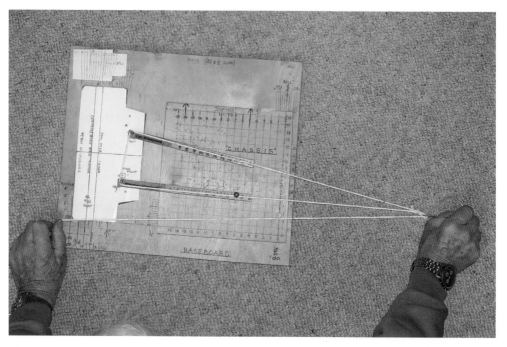

*The string computer in action for both double wishbone suspension (above) and MacPherson
strut suspension (below) layouts.* (Author)

Although this might sound a little laborious and time consuming, you will soon find that visible trends appear, with certain alterations producing particular results. And it has to be mega-quicker than trying to draw it all …

The hidden virtue is that it will give you a most useful basic appreciation of what wishbone suspension geometry can or cannot do. If you move to one of the commercial computer programs, it will prove invaluable in interpreting the results implication of what comes up on screen. Most programs are very strong on attractive coloured pictures and impressive lists of what they will do. But, some only provide bump and rebound, but not roll. Others show only a single wheel at a time. Basic datum points can vary. Data may need transfer from screen to screen with pen and ink. None of them are for the computer (or even unpractised) illiterate.

Even should you not be planning to go further than reading the foregoing, it will, perhaps, give a flavour of the questions and decisions in this area alone that face a designer up against the need to produce a winner – or find a new job. He has also to choose between a multiplicity of targets, many in total opposition to each other. These may be summed up in bare outline as:

1. Roll centre

Despite some surviving disagreement about how vital is its accurate location, a personal view is 'absolutely'. This has some powerful backing from being able to look back, computer analyse both Ligier and Tyrrell, though neither was 'Active'. Each had an accuracy of location to plus/minus .005 in vertical movement, clearly more than accident or good luck.

If we accept that a car rolling under cornering forces must be rotating about some point in space, the dissent concerns where it might be, if it has moved from a theoretical position, and why. These arguments are no reason not to make strenuous efforts to locate and pin it down. Ignorance of front or rear centres statically and dynamically will make thinking and modification to deal with problems quite impossible.

Mystery variations must result in mystery weight transfers and wheel loadings. The possible handling difficulties for a driver flat through a left–right flick would rapidly bring him back in the pits filled with bitter and reasonable complaint.

Current thinking on roll centre heights is of the order of 2 in above ground level to 1 in below at the lighter/lower end of the car, with 4 in above down to ground level at the other end. These figures normally give an inclined roll axis along the car tending to even out the various forces involved if nothing else, but are by no means a fixed approach. It is a free world.

So we will aim at a dynamically steady roll centre so far as it may be possible, or at the very least similar movement at each end of the car.

2. Outer wheel vertical in roll

With the two outer tyres doing the major part of the work in accepting cornering forces, this gives the tyre contact patches their best chance in life. Many cars, from a Mini to a Formula One, do not do this at all well geometrically and need the wheels set with a negative camber so that roll pushes them out towards vertical.

3. Wheel angle in bump/droop

In direct opposition to (2), this has become ever more important in heavy braking and acceleration with wide flat slicks. In both situations there is a tendency under pitch forces for wheels to go into bump at one end and droop at the other, doing grip no good at all. A number of experiments over the years saw tyre companies (Dunlop for the Mini, Pirelli for Toleman and Ferrari) producing asymmetric tyres with radiussed inner shoulders to try and alleviate this.

4. Track variation (scrub)
This means that individual wheels will, under certain circumstances, follow a private wavy path rather than a straight line. Most important when running straight, but may be a contribution to momentary under or oversteer lurch on turn-in to a corner.

For the intrepid souls who are going ahead with the String (or any other) Computer, a few guidelines.

From scratch, work from a bottom link parallel to the ground and as long as practicable, combined with a top link two-thirds of the bottom running downhill from wheel to chassis at 15 degrees or so from horizontal. Note every experiment in detail as you carry it out. Trying to remember results and then compare them will only lead to a hopeless muddle.

Operations and effects:
1. Alteration of wishbone lengths – a little major effect.
2. Lengthening both at once – often poorer.
3. Vertical movements of chassis mounts – major effects.
4. Scrub – rarely any problem in roll, can be serious in bump/droop.
5. 'Skewed roll' – this may, for instance, combine 2 degrees of roll with 1 in of bump on front or rear wheel and can often give excellent results in terms of outer wheel angle.

All the variations we have considered here will, of course, be reduced by restricting the actual movement of the vehicle, a basic approach explored to the full both in Indy Cars and Formula One, giving minimal roll (controlled by extremely strong bars) and almost fixed ride heights (very hard suspension and high wheel frequencies). Having said this, one has to admit that several newest generation Formula One cars have only a modest front bar and no rear bar at all, the inference being that wheel frequencies are rising substantially and coils are taking back much of the task of roll resistance.

Such a simplistic method transfers much of the suspension's task onto the tyre carcass – and if you thought geometry was a little tricky it pales beside the mysteries of what a tyre may be doing in ten thousand situations, all different.

Here are some general pointers (irrespective of the method used).

1. Very short swing axle lengths (20–40 inches):
a. Roll centre (RC) generally high.
b. RC location generally good.
c. RC sideways movements at a minimum.
d. Very good wheel angle control in roll.
e. Camber variations in bump/droop very bad (almost linear with roll in some cases).
f. Bad performance in scrub.

2. Long swing axle lengths (70–180 inches):
a. RC low.
b. RC location reasonable, subject to (c).
c. RC can move considerable distances sideways due to the shallow angles involved.
d. Mediocre wheel angle control in roll (worst on inner wheel).

  e. Camber alterations in bump/droop good.
  f. Good performance in scrub.

3. Medium swing axle lengths (40–70 inches):

As might be expected, the results lie between short and long.

4. Ultra-long swing axle lengths (effectively out to infinity, with certain near-parallel designs):

  a. RCs very low, at or below ground level.
  b. RC location very good in vertical terms.
  c. RC sideways movement can be very great, with a reversal from inside to outside of the corner possible due to the very narrow, near parallel angles.
  d. Wheel angle control poor – may be near direct equivalency to car's roll angle.
  e. Camber alterations in bump/droop very small.
  f. Scrub – good.

Current computer programs are still not the full answer to everybody's suspension problems, although some will not only analyse roll centre location and movement in an existing vehicle or design, but will also provide a wishbone layout that will give a perfect specific centre, perfectly controlled.

Before the cries of 'Eureka!' ring out, the required location of suitable pick-ups in space to provide this idyllic situation may not only prove impossible to build for physical or mechanical reasons, but can also wreck your plans for wheel angle performance in roll, bump, droop or combinations of these.

So back on 'the road to that horizon with its load of compromisin', as the Rhinestone Cowboy discovered – even if the question is the right one, the answer may be no help at all.

There is still, for the time being, not only room but also an overwhelming demand for thinking and the human brain to sort through the figures and the pretty coloured graphs for suitable solutions.

Appendix 2

Setting up

SETTING UP A CAR is much less of a black art than a laborious long day, preferably with another person and relatively simple equipment. All it amounts to is making certain that all the wheels are pointing in the correct direction, especially relative to each other, that ride heights loaded are correct, roll bar links not under load, and the weight on each pair of tyres front or rear is split equally between them.

This is not only an essential basis on which to do any further development and testing, but should ensure that the car will have reasonable balance and handling first time out. It is by no means what you may end up with after experiment, but yet again, you have to start someplace.

Should you never have need or interest in doing this, it may still illuminate a walk round the pits seeing what the experts get up to.

1. First requirement is a level surface, or four level pads on which the wheels can rest. A decent concrete floor is by its manner of construction often excellent. Otherwise make four pads from plywood or hardwood, using a builder's spirit level and a long straight piece of wood or steel tube to level them before being numbered and a painted rectangle put on the floor to locate them in the future.
2. Make up four wooden blocks, two for the front and two for the rear, to ride height plus the thickness of the corner pad. Make four more that will sit on top of the first blocks, thick enough to hold all four wheels clear of the ground.
3. Roll car onto the pads, disconnect anti-roll bars, remove springs (but leave dampers, wishbones, etc connected) and set on ride height blocks.
4. Set front caster angle. Use 3 degrees if you have no guide figure.
5. Set front and rear camber angles. Use vertical –1 degree negative if no guide figures are available.
6. Check rack and pinion is parallel to the ground and at right angles to the centre line of the car. Measure its height. Disconnect trackrod ends and centre rack bar in its housing.
7. Set toe-in on front wheels, and pointing straight ahead. Check lengths of trackrods and adjust if necessary to fit between rack and steering arm. Reset steering wheel spokes if required.
8. Check that each rear wheel has the same toe relative to the centre line of the car, or is parallel to it. Run string or length of tube from each wheel to the front. 'A' must equal 'B'.
9. Set rear toe. Normally toe-in. Use 3/16–3/8 in (5–9 mm) total if you have no guide figures.
10. Check springs for pairs, both in free length and rate.

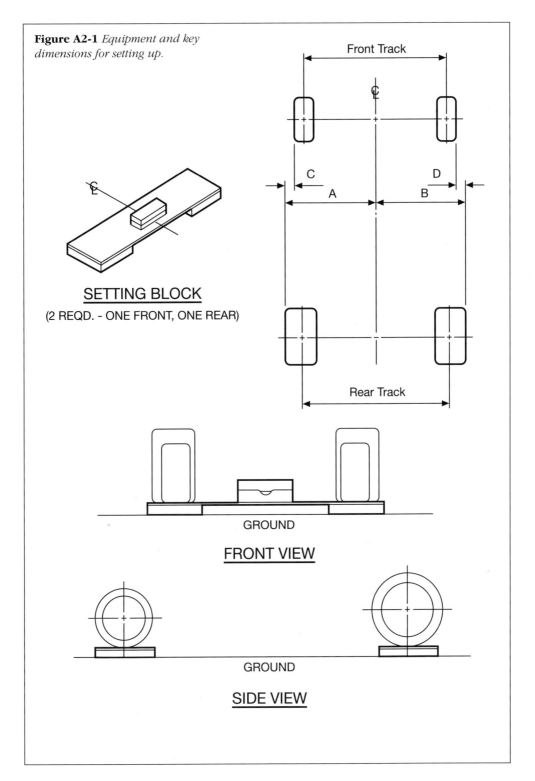

Figure A2-1 *Equipment and key dimensions for setting up.*

SETTING BLOCK

(2 REQD. - ONE FRONT, ONE REAR)

Front Track

Rear Track

GROUND

FRONT VIEW

GROUND

SIDE VIEW

11. Remove dampers and check for pairs in open/closed lengths, any coding or part numbers, good end bushes or bearings, and no leaks. Set any adjustments to full soft and paint mark at 12 o'clock. Grease and free adjustable collars and lock rings.
12. Refit all spring/dampers and lower car onto wheels without blocks.
13. Set correct ride heights, front and rear, with driver, all liquids and half tank of fuel.
14. Set corner weights to give two equal fronts and two equal rears. (This applies to single seaters. For any assymetric car – saloon, GT, sports racer – with offset driver, use the approach shown in Figure A2-2 below.) A 'heavy' corner will need the spring platform lowering, and vice versa. Adjustments at one end will certainly affect the opposite end and may enforce a series of adjustments as you approach perfection. It is strongly recommended that you adjust two corners (diagonally opposite to each other) at a time. It guards against the depressing result of getting one end perfect, only to find it ruined by attempts to get the other end correct. With any car using rubber bushes in shear in the damper or wishbone eyes, mounting bolts should be loosened and greased to have any hope of reasonable results. Even new rod ends with current PTFE interliners have enough 'stiction' to make electronic scales read erratically with every adjustment.
15. Check for bump-steer and adjust rack height and/or trackrod end positions to eliminate or reduce to absolute minimum.
16. Connect anti-roll bar links adjusting the lengths so they do not exert any force whatever on the bars.
17. With car set at correct ride height and attitude measure and mark (or note adjustment dimensions) of front and rear wing angles of attack, what flat adjustments does, etc.

And make a note of everything, including all the later alterations which will probably be many.

Figure A2-2 *Corner weight bias calculations. Check and note corner weights before any attempts at bias adjustment. Aim for perfection. In reality you may be hard put to achieve better than ±10–15 lb, unless using four electronic remote read-out platforms!*

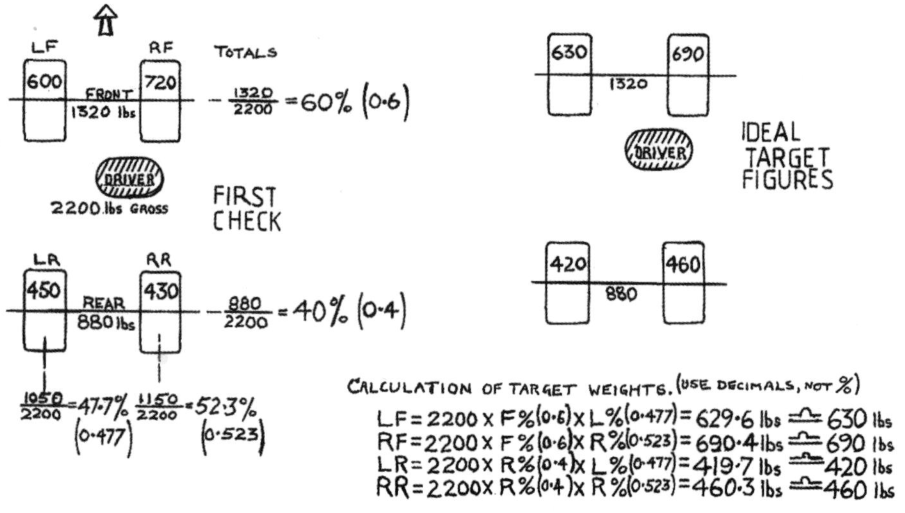

LF
RF
TOTALS
600
720
FRONT
1320 lbs
1320/2200 = 60% (0·6)
DRIVER
2200 lbs GROSS
FIRST CHECK
LR
RR
450
430
REAR
880 lbs
880/2200 = 40% (0·4)
1050/2200 = 47·7% (0·477)
1150/2200 = 52·3% (0·523)
630
690
1320
DRIVER
IDEAL TARGET FIGURES
420
460
880
CALCULATION OF TARGET WEIGHTS. (USE DECIMALS, NOT %)
LF = 2200 x F%(0·6) x L%(0·477) = 629·6 lbs ≏ 630 lbs
RF = 2200 x F%(0·6) x R%(0·523) = 690·4 lbs ≏ 690 lbs
LR = 2200 x R%(0·4) x L%(0·477) = 419·7 lbs ≏ 420 lbs
RR = 2200 x R%(0·4) x R%(0·523) = 460·3 lbs ≏ 460 lbs

Figure A2-3 *This page provides an alternative interpretation of identical data for calculations to be found in Chapter 9 on page 150.*

```
WEIGHT TRANSFER, DISTRIBUTION & ROLL RESISTANCE         dsg        12Apr94
═══════════════════════════════════════════════════════════════════════════
Client    : Mr R Sole                        Car : Squire Mk 1
═══════════════════════════════════════════════════════════════════════════
              FRONT    REAR               FRONT    REAR     TOTAL
DIMENSIONS
CoG Ht(agl)  13.000   16.000 Mean CoG Ht                    15.00 in
RC Ht (agl)   1.500    3.000 Mean RC Ht                      2.50 in
Track        58.000   55.000 Mean Track                     56.00 in
Axle Height  10.000   12.000 Roll Couple                    12.50 in
ROLL BARS ══════════════════
Diameter       .750     .750
Bore           .650     .650
Length       36.000   14.000 AngularRate      75      194          lb"deg
LeverLength   7.000    7.000 Linear Rate      88      227          lbs"
Wheel Mov't   1.000    1.000   Eff. FLA       .90      .36
BarPU Mov't    .950     .600 Resistance    4,676    4,313          lb"deg
SPRINGS ════════════════════
Spring Rate     175      400   Eff. LAR      1.78     2.78          : 1
Wheel Mov't   1.000    1.000 Wheel Rate    98.44   144.00          lbs"
DamperMov't    .750     .600 Resistance    2,890    3,801          lb"deg
WEIGHTS ════════════════════
Each Corner     200      360    Totals        400      720    1,120 lbs
Unsprung  "      50       60 Distributed    35.7%    64.3%
                                Unsprung      100      120      220 lbs
                                  Sprung      300      600      900 lbs
               Sprung Distribution          33.3%    66.7%
ROLL RESISTANCE AT 1G ═══════════════════════════════════════════════════════
                             Roll Moment                   11,250 lbs"
                             Bars & Springs 7,565    8,114  15,679 lb"deg
                               Distributed  48.3%    51.7%
                                 Roll Angle                    .72 deg
WEIGHT TRANSFER ════════════════════════════════════════════════════════════
                                 Unsprung   17.24    26.18   43.42 lbs
                             Via Roll Axis   7.76    32.73   40.49 lbs
                      Via Springs and Bars  96.93   103.96  200.89 lbs

                                   Totals  121.93   162.87  284.80 lbs
DISTRIBUTION ═══════════════════════════════════════════════════════════════

Outer With Bars &
Springs Balanced      Outer              Inner
as Static Distrib     Wheels             Wheels
─────────────────     ──────             ──────
    200 lbs             200 lbs             200 lbs  Static Corner Weight
    102 lbs             122 lbs            -122 lbs   Weight Transferred
    ───────             ───────    FRONT
    302 lbs             322 lbs              78 lbs  Dynamic Weight at 1G
     20 lbs Diff         28.7%              7.0%     Percent of Total Wt

    Outer Wheels         3.6%
        Dynamic           to
    Wt Transfer         FRONT
    360 lbs             360 lbs             360 lbs  Static Corner Weight
    183 lbs             163 lbs            -163 lbs   Weight Transferred
    ───────             ───────    REAR
    543 lbs             523 lbs             197 lbs  Dynamic Weight at 1G
    -20 lbs Diff         46.7%             17.6%     Percent of Total Wt
```

Appendix 3

Data logging

YOU MAY WELL QUITE reasonably enquire as to what data logging – something that in a remarkably few years has come to mean all things to a growing number of drivers, designers and computer nerds at the higher levels in motorsport – actually has to do with suspension.

Usually considered more in the area of engine management and tuning, it does of course cover a very wide field, but this apparently sudden sidetrack is intended to offer a decently simplified approach to what some of the huge range of electronic equipment can and cannot do. It also considers what is perhaps the biggest question of all – what do you want it to do?

Laptop screens can be difficult or impossible to read on a sunny day. A tailored and curtained cardboard box may cause laughter – even scorn – but ignore the spectators and download a file of your information for every run. Author shown doing exactly this for later study and consideration. (Author)

Figure A3-1 *Schematic layout of basic multi-channel data acquisition system.* (Illustration courtesy of Simon McBeath, taken from *Competition Car Data Logging*)

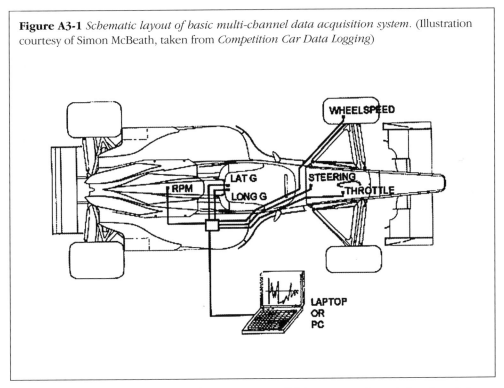

The fairly obvious answer in this context is: 'Make me go faster', but how? Some sort of instrument panel, although not electronic and almost totally lacking in any ability to record or recall, has been used since the earliest days to inform the driver what might be happening in hidden and invisible corners of, almost exclusively, the engine.

Ammeters for electric supplies to lights and battery, rev counters for engine speed, oil pressure gauges and later, water temperature gauges, as well as distance covered and trip meters were slowly added to the instrument display. Over the years, many of them barely altered in the information they were able to provide, and were only developed in the manner of presentation. Again, the alterations were not huge, but in due course, took in the fuel reserve as well as brake fluid and oil levels. The backlighting of dials ranged from superb to revolting. Possibly the most unloveable bit of advancing technology was the taped voice admonishing you to a range of activities, which most motorists who had already mastered switching on the light when entering a darkened room, could be relied on to carry out in their car without being simpered at by a manufacturer's recorded nanny, happily now rare or vanished.

Came the day of the transistor, transducer, digital displays, and dashboards exploded – now able and willing to supply fuel usage, and average speed every few seconds, remaining time to destination (constantly recalculated) or a warning that a service is shortly due which it will be impossible to carry out yourself any more, as you will not have the multi-pin plug and associated diagnostic software essential to carry out such a task without obscurely stopping the car permanently in its tracks.

Should any hint of suspicion and wariness of electronics and computers in general show at this point, ignore it, as it will not be allowed to corrupt the attempts at honesty now to follow.

204   COMPETITION CAR SUSPENSION

Figure A3-2 *Typical traces produced by a four-channel data logging system during a lap of Thruxton.* (Illustration courtesy of Simon McBeath, taken from *Competition Car Data Logging*)

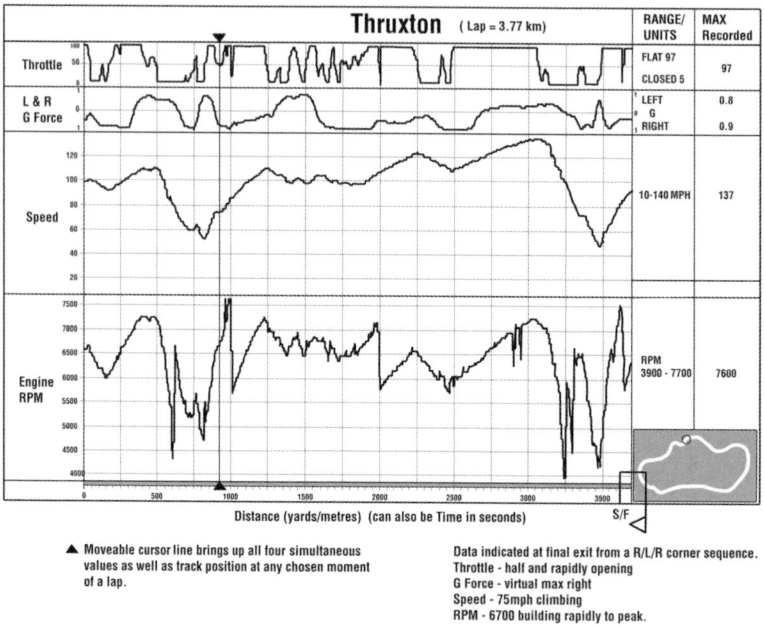

Thruxton (Lap = 3.77 km)

	RANGE/ UNITS	MAX Recorded
Throttle	FLAT 97 / CLOSED 5	97
L & R G Force	LEFT / G / RIGHT	0.8 / 0.9
Speed	10-140 MPH	137
Engine RPM	RPM 3900 - 7700	7600

Distance (yards/metres) (can also be Time in seconds)

S/F

▲ Moveable cursor line brings up all four simultaneous values as well as track position at any chosen moment of a lap.

Data indicated at final exit from a R/L/R corner sequence.
Throttle - half and rapidly opening
G Force - virtual max right
Speed - 75mph climbing
RPM - 6700 building rapidly to peak.

At the heart of all to be discussed is what has come to be generally labelled, whatever its colour, as a 'black box'. These extraordinary pieces of equipment, seemingly incomprehensible to most of us lacking the relevant university degree, did in fact make a very early if tentative appearance in Formula One, almost certainly through the late lamented Ken Tyrrell. It suffered the almost universal testing troubles of something that new – weight, cost, unreliability, but most of all – what is it the team actually needs to know? Mere time, money and brainpower cured all the troubles.

Nearly 30 years later, would-be users in motorsport find that simple question is – or should be – still their primary enquiry. Being effectively electronic calculators and recorders with gigantic memories, they can supply tens of thousands of happenings or bytes of information in seconds, but it still comes back to: 'What is the question?'

Even having made that decision, it brings a new mega-problem in train. It will have to be a human brain (probably yours) that must attempt the sorting of good from bad, useless or unwanted information. Before we go any further, it should be made crystal clear that first and foremost it is utterly vital that you have some smattering of knowledge of using a computer, whether PC or laptop including switching it on, installing software and the basics of filing. An internet link through which you can seek help from other toilers will not be wasted. Without this modest computer literacy you are on a total non-starter, simply wasting your time and money.

As you will be able to spend £20 or £200, £1,000 or £5,000 without any undue difficulty, what follows is a modest attempt to offer a signpost or two. Lest anyone doubts the bottom end of the financial scale just mentioned, it buys a mountain bike speedometer which takes signals from a tiny magnet taped inside the rim of a carefully measured front (ie non-driven) wheel and which needs only revs-per-mile programmed in to begin giving at least five selectable functions, 24 hours a day for the next couple of years. These include split-second stopwatch, clock, distance covered (both trip and cumulative), speed in mph or kph, and a callback memory of the highest speed recorded since being zeroed. This last has, for several seasons, spelled out for me speed variations which were a revelation, but reflected again and again the final timesheets. It makes you suddenly aware that you can be innocently committing sins which can be reduced or even removed completely, with thinking and commitment during later runs or laps. This all comes from quite basic and simply obtained information. The bike speedo is also not a bad example of finding that you must, whether you like it or not, spend some of your money on facilities you do not really need, but as in the home PC, have perforce to accept an enormous number of functions 95% of which you may never know, care about, or use. More to the point is whether it will provide the bits that you do want.

These tend to fall into quite a small number of groups, the first of which, for many people, tends to be the engine, although chassis performance is going to take priority here. Let us attempt to list them and decide what real use they may be. Perhaps the very first thing to clarify with your potential supplier is what (and how many) channels it will provide, the sensors essential to each one, and whether these sensors are included in the purchase price or not. If not, determine their price and availability.

Fundamentally, most sensors turn temperature, pressure or movement, whether linear, rotating or reciprocating, into minute electric currents. These are translated by the black box into digital displays in the appropriate units of inches, degrees, psi, or whatever. They can include fuel or brake line pressures, G-force, either cornering, braking or accelerating, gas-sensing of the exhaust for mixture strength and monitoring the up-to-1,000 degrees C temperatures within an exhaust. At the same time, they are also being recorded for later study and analysis. There are also strain gauges capable of detecting and measuring what is going on within wishbones or driveshafts. These all make it important to know the lengths of real time memory available as it can vary from two or three minutes, to two or three hours. Once that time is up, they usually begin to erase and overwrite from the beginning again – something you most certainly do not want to happen.

Memory and sensors can damage your financial health over and above the first investment, but without them you may find you are unable to record all you need. This is certainly not intended to scare anyone off, only to emphasise the value of some preliminary thought and planning. You will, incidentally, look in vain for trade names or 'best buy' recommendations here, partly because they would most likely be out of date before even getting into print, and because technical specifications alter if not at the speed of light, certainly at the speed of sound. So let us consider what knowledge you are seeking – and why.

The best all-round program at an affordable price (for me) five years ago provided ten channels (primarily engine) which included three 'spare'. It ran (and is still running perfectly) on a 1/10th second time base and a memory of 2 min 51 sec, after which it automatically erases and rewrites. This means of course it is useless on a circuit car but, subject only to a hasty paddock download between runs, almost idea for hillclimb and sprint use. This airy reference to 'downloading' means the admission that as well as basic computer knowledge it is virtually essential to have, or have access to, a laptop. You certainly do not need a top-of-the-range one to manage this task as even old and well-used models easily cope with the technical requirements and lack only the clarity, colour quality and size of screen of the newest. The data, once extracted, can be transferred at leisure to the home machine where the refinements of graphing, tables, overlaying different runs and so on can be explored out of the wind and the rain. But beware the old saw, 'procrastination is the thief of time' which should now be amended to 'computers are the thieves'…there is so much on which to reflect or act. The equipment just mentioned, recording at 10 Hz, memorises time, RPM ignition timing, fuel injection period to a milli-second, (both of these last constantly modified through 256 station charts of RPM v throttle, water temperature, throttle opening and mixture strength (a Lambda sensor in the exhaust). A little quick arithmetic will show that one 60-second hillclimb will produce 4,200 items of information – and there are at least three more runs left to go.

While this basic display is in columns of figures they can be converted into a variety of alternative presentations including contrasting colours, and different manufacturers can and do choose varying presentations. In general, the more you pay the larger the number of everything and the more time and dedication will be needed to sort out what it is telling you. There is however one enormous time-saver and that is to be able to make virtually instantaneous adjustment with a keyboard to fuel mixture and ignition timing rather than embarking on replacement of chokes and jets in a bank of four Del'Ortos, or stripping a distributor for new bobweights.

It would be easy to continue on aspects of engine logging and tuning, but it is not the primary aim of this current exercise which is, in a number of ways, more difficult both to interpret and to implement. We want to be able to analyse single runs or laps, breaking them down into braking, accelerations and cornering G-forces, even, if possible, the precise line followed on the track. It is now not unusual to be able to replay a run, freezing the action at any chosen point to find exactly what was happening at that moment be it on entering or in midcorner, swerving through an 'Ess' sequence, lifting and/or braking at the end of a straight.

Furthermore, you can overlay two attempts and see where you went wrong – or right. Magical as this all seems, you must then ask yourself how things might be improved (ie go faster). Often the trouble is the lack of an exact comparison, whether with yourself or another driver. At club level the driver will be the computer man as well, but not without irony, a bigger team able to invest in one of each may well find the situation is worse, not better. The problem is that if the driver is not over-familiar with computers while the computer man, although good for handling a quick run for the groceries, does not have the same grip of Donington in the wet. They need to try to speak the same language; not necessarily easy. It can be so difficult in fact, that talking to an excellent F3 driver who also did all his own computer analysis, he admitted that given such desperately close grid and lap times, he found it almost impossible to establish from computer traces where he had lost or gained a couple of tenths, even given that his mental recall of a 10-lap practise session verged on the miraculous. (Senna was reputed to be able to do it with a complete Grand Prix – no doubt one of the reasons for his legendary four-hour debriefs and inquests.) Yet again, the sheer volume of information that has still to be weighed and assessed can become overwhelming.

Some of the newest equipment to appear in this crowded, tricky market has managed to dispense with a mass of complex wiring, appreciable weight and bulk, and a range of sensors, all in favour of one sensor on a wheel, another on a plug lead and one to a tiny stick-on aerial, and a single power feed. Quite remarkably, each unit has its own (yours in fact) singular link to a satellite. This has the capability to measure and record almost two hours of data including speed, rpm, G-forces in braking, acceleration, left and right corners and the exact position of the car within the track's width, timing to fractions of a second and, once downloaded, to be able to replay and overlap other runs for direct comparison. It even eschews nut-and-bolt attachment in favour of Velcro pads so you can remove it and find out exactly how you perform on the way home with it transferred into your road car. Price – around seven times a current hillclimb entry fee.

From the point of view of suspension geometry, coil or torsion bar springs, dampers, as well as driveshafts and aerodynamic downforce, are all now susceptible to testing, measurement and effects through a variety of sensors, particularly strain gauges. The correct types of sensor will now measure with great accuracy, damper/coil movements, both in amount and frequency, steering angles, ride-height variations, and the force within push or pullrods, driveshafts and uprights. Real-life figures for all these makes possible radical improvements in weight, materials and design, opening the way to redesign that might previously have been considered too hazardous because of the unknowns. Some things previously impossible, for instance measuring a range of suspension loads and forces ten or a hundred times a second through a 3 G, 180 mph corner, compounded by huge braking forces and temperatures rocketing to 800 degrees C have become perfectly practical propositions. Then if, instead of one computer man studying results, you have 12 or 24, concentrating on one channel each that they have studied 1,000 times before, it is not difficult to see how F1 can spend not only serious money but also draw serious quantities of previously unsuspected or unknown data for future development.

Given this somewhat complicated looking vista, it is perhaps time to consider what might be the more worthwhile in terms of handling and driving, rather than the power from the engine. Don't say it, but it will obviously depend almost totally on your chosen branch of the sport, the capability within it of both you and your machine, the level at which you are competing, what regulations require or ban, and of course, the amount of cash available. It is also vital to bear in mind that with any of this equipment, even the most basic beyond a rev counter and oil pressure gauge, it will require considerable time and effort on your part to analyse the information it provides to best effect (or even at all).

It may well be that after careful consideration you feel your money might be better spent on a full-house professional engine, a set of brand-new super-sticky rubber, or a set of double-adjust dampers, it being a rare occasion for most competitors at whatever

Two sizes of linear sensors for measurement of variations in length of coil/damper units – and thus ground clearance, bellcrank movements, coil compression for example. Ten pence coin gives size comparison, and ultra-fine length setting can be adjusted with female threaded rod ends. (Photograph courtesy of Simon McBeath, taken from *Competition Car Data Logging*)

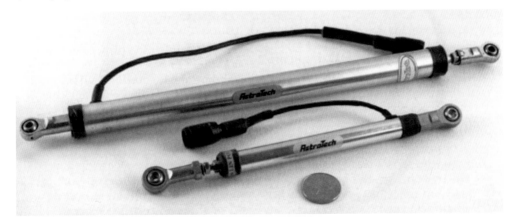

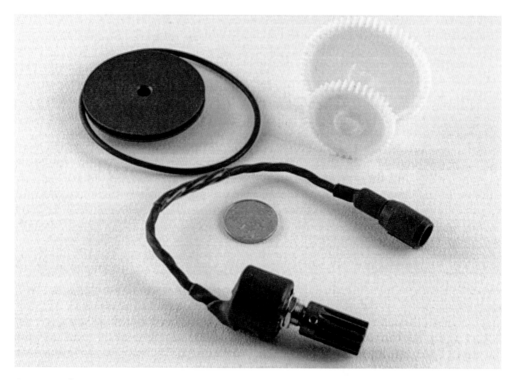

Steering column rotation sensor, coin comparison again for size. (Photograph courtesy of Simon McBeath, taken from *Competition Car Data Logging*)

level to have the finance available to do the whole lot at once. As you should have already discovered, most things on a racing car demand as much of the driver in understanding and skilled use as they can supply. This could not be more strongly the case than with data logging. So what might be the best and most helpful way to go about it? Taking solely suspension, its components and actions as a start, we break it down simply into two categories – known and unknown. In no particular order.

1. **Wishbones or other suspension links:** only monitoring by strain gauges, usually alloy wafers glued to the relevant components, will provide internal information on what is happening during frequent, varying and often violent movements. This is more in the province of the highly professional.
2. **Springs:** quantifiable and well understood these can provide vital ride-height/downforce data without hiring a wind tunnel.
3. **Dampers:** known size and shape, simple adjustability, but difficult to quantify. Internal valving can be modified, but not easily. Apart from 'driver feel' the only source is logging for actual operation effects and movement, both linear and through a range of velocities.
4. **Steering:** records of wheel angles, when, where and how much, with useful indications of understeer and oversteer. Valuable and easy to sensor off the column.
5. **Throttle position:** might be termed invaluable, not least for its cruel skill in distinguishing and making public where and for how long you really were flatout rather than cautiously feathering.

6. **RPM:** fundamental, both as a measuring and comparison baseline for much other information, and a familiar old friend to drivers for the last century or so.
7. **G-sensors:** can cover braking and acceleration as well as cornering. Current technology seems to require two, three or four to do all jobs, but this will probably be history soon. Useful and interesting, but not vital.
8. **Brakes:** apart from G-force readings, these are normally quantified in terms of line pressure. Particularly valuable for knowing really precisely when they are on or off, believe it or not. Worthwhile, but not utterly vital.
9. **Aerodynamics (see also 3. Dampers):** precise lengths of these units at accurately known speeds and track locations are the nearest you may ever get to real downforce and wing knowledge without serious, high-level wind tunnel access.
10. **Cockpit On/Off switch:** also capable of putting a marker on a trace if at all possible. Pit beacons do this for circuit racers, but any type of standing-start single-run event can be saved considerable difficulties trying to identify exactly when a car left the start line.
11. **Screen displays:** the more variations (graphs, bar charts, cumulative time addition, 3-D of fuel and ignition maps, trace-on-trace, conversion of figures to graphs etc) that are included or you can afford, the easier it will be to understand. Particularly useful will be trace superimposition and comparing several traces shown on the screen at the same time, usually one above the other on the same distance or distance base (ie throttle, rpm, steering angle and brakes). And of course, contrasting colours for everything.

G-force sensor. Depending on mounting alignment (arrow) could be used for left/right cornering or acceleration/braking measurement. (Photograph courtesy of Simon McBeath, taken from *Competition Car Data Logging*)

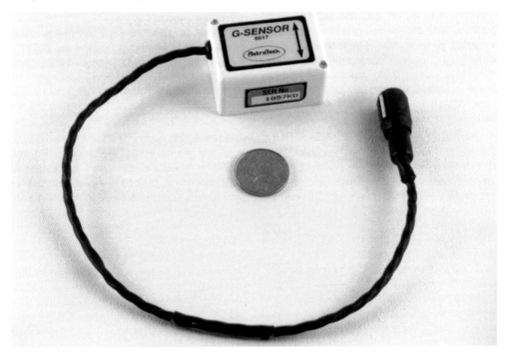

12. **Course maps:** extremely helpful and valuable. Some programs now include hillclimbs as well as most circuits. While a G-sensor sometimes enables a box to draw its own, these can look vaguely odd. These are more or less essential for really accurate point-to-point isolation of what happened and when.

Once fully embarked on your research, it is worth bearing in mind that a trawl through one of those fat catalogues put out by various electrical bits mega-suppliers may reveal some (very nice) surprises on prices of a variety of sensors, switches, warning lights and digital readout panels. Always remember, that more channels and higher recording speeds, and the increased memory they will demand, will all cost more money.

The channel nobody seems to offer, but one which has always had a personal fascination, is a heartbeat counter to run for a couple of minutes before the green light until one minute after you have won – or fallen off. Could be a nice little earner for some ingenious aftermarket supplier ...

Back to serious things. Your overall five-point plan could be as follows:

1. Choosing the gear.
2. Purchase and installation.
3. Understanding it.
4. Interpretation.
5. Acting on it.

As a large part of the foregoing has been aimed at (1), some careful techno-market research was instituted into what various other users felt were the most valuable, assuming you did not have those two dozen skilled interpreters and screens under your command already. Paddock prowling, reading, asking questions of experienced practitioners, and successive yearly pilgrimages to NEC for the Racing Car Show provided a quite surprising near-unanimity on the 'Top Five', namely:

1. Timebase at 10 Hz (0.1 second) interchangeable if at all possible with distance.
2. RPM reading to a single revolution.
3. Throttle position with settable maximum/minimum range.
4. Road speed (kilometres or miles per course).
5. Steering angle.

Honourable mention – course maps and cursor. As you can take 1 and 2 as foregone conclusions in the Box already, you are prepared to be asking pointed questions about the other three, together with any others that will be valuable, dependent on a wide range of circumstances. Any of the others may or may not of course be available, but hopefully you may now have a rough framework on which to operate. It's all yours.

Appendix 4

Rod ends and spherical bearings

IF ONE HAD TO CHOOSE a single item to be found somewhere in virtually every racing car in the world, these joints in a huge range of sizes and strengths have to be strong contenders. In consequence some consideration of what they are and how they might best be used seems to be in order. Often known collectively as 'Rose joints' – (at least in the UK, after the name of one of the earliest makers) there are now at least ten manufacturers and scores of suppliers in the market.

Rule No. 1 is to get hold of one of the makers' full catalogues. The table is based on three of these, using a single size of rod end (0.375 shank with 0.375 thru bolt) to provide a baseline with which other makes can be compared both for value and

Male and female versions of similar rod ends (below left) and a sectional view of a female version (below right). Several types of spherical joint (bottom right). These are normally pressed into a housing before being staked or circlipped in place. (Aurora)

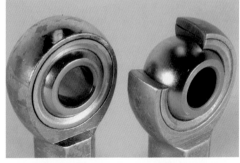

Code	Outer housing and finish
RMP 6U	Carbon steel phosphated
RM6	Carbon steel cad. plated
VCM 6	Carbon steel 'protected'
MM 6	Carbon steel 'protected'
SPM 6	Carbon steel 'protected'
RC6H	Carbon steel phosphated
CM 6	Carbon steel protected
AMPEP 2185P alloy	Med. carbon, low alloy. Phosphated
XM 5	Carbon steel 'protected'
RBJ 73	Nickel chrome moly phosphated
RMC 6NU	Carbon steel phosphated
RCA 06	Stainless
SM 6E	Stainless 17-4 PH
CM-6ET	Stainless 17-4 PH
AM 6T	Alloy steel coated
RMX 6	Chrome Moly cad. plated
RMR 6	Stainless
PRM-6T	4340 steel 'coated'
XAM 5	Alloy steel 'coated'

*Stepped – small ball with 5/16 bolt.

strength as they all specify in Imperial a figure of ultimate radial load in pounds. (Newtons in Metric). Ignore any of the meaningless phrases to be found in some – 'high strength, precision, wear resistant, alloy, general purpose, racing etc'. Stay with Radial Load.

Fortunately most current catalogues now follow quite similar designs and layouts. Not only does this permit speedy comparisons, but many now contain quite excellent detailed drawings and the required mathematical formulae for calculating loads and methods of installation.

It is possible, though by no means certain, that the stronger the joint the more expensive. When buying it is worth checking not only prices and materials but also considering the 'strength/cost ratio' which may show it is worthwhile to buy a smaller but better joint, rather than a larger and heavier, though apparently cheaper one. Females in the same thread sizes are marginally stronger than male and permit attachment with a high quality capscrew – far cheaper and easier to replace if the need arises. Keep well in mind that axial load figures (trying to push the ball out sideways) may be as low as 20% or even 10% of radial, so use big safety washers if the situation is unavoidable, or try to turn the bolt through 90 degs. Most joints are also available with left-hand threads – invaluable for making links that do not need to be dismantled for length adjustment.

Full Metric supplies are not yet in every catalogue, and some are simply Imperial converted to Metric to the thou. (Hardly practical to say the least.) Rough comparison can be made by using figures for 10 x 10mm – very slightly stronger at 0.394 diameter rather than 0.375. Remember that plated locknuts, particularly for left-hand joints are rarely included. You have to ask and make them part of your order.

Finally, the awful question. What size and quality of joint do you need for where? A personal view is that you paddock haunt to see the results of very many years research, development and breakages on other people's cars. They fall roughly into a

Ball and finish	Interliner/max angle	Radial load
1% carb. chrome plated	Acetyl Copolymer	2100
1% carb. chrome plated	Navel bronze/sintered copper	2450
Oil impreg. steel	PTFE/22°	3643
Alloy steel hard chromed	None/12°	3915
Alloy steel hard chromed	Moulded nylon/12°	4210
Stainless thru, hardened	PTFE/fibre 'Type R'	4420
Oil impreg. steel or hard chromed	None/22°	5068
Med chrome, low alloy, chromed	'Fibreglide' PTFE/fibre	5242
Stepped* alloy steel hard chromed	None/12°	5323
1% carb. chrome chrome plated	None	6300
1% cab. chrome chrome plated	PTFE/fibre	7070
Stainless hardened through	PTFE/fibre 'Type R'	7150
Stainless hard chromed	PTFE on request/12°	7363
Stainless hard chromed	PTFE liner/22°	8627
Alloy steel hard chromed	PTFE on request/12°	9544
1% chrome, chrome plated	Aluminium/bronze	9589
Stainless hardened through	PTFE/fibre	9850
AMS7440 hard chromed	Bonded PTFE/8°	10946
Stepped* alloy steel hard chromed	PTFE liner/12°	12978

Data courtesy of Aurora, Ampep and Rose

bracket between 0.25 and 0.5 in shanks and if they look a bit small to you, they almost certainly are a bit small. Consider what breakage will mean. A gearchange malfunction does not have the unpleasant implications of a suspension or steering failure. That cliché 'You get what you pay for' will never be more apt and obtain second-hand only from blood relatives or the other driver who is sharing the car ...

Appendix 5

Supporting maths/ conversion factors

$$\textbf{SIN} = \frac{\text{Opposite}}{\text{Hypotenuse}}$$

$$\textbf{COS} = \frac{\text{Adjacent}}{\text{Hypotenuse}}$$

$$\textbf{TAN} = \frac{\text{Opposite}}{\text{Adjacent}}$$

$\textbf{Hypotenuse}^2 = \text{Side } 1^2 + \text{Side } 2^2$

$$\textbf{Wheel frquency (CPM)} = 187.8 \sqrt{\frac{\text{Wheel rate lb/in}}{\text{Sprung weight (lb)}}}$$

$$\textbf{Coil rate (lbs/in)} = \frac{\text{Load (lb)}}{\text{Crush (in)}}$$

$$\textbf{Coil fitted rate (lbs/in)} = \frac{\text{Coil rate (lbs/in)}}{\text{Suspension leverage}}$$

$$\textbf{Wheel rate (lbs/in)} = \frac{\text{Coil rate (lbs/in)}}{\text{Suspension leverage}^2}$$

$$\textbf{Angular rate (roll bar)} = \frac{19700 \times \text{OD}^4}{\text{Bar length}}$$

$$\textbf{AR (tube)} = \frac{19700 \times (\text{OD}^4 - \text{ID}^4)}{\text{Tube length}}$$

$$\textbf{Lever arm ratio} = \frac{\text{Bar pickup movement (ins)}}{\text{Wheel movement (ins)}}$$

$$\textbf{Bar roll resistance (lbs/in/deg)} = \frac{\text{Bar linear rate} \times (\text{Wheel movement} \times \text{Bar PU})^2 \times \text{Track}^2 \times \pi}{180}$$

Spring roll resistance
(lbs/in/deg)
$$= \frac{\text{Spring rate} \times \text{Track}^2 \times \pi}{(\text{Wheel movement} \div \text{Spring movement})^2 \times 2 \times 180}$$

Springs in parallel Combined rate = Rate coil A + Rate coil B

Springs in series $\text{Combined rate} = \dfrac{\text{Rate coil A} \times \text{Rate coil B}}{\text{Rate coil A} + \text{Rate coil B}}$

**Effect of anti-roll bar
on single wheel bump.** $= \text{Rate of coil A} + \left(\dfrac{\text{Rate coil A} \times \text{Bar rate}}{\text{Rate coil A} + \text{Bar rate}} \right)$
(Rate of spring in bump)

Glossary

A-arm
See wishbone.

Acceleration
What happens to a human being or other object in bump (vertical) cornering (lateral) and in braking/accelerating (longitudinal).

Accelerometer
Device which measures acceleration.

Ackermann (angle)
Method devised by one Herr Langensburger which turns an inner front wheel into a tighter circle than the outer to minimise or eliminate scrub in a corner.

Active suspension
'Live' or 'thinking' pre-programmable, on-board computer control of suspension to retain virtues while eliminating undesirable aspects. Much easier said than done.

Actuator
Hydraulic ram that translates pressure into movement (displacement).

Amplifier
Not Hi-Fi in our context – see servo.

Anti-dive (angle)
Geometric method of reducing attempts by car to scrape its nose on the ground under braking by tilting inboard suspension pick-up points (see also Anti-squat).

Anti-roll bar (ARB)
Length of tube or rod linked to the suspension in such a way that if a car wishes to roll in a corner it must twist the bar (see Blades).

Anti-squat
As anti-drive, but applied to the rear of the vehicle to reduce or prevent 'sitting down' under acceleration.

Axle weight
Portion or percentage of the gross weight borne by the front or rear pair of tyres.

Ballistic recoil
Opposite reaction to a mechanical load input.

Beam axle
Early method (not to mention commercial vehicles in 2006) of mounting the front wheels at each end of a solid steel bar or one-piece rear steel casing.

Blades
Flat, tapered steel arms on one or both ends of anti-roll bars. Rotation flat to edge-on increases, and the reverse decreases the roll resistance of the bar in a complex fashion.

Bump
(Also jounce, heave, bounce) Total upward movement of wheel from static ride height (see also Droop).

Bump steer
Front wheels altering their direction without the driver moving the steering wheel. Can also occur with certain linkages on rear suspension, when it feels very peculiar.

Camber
Wheel angle seen from head-on. 'Bow legged' (or tops wider apart than bottoms) is positive, 'knock kneed' is negative. Positive in road cars but normally nil–2.5 degrees negative in race cars.

Caster
'Lean back' angle of top pivot behind bottom pivot of a front upright seen from the side of the car. Ranges from zero to eight or more degrees. Less you can get away with the better as extreme caster gives heavy steering.

Canard
Small wing mounted low down at front of car.

Centre of gravity
Point at which the whole vehicle would always stay perfectly balanced whether on its side, nose, or even upside down. Difficult to locate precisely but close estimates are practical.

Channel
Route along which a single set of electronic signals travels back and forth.

Chapman strut
Chapman's adaptation of the MacPherson strut to use on the rear of the original Elite. The coil spring and damper are mounted integrally and above the hub, which has bottom locating links to the chassis.

Chip
Nothing to do with fish. Slang; see Integrated Circuit.

Closed loop
Sometimes called 'feedback loop': a circuit that allows an actuator's or sensor's own actions to trigger what it will do next.

Coil
See spring.

Compound
See Tyres.

Contact patch
Area of a tyre that actually touches the road. Surprisingly small.

Corner weight
Portion of a car's total weight on any particular tyre contact patch. Fronts should match each other, as should rears on single seaters.

Damper
(Shock, shocker, shock absorber) Device to control the natural oscillation of a spring. Usually a piston forcing oil through carefully designed valves. Sometimes combined with remote gas/fluid reservoir. Valving can be fixed or widely adjustable.

Digital process(ing)
Translating signals from the suspension's movement into computer language.

de Dion axle (or tube)
Rear axle design devised by the French count of that name (or possibly by one of his mechanics, M Bouton) in which the differential is chassis mounted with drive shafts out to the hubs which are joined together by a solid but light tube.

Droop
Total downward movement of a wheel from static ride height (see also Bump).

Flap
Adjustable section mounted on the trailing edge of a wing to alter its effective angle of attack and thus its downforce.

Gross weight
Total weight of vehicle. Regulations may define this as 'dry' without fuel or even water and oil, and without driver. For real life calculations, add them all in.

Gurney flap
Small vertical flange on a wing or flap trailing edge producing a vortex to help air below the wing keep its flow pattern – named after American driver Dan Gurney who (perhaps) did it first.

Hardware
Boxes, wires, screens, etc, that make up the physical equipment in a computer installation.

Health monitoring
Nothing to do with the driver's wellbeing. The computer switches on its own warning light if all is not well.

Heave
One of four modes used in Lotus Active suspension control. When all four wheels move up or down at equal speed. Four wheels at a time version of bump and droop.

Instantaneous roll centre
Another of those theoretical points in space, both invisible and moving; where lines projected from the suspension links intersect, and about which a wheel is considered to rotate when moving in bump and droop. See also Roll Centre and Swing Axle Length.

Integrated circuit
A number of components forming a circuit in one package, usually silicon and miniaturised. A collection of such circuits becomes a 'chip'.

Interface
Trendy word for a joint or connection between two pieces of compatible electrical equipment. Very often two matching plugs.

Intermediate
See tyres.

Jacking
Effect of certain suspension geometries with high roll centres (notably swing axles) which cause a car to lift as it attempts to rotate around the outer tyre contact patch and eventually roll over.

King Pin Inclination (KPI)
Angle between vertical and a line connecting top and bottom pivots of a front suspension upright seen from head on.

Leaf
See Spring.

Loop gains
Amplifying a tiny signal into a bigger one in a loop circuit.

Microcomputer
Very small computer. Followed mini-computer into use as computers shrank from room size to large desk to small box and less (also laptop).

Microprocessor
Chip inside a computer which controls its activities and the instructions it sends out.

Modal
In particular, the Lotus approach to suspension analysis and control by breaking all movements down into four basic modes (see also Heave, Pitch, Roll and Warp).

Monostable
Electronic equivalent of a headlight flasher switch: always in condition 'A' but can be ordered temporarily to 'B'.

Panhard rod
After the Frenchman of Panhard and Levassor (very early car builders) fame. A transversely mounted rod, from chassis on one side to solid axle on the other to prevent sideways movement.

Pitch
Rotation of a vehicle about its transverse axis in nosedive or squat.

Programme
Set of instructions which tell a computer what to do in any particular situation.

Pullrod
Link from top of an upright in tension to bottom of a spring suspension unit (usually through a pivot bar or bellcrank of some type).

Pushrod
Same as pullrod, except working upwards under compression from the bottom of an upright to a spring suspension unit.

Roll
Rotation or lean of a vehicle under cornering forces.

Roll axis
Longitudinal line around which a vehicle rolls (joins front and rear roll centres).

Roll centre
Invisible moving point about which a vehicle is considered to rotate in a corner. Easy to plot in static situation, but far from easy once the vehicle is moving.

Roll moment
Leverage exerted by a car attempting to roll.

Roll stiffness
Resistance to roll of a vehicle when cornering, exerted mainly by the anti-roll bars and to a lesser degree by the suspension springs.

Rack and pinion
Steering mechanism – toothed bar pushed from side to side when a small cog connected to the steering wheel is rotated. Universal in sports and racing cars.

Rake (angle)
When a vehicle is set other than parallel to the ground. Normally nose-down to some degree for aerodynamic reasons.

Ride height
Static clearance of a vehicle above the ground which controls the vertical height in space of the inboard suspension pick-up points, as well as all bodywork heights that might be specified by the regulations.

Rocking arm
A stressed top wishbone working like a see-saw with the wheel at one end and a coil/damper unit at the other.

Scoop
Nose rise under braking. A phenomena available with Active suspension, but not in popular use.

Self-centre
Tendency of the front wheels to return to the straight-ahead position during and after a turn, caused geometrically by the caster angle.

Sensor
Device which translates a physical happening (eg movement, speed, temperature rise and fall) into an electrical signal.

Servo amplifier
Boosts the signals to/from a servo valve.

Servo valve
High speed hydraulic switching valves which change push into pull and vice-versa within an actuator.

Shock absorber
See Damper.

Slick
See Tyre.

Software
Collection of instructions for a computer stored in various ways including on magnetic disc and tape.

Solid axle
Alternative name for beam axle but more for generally a steel rear axle case containing crown wheel, pinion, differential, bearings, etc, and carrying the brakes, drums and drive shafts.

Splitter
Thin horizontal ledge, often adjustable for width, on front bottom edge of bodywork designed to persuade as much air as possible over the top of the vehicle rather than underneath it.

Spoiler
Usually a lip or ridge on the bodywork designed to enhance, alter or destroy smooth airflow at a particular point.

Spring
Coil, leaf, torsion bar, rubber block, etc, which provides the squashable cushion in a suspension.

Spring rate
Load necessary to deflect any spring by a given distance (usually lbs/in or newtons/mm).

Sprung weight
See weight.

Steering arm
Lever on the front upright through which the steering forces are exerted (usually a forged finger or a pair of bolt-on alloy plates) attached to the trackrod end.

Swing axle
Suspension design in which the wheel mounts on a single solid link attached near to, on, or beyond the centre line of the vehicle.

Swing axle length (SAL)
Distance between the Instantaneous Roll Centre and the wheel. Varies continually during suspension movement.

Synthetic spring
Word for what an actuator becomes when working.

Toe-in
When a pair of wheels seen in plan view are not parallel but are closer at the front than at the rear.

Toe-out
Reverse of toe-in.

Toe control link
Strut between chassis and rear upright (usually threaded left/right each end for rapid adjustment) giving control of rear toe.

Top hat
Bush with bigger diameter flange at one end.

Torque tube
A tubular extension bolted to the front of a solid axle differential housing, which locates it fore and aft, and also deals with braking and acceleration twisting loads.

Track
Distance between the centre lines of a pair of tyres (front or rear).

Trackrod
Bar connecting a rack and pinion to the steering arm.

Trackrod end
Spherical joint at the outboard end of a trackrod.

Transducer
Device which translates movement into electrical signals.

Transient manoeuvre
The move from one state or condition to another, usually by a steering movement – the perfect vehicle example is taking an 'S' bend.

Tyre
Round, black and one on each corner. But also
- compounds; specific rubber mix on the working face
- slicks; completely smooth surfaced with only wear check slots
- intermediates; light/medium cut tread for damp/dusty surfaces
- wets; complex and deep pattern designed to clear substantial water from beneath the tyre
- control; type, pattern or make designated in the rules as the only type to be used
- cross ply; carcass in which the fabric layers run from side to side but at varying angles
- radials; carcass in which the main load bearing layer (often of steel wire rather than fabric or synthetic weave) runs completely round the tyre beneath the tread compound.

Upright
Casting or fabrication which carries the hub, bearings, oil seals and often single or twin brake callipers for independent suspension.

Warp
Mode of Lotus Active when the front and rear axle roll opposite ways and amounts.

Watt's linkage
All too often written without the apostrophe, but James Watt invented it for his steam engines. Automotively it is usually employed to locate a solid rear axle transversely with great accuracy while still permitting it to rise, fall or tilt freely.

Weight
Sprung; parts of a vehicle supported by the springs. Generally taken as gross weight, less unsprung weight. *Unsprung;* normally taken as wheel, tyres, hubs, outboard brakes, etc, plus half the weight of any linkages, outboard coils, dampers, etc.

Wet
See Tyres.

Wheel frequency
Rhythmic speed at which a wheel/hub/upright will bound up and down if not damped. In CPM (cycles per minute) or Hz (hertz, or cycles per second). Low is soft, high is hard in suspension terms.

Wheelbase
Distance between front and rear wheel hub lines.

Wheel rate
Spring rate as seen by the wheel after suspension leverage effects.

Wing
Precisely what you see on an aircraft but upside down so that it will press down rather than lift when moving through the air.

Wishbone
Roughly vee-shaped link joining an upright to the car. Deceptively simple in appearance but with much know-how in its material, stressing and manufacture. Also A-frame.

Yaw
Rotation of a vehicle about its vertical axis – 'hanging the tail out' in most people's terms but also sideways lurch in strong crosswinds.

Index